Introduction To Latin

Revised First Edition

Study Guide and Reader

Introduction To Latin

Revised First Edition

Study Guide and Reader

Ed DeHoratius

Wayland High School

Focus Publishing
R. Pullins Company
Newburyport, MA
www.pullins.com

ISBN 10: 1-58510-283-0
ISBN 13: 978-1-58510-283-9

10 9 8 7 6 5 4 3 2 1

1107TS

Table of Contents

Acknowledgments ix

Preface for Students xi

Preface for Instructors xiii

Authors and Text xvii

Chapter One 1

    1. The Sentence 1

    2. Parts of Speech 1

    3. Function (What Words Do) 2

    4. Sentence Patterns 3

    5. The Verb 4

    6. Principal Parts 10

    7. Indicative and Infinitive Uses 10

Chapter Two 11

    8. Latin Cases and Case Uses 11

    9. The Noun 13

  10. Gender 14

  11. Dictionary Entry 14

  12. First Declension 14

  13. Second Declension 15

  14. The Conjunction 18

  15. Reading Latin: Using Expectations 19

Chapter Three 21

  16. Genitive Case 21

  17. Dative Case 23

  18. Expectations 26

  19. Sentence Pattern: Special Intransitive 26

Chapter Four 29

  20. The Adverb 29

  21. Ablative Case 31

  22. The Preposition 34

  23. Expressions of Place 35

  24. Word Order 39

Chapter Five 41

  25. The Adjective 41

  26. Agreement 41

  27. The Gap 45

  28. *Sum*: Present Indicative and Infinitive 46

  29. Sentence Pattern: Linking 47

  30. More Uses of the Ablative 49

Chapter Six 53
   31. Imperfect Active Indicative (First and Second Conjugation) 53
   32. Future Active Indicative (First and Second Conjugation) 57
   33. Commands: The Imperative 61
   34. Vocative Case 61
Chapter Seven 65
   35. Third Declension Nouns 65
   36. Imperfect and Future of *sum* 71
   37. Dative of Possession 73
Chapter Eight 75
   38. Perfect Active Indicative 75
   39. Perfect Active Infinitive 77
   40. Forms of *possum* 77
   41. Infinitive as a Noun 80
Chapter Nine 85
   42. Third Conjugation 85
   43. The Pronoun 93
Chapter Ten 99
   44. Demonstrative Pronouns 99
   45. Special Adjectives in -*īus* 106
   46. Sentence Pattern: Factitive 107
Chapter Eleven 111
   47. Imperfect Active Indicative (Third Conjugation) 111
   48. Future Active Indicative (Third Conjugation) 112
   49. Numerals 115
   50. Expressions of Cause 119
Chapter Twelve 123
   51. Third Declension Adjectives 123
   52. Expressions of Time 126
Chapter Thirteen 129
   53. Fourth Conjugation 129
   54. Interrogative Pronouns 129
   55. The Reflexive Pronoun 136
   56. Possessive Adjectives and Possession Using *eius* 140
   57. Ablative of Specification (= Ablative of Respect) 141
Chapter Fourteen 145
   58. Imperfect Active Indicative (Fourth Conjugation) 145
   59. Future Active Indicative (Fourth Conjugation) 145
   60. Accusative of Extent and Degree 147
Chapter Fifteen 149
   61. Perfect Active Indicative 149
   62. Pluperfect Active Indicative 153
   63. Future Perfect Active Indicative 157
   64. Perfect Active Infinitive 158

Chapter Sixteen 161
  65. Fourth Declension Nouns 161
  66. Fifth Declension Nouns 165
  67. Locative 166
Chapter Seventeen 169
  68. Passive Voice 169
  69. Present Passive Indicative 170
  71. Future Passive Indicative 174
  72. Present Passive Infinitive 174
  73. Sentence Pattern: Passive 180
  74. Ablative of Agent 180
Chapter Eighteen 183
  75. Dependent Clauses 183
  76. Dative with Adjectives 189
Chapter Nineteen 191
  77. Relative Pronoun 191
  78. Relative Clause - Adjectival Use 192
  79. Relative Clause - Noun Use 199
Chapter Twenty 201
  80. Perfect Passive Indicative 201
  81. Pluperfect Passive Indicative 202
  82. Future Perfect Passive Indicative 203
  83. Perfect Passive Infinitive 204
  84. Paradigm of *vīs, vis,* f. 206
Chapter Twenty-One 207
  85. Irregular Verbs: *volō, nōlō, mālō* 207
  86. Negative Commands with *nōlō* 209
  87. Noun Clause: Objective Infinitive 210
Chapter Twenty-Two 211
  88. Infinitive Forms 211
  89. Noun Clause: Indirect Statement 215
  90. Tenses of the Infinitive in Indirect Statement 215
Chapter Twenty-Three 223
  91. Intensive Pronoun: *ipse, īdem, quīdam* 223
  92. Deponent Verbs 228
  93. Special Intransitive: Verbs used with an Ablative Object 232
Chapter Twenty-Four 233
  94. Participles 233
  95. Tenses of the Participle 240
  96. Participle Uses 240
  97. Ablative Absolute 240
Chapter Twenty-Five 245
  98. *eō, īre, iī (ivī), itūrus* (to go) 245
  99. *ferō, ferre, tulī, lātus* (to carry, bear) 246

Chapter Twenty-Six 247
   100. Comparison of Adjectives 247
   101. Declension of Comparatives 249
   102. Irregular Comparison 249
   103. Comparison with *quam* and Ablative of Comparison 251
   104. Comparison of Adverbs 253
Chapter Twenty-Seven 255
   105. Present Active Subjunctive 255
   106. Perfect Active Subjunctive 260
   107. Subjunctive of *sum* 262
   108. Independent Uses of the Subjunctive 262
Chapter Twenty-Eight 267
   109. Imperfect Active Subjunctive 267
   110. Pluperfect Active Subjunctive 269
   111. Subjunctive of *sum* 272
   112. Tenses in Independent Uses of the Subjunctive 272
   113. Tenses in Dependent Uses of the Subjunctive: Sequence of Tenses 272
   114. Dependent Uses of the Subjunctive 275
Chapter Twenty-Nine 281
   115. Present and Imperfect Passive Subjunctive 281
   116. Perfect and Pluperfect Passive Subjunctives 281
   117. Dependent Uses of the Subjunctive - Noun Clauses 281
   118. Forms of *fiō, fierī, factus* 291
Chapter Thirty 293
   119. Subjunctive of *possum* 293
   120. Clauses of Fearing 293
   121. Conditions 295
Chapter Thirty-One 301
   122. Gerund 301
   123. Gerundive 304
   124. Passive Periphrastic 313
Chapter Thirty-Two 317
   125. Supine 317
   126. *Ut* + the Indicative 319
   127. More on Relative Pronouns 322
   128. Additional Uses of the Subjunctive 324
   129. Impersonal Constructions 325
Citations by Author...328
Citations by Chapter 332

MAGISTRIS LINGUAE LATINAE OMNIBUS

PRAESERTIM
Dan Algeo, Rosemont School of the Holy Child
Charles Kling, St. Joseph's Preparatory School (Retired)
Henry Bender, The Hill School
Francis Newton, Duke University (Emeritus)
Paul Gwynne, The American University of Rome
Fr. Reginald Foster

Acknowledgements

First and foremost, I want to thank my colleagues in the Wayland High School Language Department for their patience and support. I especially want to thank my fellow Latin teachers, Tim Casey and Lee Krasnoo, for their assistance in identifying sources and their willingness to help pilot the exercises and fact check some of the texts, e.g. the result clause from the Scholiast on Juvenal came from one of Tim's Latin 3 projects, and Lee's Latin 4 class helped me identify a miscited line from the *Aeneid*.

I also want to thank the audience at the Classical Association of Massachusetts spring 2007 meeting, where the theory behind some of the exercises and some examples were presented. Their discussion and insight were invaluable in the completion of the final manuscript. I especially want to thank Ken Kitchell of the University of Massachusetts at Amherst for catching a mistake in one of the translations.

The following people and institutions also assisted in the completion of the manuscript: the College of the Holy Cross for the use of its library; Peter Sipes and Andrew Bentley for suggesting sources; the students in my Latin 2 class, 2006-2007, for piloting some of the exercises; and Jacqui Carlon of the University of Massachusetts at Boston for her helpful and insightful comments on the final manuscript.

The team at Focus Publishing, as always, offered invaluable advice and assistance: Ron Pullins, Kathleen Brophy, and Linda Diering. And to my family, Liz, Will, and Matt: thank you as always for your love, patience, and support.

Preface for Students

It is impossible to understand a culture without understanding its language. The Latin language has nine different ways to express purpose; this linguistic detail alone reveals as much about who the Romans were as any text or artifact. But from whom should we learn the language of the Romans? Who is left to teach it? Your instructors are not native speakers. I certainly am not, nor did I learn Latin from native speakers. That's not to say of course that they or I are deficient in our knowledge of Latin, but only to say that there is a distinct difference that comes from learning from a native speaker rather than a non-native speaker. Certainly Latin is speakable and certainly there are those that speak it with near-native proficiency. But no one in centuries has grown up speaking Latin from infancy as their lone mother tongue. The only native speakers left to us, or really native users, are Latin authors. The majority of exercises in this study guide then use unadapted Latin, written by native Latin users. It is hoped that this exposure will not only improve your understanding of Latin as a language but will also increase your interest in the native users of Latin, the Romans themselves.

This book is divided into the chapters and, for the most part, the grammatical sections of your textbook. Most, though not all, grammatical sections of your textbook will have a corresponding section in this book. Each chapter in this study guide is comprised of the following elements:

- an introductory paragraph that summarizes what is covered in the chapter
- a list of Terms to Know that collects new and review terminology
- review questions that organize and highlight important information in the grammatical sections
- supplemental grammatical information that either augments the grammatical information of the textbook or introduces grammatical information that was not included in the textbook
- exercises (explained in greater detail below)

The exercises come in two forms. The more traditional form that uses the vocabulary of a chapter to drill new forms or contructions is used minimally because of the availability of similar exercises in both the textbook and the companion website. The bulk of the exercises are the text-based exercises mentioned above in the first paragraph. The goal of this approach is threefold: 1) to illustrate and increase comprehension of a particular grammatical form or construction; 2) to expose you to different Latin authors from different literary periods; 3) and to introduce the literary, cultural, and historical contexts that produced each author and text.

The texts range from the early 2nd century BCE to the 14th century CE. Each text is accompanied by an introductory paragraph that establishes the immediate context of the excerpt. Following each text is a series of tasks that focuses on the grammatical form or construction of that section. It is important to note that few of these tasks are translation-tasks. These texts weren't written with grammatical instruction or review in mind, and they certainly weren't written with the vocabulary of your textbook in mind; translation of such passages, because of the scope of vocabulary alone, often becomes cumbersome. But the absence of translation is no reason to withhold unadapted Latin from students even in their first chapter of Latin. Rather than translation, the tasks will often ask you to identify forms in the text, to complete English translations with translations of Latin constructions, or to parse forms. Vocabulary is provided when necessary, either for the identification of forms or for translation, though words already covered in the vocabulary of your textbook are not included. There are some instances, however, when the provision of vocabulary proved counterproductive to the purpose of the exercise. In these instances, though rare, you will need to rely on an external dictionary (a good, simple on-line dictionary can be found at http://archives. nd.edu/latgramm.htm). In short, these exercises will function much like any other Latin exercise, but they will use the Latin of Rome's native users rather than sentences composed by instructors or textbook writers. Thus, not only are you reviewing your grammar but you are also learning about such topics as 2nd century BCE Roman comic plays, Golden Age poetry, and mythology.

One caveat: the exercises are of course designed to help you better understand Latin. But they are also not necessarily designed to be excessively easy or straightforward. Many indeed are. But you will find some exercises that, whether because of the nature of the text or of the exercise itself, might prove difficult, frustrating, or not readily accessible at first. Such challenges are of course intentional; it is important that you understand that Latin will indeed not always be clear, and it may take two or three attempts before you understand a passage. The same will hold true for some of the exercises. Such difficulty, ideally, should not result in (excessive) frustration, but rather should serve as an appropriate challenge to both your knowledge of Latin and your intellectual acumen. Do not fear, however: both I and your instructors still face the same challenges; we use dictionaries and check grammar; we encounter passages that confuse us or do not make immediate sense. But the ability to understand such passages, to bring together both our knowledge and our intellect, is borne of focus, practice, and hard work, and is what makes Latin so enticing.

Many of the exercises will also ask you to explain why you answered the way you answered. Such questions will not always be black and white; many will be the type that have some wrong answers, and multiple right answers. The process of answering these questions is almost as important as the answers themselves. To review not only your knowledge but also the ways in which you apply such knowledge is an essential aspect to increasing comprehension and understanding; it will make you a better Latin reader.

In addition to the chapters, the following resources are included:
- a glossary of authors excerpted
- a list of texts excerpted, organized both by chapter and by author

Both resources are provided for that student who wants to explore an author or a text beyond the excerpt provided. The former provides brief biographical information about each author, as well as, in most cases, a broad summary of the text excerpted. The latter cites from where in each text each passage excerpted in this study guide comes.

I hope that you will approach this study guide as more than a supplement to your textbook. It is of course designed to be just that. But when I began writing it, I quickly realized that writing a series of drills and exercises seemed an empty endeavor; they already exist in your textbook and on-line. Rather, I started reading a lot of Latin and noting in which passages certain gramamtical forms and constructions appeared repetitively and/or in a particularly illustrative manner. And I of course could not ignore some of the iconic passages of Latin literature which, even if lacking in grammatical redundancy, often found their way into the present volume because of their inherent importance. When I piloted some of the exercises with my own students, I was pleased to find that much of what I hoped would happen did happen: not only did they review whatever form or construction we were studying, but, and perhaps more important, they became interested in the texts themselves (even if they couldn't yet understand them): they asked questions, I translated or summarized some of the Latin, we discussed Latin and the Romans beyond what the chapter dictated. In a high-school setting, where I see my students as much as four times as often as a college student might see her instructor, I have time for such freedom. You might not in your classroom, but nonetheless I encourage you to pursue those questions, whether with your instructor inside or outside of the classroom, in your library, or with your classmates. I hope that the more Latin you learn, the more you will want to learn about the Romans, and the more you learn about the Romans, the more Latin you will want to learn.

Preface for Instructors

Movie watchers of the late 1980s might recognize the name J. Evans Pritchard. He is the literary critic eviscerated, quite literally in terms of his book, by Robin Williams in *Dead Poet's Society* for suggesting that the value of poetry might be mathematically plotted on a graph. I confess, however, that in the preparation of the present volume, I often felt myself sympathizing with J. Evans Pritchard. In many ways, while I will admit that there were no graphs prepared, I nonetheless was often assessing Latin literature in a way that J. Evans Pritchard would enthusiastically embrace. My two Pritchard-ian axes were 1) grammatical value, measured by either redundancy or illustrative variation and 2) cultural, historical, or literary value. A high score in one category often offset a low score in the other, so that Martial, whose epigrammatic style often yields grammatical redundancy but whose sheer production renders many of his poems less notable among philologists, appears in almost every chapter. Conversely, the opening line of the *Aeneid* includes a mere two direct objects, but because of its literary significance, it has also been included.

The texts then used for the Text-based Exercises are intentionally varied. It is of course impossible for me to survey all of Latin literature, and perhaps one of the most difficult aspects to writing the present volume was disciplining myself against continuously adding more texts as I found them; indeed, I worry that some chapters are bloated as they are. The inclusion of some of the more capricious and arbitrary choices (e.g. Seneca's *Phaedra*), if I'm being honest, is beholden entirely to the contents of my book shelf and what I thought I could get through before my one-and-a-half-year-old and four-year-old sons needed separating.

Such texts are utilized for as many as 90 of the 129 grammar sections in the textbook and are intended 1) to illustrate particular forms or grammatical constructions, preferably in a repetitive or otherwise illustrative way; 2) to provide for the student some interaction with the text and the forms or grammatical constructions in question, often without translating the passage; 3) to expose the student to a variety of Latin authors and texts, and their cultural, literary, or historical significance.

In their most basic form, these texts should be used with the accompanying exercises to reinforce aspects of particular forms or grammatical constructions; such exercises can be done for homework, for in-class work, or for student enrichment. Perhaps more important, however, because translation is not frequently asked of students, is the potential for customization implicit in each text. More advanced classes can engage in more translation than the exercises call for; it is relatively easy for instructors or students to facilitate such work because most of the passages are relatively short. Even classes with a wide range of ability levels can use the passages at their own pace: weaker students can focus on the exercises alone, while stronger students can augment the exercises with translation or other work. The instructor can then assist the weaker students knowing that the rest of the class is busied constructively.

The texts also provide opportunities for non-language exploration: research of authors, research of the source texts from which excerpts are taken, and/or research of cultural topics introduced by the excerpts. Instructors can take advantage of these cultural opportunities to whatever extent they deem appropriate for their class, but their presence affords instructors a freedom and variety that few textbooks or workbooks do. I have provided introductions to each excerpt that give some sense of the context within which the excerpt appears. And in some instances, I have provided brief cultural digressions that explain particularly obvious or important allusions. But neither such introductions nor such explanations could begin to cover the breadth of potential discussion points or explications to be found in each text. I hope that instructors will enjoy, as I have, the variety of questions from students that each text inevitably raises.

Finally, because the texts are unedited and unadapted, students are exposed to the Latin of its native speakers or users. These texts illustrate Latin as the Romans (or Latin users) would have known it, with all the grammatical vagaries, the idioms, the alternate forms and spellings, and the nuance with which we imbue our English; I have intentionally not updated Plautus' archaisms or Medieval orthography. The sooner students can acquire the flexibility necessary to view their grammatical rules in the context of Latin users who used the language in a more natural and intuitive way than we have learned it, and who might not adhere to their grammatical rules as frequently or consistently as we might like, the more easily students will transition to understanding and approaching Latin as a dynamic language, instead of merely a system of rules to be applied.

The sheer number and variety of the texts themselves posed some logistical hurdles. I have attempted to make the text-based exercises as self-contained as possible, i.e. students should be able to complete the bulk of them without needing a dictionary; the vocabulary provided and the glossary and/or vocabulary lists from the textbook should prove sufficient. There are some exercises, however, where the provision of vocabulary would too obviously reveal the answer to a previous question. In these instances, it is likely that an external dictionary will be necessary. It is of course assumed that Latin students will have such a dictionary, if not their own then access to one via a library, but instructors can elect to skip such exercises if they wish to keep their students' work entirely self-contained within the scope of the workbook and textbook.

While the bulk of the present volume is comprised of these text-based excercises, three other types of supplements to the textbook are also included: Review Questions, Supplementary Grammar, and Exercises.

Review Questions target specific information from the textbook so that students can review the most important details and create their own summaries of each chapter's information. These questions will likely not be used in class, but are good ways for students to organize for themselves the information of each chapter.

Supplementary Grammar will either expand upon a given grammatical topic or introduce grammar that was not included in the textbook. The former tends to focus on drawing connections between Latin and English to facilitate comprehension of both or to include details that are too specific for the scope of the textbook.

Exercises will use the vocabulary of a chapter, or the recent chapters, to drill a particular grammatical point. Because of the plethora of exercises in the textbook and on-line, and because the majority of exercises in this study guide are text-based, there are few such exercises.

Each chapter also opens with an introductory paragraph and list of terms to know. Additionally, there is a biographical dictionary of authors excerpted in this volume, and a list of passages, organized both by chapter and by author.

When I wrote the first draft of Chapter 1, I found myself spent and frustrated after a fruitless few hours of trying to envision and write drills. I couldn't imagine another thirty-one chapters of this. I had used Latin texts as paradigms before in class, though sparingly (Catullus 5 for interrogatives, the *Carmina Burana* for nominatives and indicatives), and I wondered if I could incorporate such selections into the exercises of the present volume; why write sentences when the Romans themselves already had? Little did I expect my initial investigation to turn into the number and variety of texts that it has. I hope then that you will find the present volume useful not only for drilling forms and grammar, though ostensibly that is its intention, but also for exposing to your students the wonder and variety of the Romans, as evidenced through their literature, that has already captured our imaginations and that we hope will likewise capture the imagination of our students.

I also ask that if anyone has paradigmatic texts that they would be willing to share, I would be happy to add them to my growing list. Please send them to the following e-mail address: edehoratius@ alumni.duke.edu.

About the Texts

Because there are over 300 texts in the present volume, they are culled from public domain sources. While the purist in me chafed at this notion, that instructors and students would not have texts to read that represented the latest in textual scholarship, the pragmatist in me understood the need for expediency and cost effectiveness. I would suggest too a further advantage to such texts: the opportunity to discuss with students the textual tradition, the process of pre-printing "publication," the process by which modern editions are edited and finalized, and the (sub-)discipline of paleography, one that is dear to my heart after writing my senior thesis at Duke University on a 15th-century manuscript in its special collections library under the direction of Francis Newton. These are all relevant discussions, or even potential avenues of further research by students, when an instructor is faced with a text that differs slightly from the modern edition of an author with which the instructor might be familiar.

In preparing the texts, I have made few changes to the original: first words of sentences are capitalized, and consonantal "u" has been changed to "v" to follow what seems to have become largely conventional; otherwise, the original texts have not been altered, other than minor punctuation adjustments. Many of the texts in the present volume are excerpted from larger works. In these cases, I have truncated texts at clause breaks whenever possible without making the excerpt too unwieldy. Even if the clause break occurs at a semi-colon or a conjunction, the first words of most excerpts are capitalized. There are some examples where an excerpt begins, for instance, at the beginning of a relative clause. In these instances, the first word will not be capitalized, but will be preceded by an ellipsis. All translations are mine.

Authors and Text

This glossary is intended to provide a brief introduction to the authors and/or texts included in this book. Included for each author is his full name, his dates, the name of the text(s), and the chapter numbers within which each text appears (indicated by the numbers in parentheses); for authors with more than one text included, each text will be described.

I have purposely eschewed an excess of facts. Rather, I have endeavored here to provide a sense of what the author was about, what he was trying to accomplish, and any relevant historical context within which that accomplishment might take place. While each excerpt throughout this book will include a brief introduction, the information included here will serve as part of those introductions, i.e. broad summaries will be given here so that they do not need to be repeated throughout the introduction of each text. Anonymous texts or authors that do not appear frequently in the present volume are not included here; enough context is provided with the introductions of such texts that to include them here would be repetitive.

Alcuin: c.735 – 804 CE; *Farewell to his Cell* (6). A scholar and writer associated with the royal court of Charlemagne, Alcuin revised and revolutionized the educational approach of the court's school and was a pioneering figure in the Carolingian Renaissance, the first revival, albeit relatively short-lived, of a pervasive interest in the ancient world. Alcuin expanded the educational focus of the palace school to include the liberal arts and theology; students at the school included Charlemagne himself and his sons. Eventually, Alcuin left Charlemagne's service to take over the administration of the famous monastery at Tours.

Archipoeta (3). A poet of the mid-12th century CE about whom little is known. Apparently connected with the royal court of Emperor Frederick the 1st, he belongs to the poetic group known as the *vaganten*, a German name which reflects the wandering nature of their poetic performances; the French troubadours and jongleurs were of a similar type. Much of the poetry of the Archipoeta is simple and popular in nature, focusing on drinking songs and the life of the middle- and lower classes, but he elsewhere treats loftier subjects such as philosophy and theology.

Aulus Gellius: c.125 – post-180 CE; *Noctes Atticae* (5, 15, 17, 31). Little is known about Gellius' life beyond the wide range of interests he reveals in his only surviving text, *Attic Nights*. He studied in Rome before travelling to Athens, where he began collecting his material: a compilation of anecdotes and stories based on lectures he had heard and texts he had read. He later arranged these stories into the twenty book collection called *Noctes Atticae* or *Attic Nights*. Begun during a particularly long and cold winter in Attica (hence the name), the region of Greece where Athens is located, *Attic Nights* provides a unique picture of the ancient world because of Gellius' inclusion of anecdotes and information on a wide range of subjects. Gellius also provides the only surviving fragments of some texts otherwise lost.

Caesar: Gaius Julius Caesar, 100 / 102 – 44 BCE; *De bello Gallico* (13). Rome's first century BCE was characterized by political strife and chaos, as the institutions of the Roman Republic finally broke down and created a power vacuum for ambitious Roman generals to attempt to fill. Caesar is perhaps the best known of these generals, if only because of his immortalization by Shakespeare. He amassed a great fortune while conquering Gaul (modern-day France), which he used to finance his attempted takeover of Rome. While popular and successful, Caesar ultimately proved too arrogant for Rome; his bald accumulation of power alienated enough senators that they plotted his assassination, famously executed on March 15, 44 BCE, the Ides of March. As a writer, Caesar is best known for his *De bello Gallico*, a third person account of his own campaign in Gaul. Perhaps its most notable feature is its focus on the anthropology of the Gauls; Caesar goes to great lengths to chart the characteristics, customs, political structures, and society of the very people whom he was conquering.

Carmina Burana (1, 23). The name of a manuscript, written in the early 13th century and now housed in a library in Munich, that collects over 1,000 poems, mostly in Latin. The best-known of these poems are the drinking songs: short, simple poems that celebrate the pleasures of pub life, although the collection also includes love poems and religious poems (the latter lost).

Cato: Marcus Porcius Cato, 234 - 149 BCE; *De agri cultura* (17). Cato is perhaps best known for his near-legendary sternness and severity; his life and political career was largely devoted to the promotion of Roman Republican values and the criticism of the extravegence and opulence that was beginning to characterize the Roman aristocracy. He is perhaps best known for his *Origines*, now lost, that narrated the early history of Rome and Italy; it became an early model for Latin prose style, since the majority of literature produced by Romans at this time was written in Greek. His *De agri cultura*, also known as *De re rustica*, which has largely survived, functions as a manual for farming and cultivating the land.

Catullus: Gaius Valerius Catullus, c.84 – 54 BCE; *Carmina* (2, 3, 4, 5, 7, 8, 9, 11, 13, 14, 19, 21, 22, 23, 24, 26, 27, 28, 29, 32). Little is known about Catullus' life, and his biography is complicated by the autobiographical nature of his poetry; of course, it is not known (and is tantalizingly ambiguous) whether Catullus' poetry is in fact a reflection of his life or a reflection of the poetic persona that Catullus adopts. Nonetheless, Catullus' poetry marks the first conspicuous shift from the epic poetry of Ennius, an early Latin poet who emulated Homer, and whom Vergil (who post-dates Catullus) emulated, to the more personal, individualized, and emotional poetry championed by the Greek poet Callimachus and the tradition he inspired. Catullus' 116 surviving poems are in general divided into three groups, each of which comprises roughly a third of his output: poems 1 – 60 are poems of various meters; poems 61 – 68 are *epyllia*, mini-epic poems, though many of Catllus' *epyllia* do not use the epic meter of dactylic hexameter and are not as long as more traditional *epyllia*; poems 69 – 116 are all written in elegiac couplets. The most enduring poems of Catullus' *oeuvre* focus on his relationship with a certain Lesbia, a married woman with whom Catullus is engaged in a torturous relationship. Although Lesbia's identity is not known (and indeed may not be intended to be known), circumstantial evidence may identify her as Clodia, the wife of Q. Metellus Celer and the sister of P. Clodius Pulcher. The identification of Lesbia with Clodia becomes even more compelling because of Cicero's oration *Pro Caelio*, in which he defended Marcus Caelius Rufus against a number of charges that might have been brought by Clodia herself. Whether or not she brought the charges, Cicero lambasts her in his speech, and so connections between Cicero's characterization of her and Lesbia's treatment of Catullus have long been drawn.

Cicero: Marcus Tullius Cicero, 106 – 43 BCE. Best known for his embodiment of the beauty and complexity of Latin prose, a reputation cemented by scholars of the Italian Renaissance, Cicero was a lawyer and politician, many of whose speeches, treatises, and letters have survived. Cicero was a contemporary of Caesar and lived through the tumultuous demise of the Roman Republic; many of his speeches provide an invaluable primary source for this complex period of Roman history.

But Cicero ultimately would find his downfall in those same politics that provided such a forum for his rhetorical talents. He delivered a series of speeches, called the *Philippics*, that eviscerated Marc Antony in the wake of Caesar's assassination. When Antony and Augustus (then still known as Octavian) called a truce, part of their agreement was the honoring of proscriptions, i.e. lists of people that each wanted killed. Cicero was on Antony's list and, upon his death, his hands and tongue, the primary tools of the orator, were hung in the Forum; their intended message was clear.

> *In Catilinam* (7, 10, 13, 15, 17, 18, 19, 23, 24, 27, 28, 30, 31, 32). Cicero made his best known speeches against a Roman noble named Lucius Sergius Catiline. Catiline, commemorated only by his enemies, remains an enigmatic historical figure. According to his detractors, he was involved in a conspiracy to overthrow the Roman Republic because of his anger at having been passed over for the consulship. Whatever the truth might be, however, Catiline has remained (in)famous because of the sharp invective and comprehensive attack Cicero leveled against him in his four orations.

> *Pro Archia* (16, 17, 18, 22, 26, 27, 28, 30, 31). Cicero defends a Greek, Archias, against a charge that questions his Roman citizenship. The speech is often considered anamolous for Cicero because of its focus on the humanities and their role in public life; Archias was a poet, and part of Cicero's defense focuses on the importance of Archias' work for the public good.

Damian, Peter: c.1007-1072; (2). An Italian theologian, born in Ravenna, becoming a Cardinal in his lifetime and a Doctor of the Church in the 19th century, Peter Damian is perhaps best known for his tract on the omnipotence of God, in which he defends God's omnipotence by discussing whether God can restore a woman's virginity, and whether God can change the past. The text included here is a short poem, titled from its first line, *Ad perennis vitae*, likely intended to be accompanied by music.

Horace: Quintus Horatius Flaccus, 65 – 8 BCE; *Carmina* (3, 5, 8, 11, 19, 26, 27, 29, 31). The emperor Augustus patronized a number of poets via his cultural attache Maecenas; Horace was one of those poets. He wrote a wide range of literature, from odes to satires to a treatise on writing poetry, but his odes are by far the most famous. Horace consistently incorporates into his odes the theme of the brevity and unpredictability of life, and the values and benefits of the country life vs. the complexity and excess of the city life.

Livy: Titus Livius, 59 BCE – 17 CE; *Ab urbe condita* (5, 16, 22, 24, 28, 29, 31, 32). Livy undertook a vast history of Rome that stretched from the flight of Aeneas from Troy to Livy's contemporary Rome; the opus filled 142 books. Only, however, 35 of these 142 books have survived. The first five books cover the Roman monarchy, which stretched from the traditional founding of Rome in 753 BCE with Romulus as its first king, to the fall of the monarchy in 509 BCE. Livy's history of the monarchy focuses on stories that are likely more legend than true history and that are included as much to promote the values that characterized early Rome (values that would be maintained through the early Republic) as to provide a chronicle of early Roman history.

Martial: Marcus Valerius Martialis, c.40 – 103/104 CE; *Epigrams* (1, 2, 3, 4, 5, 6, 7, 8, 9, 10, 11, 12, 13, 14, 15, 16, 17, 18, 19, 20, 21, 22, 23, 24, 25, 26, 27, 28, 29, 32). The poet Martial made his career out of writing usually short, succinct, vivid, and often acerbic poetry. Apparently not a successful writer until later in life, Martial nonetheless produced more than 1,500 short poems, or epigrams. These epigrams remain simple and straightforward, often without the self-conscious poetics of the better-known poets; Martial tends to eschew allusion and excessive rhetoric in his poetry. Nonetheless, he is lauded by Pliny (the younger) and counts as poetic addressees other notable contemporary writers.

Miraculum Sancti Nicholai **(5, 6, 9, 13).** A miracle play of the 13th century in which the son of King Getron is kidnapped by the pagan King Marmorinus. Through prayer to St. Nicholas, the boy is taken from the court of King Marmorinus and returned to his parents.

Ovid: Publius Ovidius Naso, 43 BCE – 17 CE. Ovid's life is perhaps defined by its close: in 8 CE he was exiled by the emperor Augustus to Tomis, a town on the western coast of the Black Sea, where he died nine years later. His exile, however little is known about the specifics of its cause, captures the spirit of a poet who lived at least his literary life, and perhaps too his political / social life, on the edge of decorum and acceptability. Ovid himself tells us that he was exiled for a *carmen* and a *crimen*, the former likely his *Ars amatoria*, the latter likely some indirect role (a direct role surely would have led to death) in the promiscuity of the emperor Augustus's granddaughter Julia. Nonetheless, Ovid is a poet defined by his pervasive irony and wit, and his interest in exploring unheralded or innovative perspectives on traditional stories or themes.

> *Metamorphoses* **(3, 4, 6, 8, 9, 10, 11, 12, 17, 18, 20, 22, 23, 24, 26, 29, 30, 31, 32).** Ovid undertakes epic poetry with the *Metamorphoses*, a sprawling compendium of mythology and legend whose unifying theme is change or transformation. While Ovid cloaked the *Metamorphoses* in the guise of epic, as with much of Ovid's *oeuvre*, his epic reveals his interest in both exploring the limits of and experimenting with genre. The epic tradition, as established by Homer and emulated by Ovid's near-contemporary Vergil, focused on a main, heroic character, chartered that character's trials and successes, and told much of its story through narrative flashbacks. Ovid's *Metamorphoses*, however, has no main character and moves through its complex narrative structure in rough chronological order, beginning with the creation of the world and ending with Ovid's contemporary Rome. Ovid's epic in many ways is the anti-epic. The stories summarized below are used throughout the present volume. Introductions to specific episodes are provided with each excerpt, but these general introductions are provided to avoid having to repeat background information with each excerpt.

>> **Apollo and Daphne.** The god Apollo has just killed the monstrous snake Python and brags about his prowess with the bow and arrow to the god Cupid, who also wields the bow and arrow. Cupid, offended by Apollo's bravado, takes revenge on Apollo by shooting him with an arrow that will cause him to fall in love. He shoots the unsuspecting and innocent nymph Daphne, who has sworn off men in allegiance to the goddess Diana and her virginity, with an arrow that will prevent her from falling in love. Apollo pursues Daphne, at first almost naively but eventually with greater fervor, until she pleads to her river-god father Peneus to save her. He responds by changing her into the laurel tree, which Apollo, unable to have Daphne herself, adopts as his signature tree. The story for Ovid then becomes an aetiology for the use of the laurel wreath as a triumphal crown.

>> **Daedalus and Icarus.** The Athenian craftsman Daedalus, imprisoned with his son Icarus for his role in the conception of the Minotaur, creates wings for himself and his son to escape from the island kingdom of Crete. He instructs his son not to fly too high or too low; the wings will fail. But Icarus, the rash youth, does not listen, and the heat of the sun melts the wax bindings of his wings so that he plummets to his death. The myth is an illustration of hubris, or excessive pride.

Orpheus and Eurydice. The hero-poet Orpheus married Eurydice, but she was killed immediately after the wedding by a snake hiding in the grass. Orpheus, beset with grief, resolved to journey to the underworld to recover her. He assuaged Cerberus, the three-headed guard dog to the underworld, and eventually charmed with his song Hades and Persephone, the king and the queen of the underworld. They agreed to release Eurydice to Orpheus but leveled one condition: that she follow him out and that he not turn to see her until they are both out of the underworld. Orpheus, of course, cannot resist the temptation to see her and, at the last moment, turns; Mercury, the god who ferries souls to the underworld, immediately appears and returns her there forever. The myth can be read as a metaphor for the grieving process, i.e. Orpheus was so grief-stricken that he would do anything to get his wife back, but in the end, nothing can bring her back. In this reading, his turning to look at Eurydice was inevitable: her death is final; she cannot be brought back, however much Orpheus wants her to be.

Pygmalion. The famous Cypriot sculptor removed himself from society after being horrified by the behavior of the first prostitutes, the Propoetides, whom Venus changed to stone. Pygmalion in response sculpted the perfect woman. He fell in love with his statue and treated it like his girlfriend: dressing it, undressing it, bringing it gifts, caring for it. At a festival of Venus, he prayed to Venus that he might find a woman similar to his statue, but Venus knew what he really wanted. When he returned home, his sculpture came to life, and Pygmalion and Galatea (a name conferred upon the statue by later readers) had a daughter Paphos, from whose name Cyprus took its ancient name.

Pyramus and Thisbe. The ancient antecedent for Shakespeare's *Romeo and Juliet*, also appearing in Shakespeare's *Midsummer Night's Dream*, the story of Pyramus and Thisbe focuses on the tragic forbidden love of two Babylonian youths. Forbidden by their fathers to meet or talk, they formulate a plan to meet at night in the woods outside Babylon. Thisbe arrives first at the same time as a lionness, bloodied from killing cattle. She flees but drops her shawl, which the lioness mangles with her bloody mouth. Pyramus arrives and, finding the bloody shawl, assumes Thisbe has been killed, and kills himself. Thisbe returns to find Pyramus dead, and kills herself in response.

Amores **(5, 7, 10, 15, 19, 23, 24, 31, 32).** Ovid's earliest published endeavor saw him delve into elegiac poetry, that poetry that focused on the emotional, the personal, and the individual. Ovid ostensibly writes a series of poems centered around a likely fictional love affair with a woman named Corinna. (As with other elegiac poetry, not all of the *Amores* involve Corinna, but she is the thread that binds the collection together.) However, even in this early poetry, Ovid is already revealing many of the trends that will characterize his entire *oeuvre*: the exploration of genre, the often ironic incorporation of literary predecessors, and the fascination with the mechanics of emotion and the creative process, two ostensibly disparate themes in which Ovid sees vast similarities.

Petronius: Petronius Arbiter, c.27 – 65 CE; *Satyricon* (3, 6). The specific identity of Petronius is unknown. Manuscripts of the *Satyricon* identify him as Titus Petronius, but the Petronius at work in the emperor Nero's court as his *arbiter elegentiae* (arbiter of good taste) has become generally accepted as the author of the *Satyricon*. The *Satyricon* is one of the few, and certainly the most prominent, examples of ancient prose fiction. A collection of different stories interwoven with the humorously ill-fated travels of its two main characters Encolpius and Giton (a third, Ascyltus, disappears from the text midway through), the *Satyricon* is best known for the character Trimalchio and the extravagant dinner party he throws, which Petronius describes in lavish detail; Trimalchio, an ex-slave who has made his fortune, is a classic satire of the *nouveau riche*. The selections in this volume come from the story of the Matron of Ephesus, in which a faithful woman mourns her recently dead husband but is tempted by the advances of a soldier.

Plautus: Titus Maccius Plautus, c.250 – 184 BCE. Plautus wrote comic plays based on Greek originals of the 4th and 3rd centuries BCE. The humor of his plays lies in the satirizing of Roman character-types and Roman daily life, rather than contemporary politics; while the basic narrative and even setting often reflects the plays' Greek origins, Plautus adapted many of the cultural aspects of his models to reflect Roman *mores*. Over 130 plays have been attributed to Plautus, but the Roman author Varro identifies only 21 as authentically Plautine (the others would have been said to have been written by Plautus to attach to them the cachet that Plautus' name carries with it).

Menaechmi **(1, 7, 8, 9, 10, 15, 16, 17, 20, 22, 23, 24, 25, 27, 28, 29, 30, 31, 32).** Identical twin sons, Menaechmus and Sosicles, journeyed to Tarentum where Menaechmus was kidnapped. The other brother, Sosicles, returned home where he was renamed in honor of his lost, and presumed dead, twin. When Sosicles was grown, he decided to travel the Mediterranean to find evidence of his brother Menaechmus, whether dead or alive. When the play opens, he and his slave Messenio have arrived in Epidamnus, coincidentally the town where Menaechmus lives. The play then becomes a series of confusing interactions and misidentifications as each brother functions in Epidamnus without knowing that his identical twin is also in the town. Eventually, the brothers are of course reunited. *Menaechmi* is the classical antecedent for Shakespeare's *A Comedy of Errors*. (A textual note: The identical names of the twin brothers, the very device on which the comedy of the play rests, itself poses problems when publishing the play. Editors tend to refer to the brothers as Menaechmus I and Menaechmus II, or as Menaechmus and Sosicles. In the present volume, the latter convention will be used, if for no other reason than because the play is excerpted in short segments, it becomes even more important to distinguish between the twin brothers and their roles in a given scene.)

> **Erotium.** The mistress of Menaechmus.
> **Menaechmus & Sosicles.** Twin brothers. Menaechmus was kidnapped as a youth and Sosicles was renamed Menaechmus in his honor. Sosicles has been travelling the Mediterranean looking for evidence of Menaechmus and, having arrived in Epidamnus, has unwittingly found it.
> **Messenio.** The slave of Sosicles.
> **Peniculus.** The mooch of Menaechmus.

Miles Gloriosus **(1, 2, 4, 9, 10, 11, 13, 22, 30, 31, 32).** An arrogant soldier has arrived in Ephesus with the lover of an Athenian who is out of town. The Athenian's slave travels to tell him, but is captured and is presented to the arrogant soldier as a gift. Reunited with his master's lover, the slave writes to his master in Athens and schemes to reunite them without incurring the wrath of the soldier. *Miles Gloriosus* is one of the ancient comedies upon which the musical *A Funny Thing Happened on the Way to the Forum* is based; one of the main characters in the musical is named Miles Gloriosus.

Pyrgopolynices. The *Miles Gloriosus* of the title.

Artotrogus. The mooch of Pyrgopolynices.

Periplectomenus. The kindly old man who lives next door to Pyrgopolynices and will conspire with Palaestrio to reunite Philocomasium with Pleusicles.

Palaestrio. The current slave of Pyrgopolynices and the former slave of Pleusicles.

Philocomasium. The current but unwilling girl of Pyrgopolynices and the former girl of Pleusicles.

Pleusicles. Philocomasium's boyfriend, with whom Palaestrio is trying to reunite her.

Pliny: Gaius Plinius Caecilius Secundus, 63 – c.113 CE; *Epistulae* **(4, 12, 17, 22, 23, 28, 29, 30, 31).** After his father died young, Pliny traveled to Rome to further his education with, among others, Quintillian, a famous Roman teacher whose writings have survived (but have not been included in the present volume). Although Pliny was a prolific writer, most of his writings have been lost. What has survived is Pliny's *epistulae* or letters, a voluminous collection of letters that he wrote to his friends and colleagues that preserves a unique window into Roman daily and administrative life. The letters survive in ten books, the first nine of which became literary epistles, i.e. Pliny prepared them and envisioned them, even if not originally, for publication. The last book is comprised of letters between Pliny and the emperor Trajan about Pliny's duties as governor of Bithynia-Pontus, a region of ancient Rome in modern-day Turkey; it is in Book 10 that the famous Christian letters appear, in which Pliny and Trajan discuss how Pliny should handle the Christians in his region.

Seneca: Lucius Annaeus Seneca, c.4 BCE – 65 CE; *Phaedra* **(7, 9, 10, 11, 12, 15, 16, 17, 19, 20, 23, 24, 26, 28, 32).** Phaedra is a tragic heroine of ancient literature. The wife of the Athenian hero Theseus, she fell in love with Hippolytus, Theseus' son by a previous marriage. Ultimately rejected by Hippolytus, Phaedra commits suicide, whether because she was afraid that Theseus would discover her feelings or out of shame over Hippolytus' rejection of her (different authors tell different stories). The Roman philosopher (and lesser known tragic playwright) Seneca characterizes Phaedra less sympathetically than the Greek playwright Euripides. In Seneca, Phaedra herself (instead of her nurse) tells Hippolytus of her feelings and, upon his rejection of her, tells Theseus of his (fabricated) rape of her. She then kills herself and dies over Hippolytus' body.

Vergil: Publius Vergilius Maro, 70-19 BCE. The most famous Roman poet, Vergil was born near what is today Milan, Italy and eventually travelled to Rome. There, after publishing his first set of poetry, the *Eclogues*, he was accepted into the literary coterie of Augustus' patron of the arts, Maecenas; Vergil would introduce the poet Horace into the same group. Vergil next published a series of poems, the *Georgics*, that ostensibly provided practical advice for farming and animal husbandry but in reality did so as a glorification of the simple life of the country. The *Aeneid*, Vergil's final and most famous text, cemented his reputation as Rome's most famous poet; in the Middle Ages, his fame took on a spiritual component: the *Aeneid* was used as means for foretelling the future (the so-called *Sortes Vergilianae*), and the Italian poet Dante made Vergil his guide through hell in his *Inferno*.

Aeneid **(1, 2, 3, 4, 5, 6, 8, 11, 13, 15, 16, 17, 21, 23, 24, 27, 32).** Vergil's epic poem of twelve books charts the heroic journey of the Trojan Aeneas from Troy to the shores of Italy. The first six books of the *Aeneid* are Vergil's "Odyssey", i.e. the journey of Aeneas from Troy to Italy, while the second six books are Vergil's "Iliad", i.e. the protracted conflict and battle between Aeneas and his Trojans and the indigineous Italians who oppose his settlement. The first six books of the *Aeneid* are by far the more popular. Book 1 finds Aeneas stranded in a storm at sea sent by Juno who hates Aeneas because the Romans, in whose founding Aeneas will play a part, will conquer the Carthaginians, Juno's chosen people; the book ends with Aeneas arriving in Carthage where he is welcomed by queen Dido, who invites Aeneas to tell the tale of his journey. Book 2 then begins Aeneas' tale to Dido and the Carthaginians and details the fall of Troy. Book 3 covers Aeneas' journey from Troy to Carthage and the stops he made along the way. Book 4, Aeneas' tale completed, narrates the tragic love affair of Aeneas and Dido, which culminates in Aeneas' sudden departure from Carthage and Dido's suicide. Book 5 describes Aeneas' journey from Carthage to Italy and Book 6 follows Aeneas to the underworld, whose gateway is in Italy near Naples, where Aeneas meets his father, who died on the journey to Italy, and sees the future leaders of Rome.

***Eclogues* (4, 24, 28, 29, 30).** Vergil wrote his ten Eclogues in imitation of the pastoral poems of the Greek poet Theocritus. Pastoral poems, or bucolics as they are also known, most commonly have shepherds reciting their own tales of love, mythology, and the art of their own singing / poetry. Vergil's most famous Eclogue, the fourth, with no precedent in Greek literature, tells of a young boy, not yet born, who will save Rome from the state of degredation into which she has sunk. Later Christian readers, because of its connection with the birth of Christ, used this poem to confer upon Vergil a quasi-Christian status. Though by no means Christian, Vergil, and more important, his texts, were considered more acceptable because of this poem than many of his fellow pagans, whose texts were routinely destroyed or reused for the copying of Christian texts.

CHAPTER 1

Chapter One introduces both the verb and important terminology for learning and understanding a language. The verb is the most important aspect of the Latin sentence, and will carry more information than the English verb does. Thus it is essential to understand how the Latin verb works in order to understand how a Latin sentence works.

The list of **Terms to Know** is conspicuously long: this chapter introduces a lot of terminology that will be used throughout the book and in many cases will be reintroduced and expanded upon in later chapters; subsequent lists of Terms to Know will not be this long.

1. The Sentence

    1. Why is it important to know Latin endings?

2. Parts of Speech

    1. What English part of speech does Latin not have?

    2. What are the three things that a verb expresses?

    3. What are the five things that a noun names?

    4. Which two types of words does an adjective modify?

    5. What kind of word does an adverb modify?

   • An adverb can also modify adjectives or other adverbs.

    e.g. The really tall man runs very fast.

       "Fast" is an adverb modifying the verb "runs,"
          i.e. how does the man run? Fast.

       "Really" is an adverb modifying the adjective "tall,"
          i.e. how tall is the man? Really tall.

       "Very" is an adverb modifying the adverb "fast,"
          i.e. how fast does the man run? Very fast.

Terms to Know

sentence
part of speech
verb
noun
adjective
adverb
preposition
pronoun
conjunction
interjection
subject
direct object
intransitive
transitive
conjugation
stem
personal endings
person
number
finite forms (verbs)
tense
voice
mood
infinitive
principal parts
complementary
  infinitive

6. What four types of information does an adverb give?

7. What does a preposition do?

- Prepositions and the relationships they convey vary from language to language, so where Latin might use the preposition "in" (same word in both English and Latin), English might translate that preposition with "in," "on," "to," "against," etc.

- It is essential then to understand the context within which a prepositional phrase occurs to be able to best translate that preposition into English

- Relying on a list of definitions to translate a preposition from a glossary or dictionary is not enough in some instances. Context and successfully capturing the meaning of the Latin in English will ultimately determine the translation of a preposition.

8. What does a pronoun do?

9. What does a conjunction do?

10. What is an interjection?

3. Function (What Words Do)

1. What is a subject?

2. What is a direct object?

Function (What Words Do) Text

Anonymous, *Carmina Burana, In Taberna* 33-48. In this excerpt from a descriptive poem about a Medieval bar, the types of people drinking are described.

- In the excerpt, the subjects are italicized and the verbs are underlined.

- Based on your observations of these subects and verbs and on what you know of how Latin conveys meaning, complete the following:

  □ Make at least two observations about how Latin works, or the differences between Latin and English. These observations should reflect a deliberate and insightful interaction with the language. You are not, however, necessarily expected to understand the meaning of the excerpt as a whole.

  □ Attempt to identify the part of speech of one of the words neither underlined nor italicized.

Bibit hera, bibit herus,
bibit mīles, bibit clerus,
bibit ille, bibit illa,
bibit servus cum ancillā,
bibit vēlox, bibit piger,
bibit albus, bibit niger,
bibit constans, bibit vagus,
bibit rudis, bibit magus.

Bibit pauper et egrōtus,
bibit exul et ignōtus,
bibit puer, bibit cānus,
bibit presul et decanus,
bibit soror, bibit frāter,
bibit anus, bibit māter,
bibit ista, bibit ille,
bibunt centum, bibunt mille.

Bibit *hera*, bibit *herus*,
bibit *mīles*, bibit *clerus*,
bibit *ille*, bibit *illa*,
bibit *servus* cum ancillā,
bibit *vēlox*, bibit *piger*,   5
bibit *albus*, bibit *niger*,
bibit *constans*, bibit *vagus*,
bibit *rudis*, bibit *magus*.

Bibit *pauper* et *egrōtus*,
bibit *exul* et *ignōtus*,   10
bibit *puer*, bibit *cānus*,
bibit *presul* et *decanus*,
bibit *soror*, bibit *frāter*,
bibit *anus*, bibit *māter*,
bibit *ista*, bibit *ille*,   15
bibunt *centum*, bibunt *mille*.

4. Sentence Patterns

1. What is the difference between the transitive sentence pattern and the intransitive sentence pattern?

Sentence Patterns Text

Carmina Burana. [Refer to the poem above for the questions below.]

2. Is the verb of the above excerpt, *bibit / bibunt*, used transitively or intransitively? Explain your answer.

3. In line 13 above, if *bibit* means "drinks," *soror* means "sister," and *frater* means "brother," what would those two clauses mean?

4. A transitive sentence based on the poem above would be:

   a.   Bibit soror **aquam**, bibit frāter **lac**.

5. If *aquam* means "water" and *lac* means "milk," what would the transitive sentence above mean?

Sentence Patterns Exercise

6. Identify which of the following English sentences are grammatically correct. Your determination will be based on whether or not the verbs of the English sentences are transitive or intransitive.

    a. The man was lying in bed.

    b. The man was lying the book on the table.

    c. The man was laying in bed.

    d. The man was laying the book on the table.

    e. The woman's arm itched.

    f. The woman's arm scratched.

    g. The woman itched her arm.

    h. The woman scratched her arm.

5. The Verb

1. What is a conjugation? How many does Latin have?

2. In the vocabulary list on page 11 of your textbook, you will notice that each verb has four Latin forms listed; these forms are the verb's principal parts.

3. The stem of a verb is formed by removing the *-re* from the second principal part of a verb.

    a. amāre → [*subtract the* -re] → amā(re) → amā- = stem

    b. docēre → [*subtract the* -re] → docē(re) → docē- = stem

4. Onto the stem of a verb are added personal endings. Why are they called personal endings?

5. What are finite forms or verbs? Why are they called this?

6. What are the three translations for the present tense?

7. Why is an infinitive called an "infinitive?"

The Verb Exercise

8. Form the stems for the following verbs from the vocabulary list on page 11 of your textbook.

    a. iuvāre

    b. labōrāre

    c. superāre

    d. tacēre

    e. timēre

    f. vidēre

    g. vocāre

The Verb Text, Indicative

Brown University Motto

In Deō spērāmus.

Vocabulary

Deus, -ī. god   **spērō, -āre.** to trust, to hope

1. Translate the motto.

The Verb Text, Indicative

Vergil, *Aeneid* 4.208-210. When Dido founded Carthage, she had fled from her murderous brother who had killed her husband. In honor of her husband's memory, she foreswore men (a pledge she will later break with Aeneas). One of Dido's suitors was a local ruler named Iarbas. When he heard of Dido's relationship with Aeneas, he angrily prayed to Jupiter for justice.

> An tē, genitor, cum fulmina torquēs
> nēquīquam horrēmus, caecīque in nūbibus ignēs
> terrificant animōs et inānia murmura miscent?   210

1. Identify one verb with "we" as the subject.
2. Identify two verbs with "they" as the subject.

The Verb Text, Indicative

Plautus, *Menaechmi* 551. The maid of the mistress of Menaechmus has just given Sosicles her mistress' bracelet to take to the jeweler. Sosicles, of course, not recognizing the maid, is thankful that he has just received a free bracelet, and muses here about how fortunate he is.

Sosicles. Dī mē quidem omnēs adiuvant, augent, amant.

Plautus, *Menaechmi* 966-967. Menaechmus has just finished speculating on the strange day he's had; his father-in-law and doctor have just accused him of things that he did not do. Messenio, the slave of Sosicles, hears Menaechmus' soliloquy and responds with his own about the duty of a slave to his master, the opening of which is excerpted here. The irony of course is that the man for whom Messenio will perform such duties is not in actuality his master.

Messenio. Spectāmen bonō servō id est, quī rem erīlem
prōcūrat, videt, collocat cōgitatque,…

1. Identify the seven verbs in the previous two excerpts, three in the first and four in the second. (In the second excerpt, in line 966, *est* is a verb but, because it is an irregular verb, it is not included in the four to be found.)
2. Identify each of the verbs' conjugation.
3. Identify each of the verbs' subjects, based on its ending.

The Verb Text, Indicative

Martial 1.89. Martial criticizes a certain Cinna for talking too much. He ends the poem by wondering whether Cinna's garrulousness affects how his praises of the emperor are received.

Garrīs in aurem semper omnibus, Cinna,
garrīs et illud teste quod licet turba.
Rīdēs in aurem, quereris, arguis, plōrās,
cantās in aurem, iūdicās, tacēs, clamās,
adeōque penitus sēdit hic tibi morbus,　　　　　　5
ut saepe in aurem, Cinna, Caesarem laudēs.

1. Identify the twelve finite verbs in the poem. Use a combination of characteristic vowels and personal endings to identify the verb forms.
2. There is one infinitive in the poem. Identify it, based on the infinitive ending.

The Verb Text, Indicative

Plautus, *Miles Gloriosus* **206-210.** The slave Palaestrio and the kindly old man Periplectomenus are conspiring to bring together a young woman who is the consort of Pyrgopolynices, Palaestrio's master, the Miles Gloriosus of the title, and her former lover, who happens to be living in Periplectomenus' house next door. In this excerpt, Periplectomenus, the old man, is observing the physical manifestations of Palaestrio's mental scheming.

Periplectomenus. Concrepuit digitīs: labōrat; crēbrō commūtat statūs.
Eccere autem capite nūtat: nōn placet quod repperit.
Quidquid est, incoctum nōn exprōmet, bene coctum dābit.
Ecce autem aedificat: columnam mentō suffīgit suō.
Apage, nōn placet profectō mī illaec aedificātio;   210

1. Fill in the following table with the requested information based on the finite verbs in the excerpt above.

Line #	Verb	Conjugation	First 2 Principal Parts
206	labōrat		
206	commūtat		
207	nūtat		
207	placet		
209	aedificat		
210	placet		

2. A number of verbs from the excerpt whose forms you have not yet learned were left out of the table. They are explained below.

   concrepuit (206) = the perfect tense, from the third principal part

   reperrit (207) = the perfect tense, from the third principal part

   exprōmet (208) = the future tense of a third conjugation verb

   dābit (208) = the future tense of a first conjugation verb

   suffīgit (209) = the perfect tense, from the third principal part

The Verb Text, Indicative

Martial 6.60. Martial sees all of Rome praising his poetry to such an extent that one Roman gentleman is overcome physically.

Laudat, amat, cantat nostrōs mea Rōma libellōs,
    mēque sinūs omnis [habent], mē manus omnis habet.
Ecce rubet quīdam, pallet, stupet, oscitat, ōdit.
    Hoc volō: nunc nōbīs carmina nostra placent.

---

1. The *habent* of line 2 is not in Martial's original poem, but is included to assist with the exercise below.
2. Finish the translation below by translating the verbs in brackets.

    My home city Rome _____ [*laudat*] my poetry, _____ [*amat*] my poetry, and _____ [*cantat; cantō, -āre* = "sings about"] my poetry / and every lap _____ [*habent*] me, every hand _____ [*habet*] me.

3. Identify the conjugation of all of the verbs in line 3. What is the one verb whose conjugation you can't identify?
4. There are two verbs in line 4, one irregular and one second conjugation. Identify them both.

The Verb Text, Infinitive

Marist College (NY) Motto

Ōrāre et labōrāre.

Vocabulary

ōrō, -āre. to pray

---

1. Translate the motto.
2. What is the understood question that the motto answers?

The Verb Text, Infinitive

Martial 7.60. Martial slyly draws a distinction between the god Jupiter, whom he addresses in the first line, and the emperor, wondering what good it does him to praise Jupiter, when it is the emperor who will exert the most salient and direct influence over his life.

Tarpēiae venerande rector aulae,
quem salvō duce crēdimus Tonantem,
cum vōtīs sibī quisque tē fatīget
et poscat dare quae deī potestis:
nīl prō mē mihi, Iuppiter, petentī   5
nē suscensueris velut superbō.
Tē prō Caesare dēbeō rogāre:
prō mē dēbeō Caesarem rogāre.

---

1. Identify the three infinitives in the above poem. (One is repeated.)
2. Complete the translation of lines 7-8 below by translating the infinitives in brackets.

   > I ought _____ [*rogāre*] you [i.e. Jupiter] on behalf of Caesar: / I ought _____ [*rogāre*] Caesar on behalf of myself.

The *Tarpēiae* of line 1 refers to the Tarpeian rock, located on the Capitoline Hill next to the temple of Jupiter Optimus Maximus. Tarpeia was a Roman woman who lived during the Roman monarchy and who betrayed Rome by letting Rome's enemy into the city. The deal she had struck with the enemy was that she would receive what they wore on their wrists, i.e. their jewelry, in return for her faithlessness. Indeed, she did receive what they wore on their wrists, but in this case it was their shields, because they were in full military gear: they crushed her under the weight of them.

The Verb Text, Infinitive

Vergil, *Aeneid* 2.10-13. Dido, smitten with Aeneas, invites him to recount to her and her dinner guests his travails. Aeneas agrees because she so wants to hear the tale but admits that it will be difficult for him to recount such sadness.

Sed sī tantus amor cāsūs cognōscere nostrōs   10
et breviter Trōiae suprēmum audīre labōrem,
quamquam animus meminisse horret lūctūque refūgit,
incipiam.

1. Complete the following translation of lines 10-11 by translating the verbs in brackets.

> But if there is such a desire in you _____ [cognōscere; cognōsco, -ere = know] my misfortunes / and _____ [audīre; audiō, -īre = hear] briefly the final struggle of Troy...

2. What are the two third-person verbs in line 12?

3. Which of them is a second conjugation verb? Explain your answer.

6. Principal Parts

- The three principal parts of English verbs are: 1. the infinitive form (without the "to"); 2. the perfect indicative or simple past form; and 3. the past participle.

  - for regular verbs, principal parts are formed by adding -ed to the infinitive

    walk, walked, walked

  - for irregular verbs, -ed is generally not used

    run, ran, ran
    fall, fell, fallen

  - the English verbs "lie" and "lay" are often confused because their principal parts overlap:

    lie, lay, laid
    lay, laid, lain

  Do the principal parts above change any of your answers to exercise 4.6 (on page 4)?

- From the vocabulary list on page 11 in your textbook, write out the four principal parts of six verbs of your choice, three from the first conjugation and three from the second conjugation.

7. Indicative and Infinitive Uses

1. What is an indicative verb used for?

2. What is the difference between the way Latin and English express questions?

3. What is a common use of the infinitive?

4. What is the term for this use?

CHAPTER 2

While Chapter 1 introduced the Latin verb, Chapter 2 introduces the Latin noun. The two most common cases are presented: the nominative and the accusative cases, used for the subject of a sentence and the direct object of a sentence, and equivalent to the English subjective and objective cases. The concept of declension, the category into which each Latin noun is placed, and the concept of grammatical gender are introduced, as well as the endings of the first two declensions. The concept of sentence structure is also introduced, with looks at the conjunction and using expectations, both of which are important first steps for understanding Latin.

> **Terms to Know**
>
> case
> nominative
> accusative
> declension
> number
> gender
> dictionary entry
> coordinating
>   conjunction

8. Latin Cases and Case Uses

1. How many cases does Latin have (including the final, less common case)?

2. List along with each case its primary usage.

- English has three cases: the subjective, the possessive, and the objective.

    □ The English subjective is equivalent to the Latin nominative.

    □ The English possessive is equivalent to the Latin genitive.

    □ The English objective is equivalent to the Latin dative, accusative, and ablative.

    □ English cases are in general not visible in most nouns:

    The servant sees the Gauls.
    The Gauls see the servant.

    – The servant and the Gauls change grammatical function (from subject to direct object and vice versa) because they change word order.

    – Their forms, i.e. the spelling of the words themselves, remain exactly the same even when their grammatical function changes.

□   Latin cases and so grammatical function are visible in their noun forms, and the endings that represent these cases must be known and recognized.

Servus videt Gallum.
Gallum videt servus.

–   Do these two Latin sentences mean the same thing?

Serv**us** videt Gall**um**.
Gall**um** videt serv**us**.

–   Because the endings on the nouns remain the same, even though the order of the nouns is different, the meaning of these sentences is the same.

Servus videt Gallum.
Servum videt Gallus.

–   Do these two Latin sentences mean the same thing?

Serv**us** videt Gall**um**.
Serv**um** videt Gall**us**.

–   Because the endings on the nouns are different, even though their order remains the same, the meaning of these sentences is different.

□   The way Latin cases work is still evident in the forms and usage of English pronouns.

"Him followed his next mate."
(John Milton, *Paradise Lost* 1.238)

–   In the above sentence, who followed whom? Or, of the two nouns, "him" and "mate," which is the subject and which is the object?

–   The sentence might not make immediate sense because English speakers are accustomed to using word order rather than case or forms to understand a sentence.

–   The word order in the Milton quote violates our grammatical expectations because "him," which we want to make the subject, comes first.

–   But, because English pronouns do indicate meaning through form, "him" can come first and not be the subject; the form "him," rather than placement, indicates its meaning. If it were the subject, its form would have to be, as you know, "he".

–   Indeed, "him" is the object and "mate" is the subject, despite their word order; his next mate followed him.

–   The process of understanding this type of English, while unnatural at first, becomes easier with practice. (Remember that Yoda speaks perfectly understandable

English even though he speaks in a very non-traditional word order.) The same will hold true for Latin. You will have to retrain your brain to rely not on word order for meaning but rather on case. In Latin, the ending, rather than the word order, will yield meaning.

English pronouns are the source of constant grammatical confusion because of the unfamiliarity of a case system to English speakers.

Commonly, the English subjective pronoun, especially "I," will be used more frequently than is grammatically correct because it is perceived to sound more intelligent or more cultivated (when in reality it has the opposite effect, because it is wrong).

— "between you and I" = "between you and me," because "between," as a preposition, requires the objective case "me"

Question words are commonly mistaken as well, because of their required violation of word order (relative pronouns also, but both of these will be discussed in a later chapter).

— "Who did you see at the party?" = "Whom did you see at the party?", because "whom" is the object of "see" and as the object requires the English objective case. The "m" ending of the objective case here is the same "m" of "him" and "them" and of the Latin accusative singular.

9. The Noun

1. What is a declension?
2. How many declensions does Latin have?
3. How is the base of a Latin noun formed?

- It is a common mistake to view the nominative singular as a more important form than the genitive singular. The genitive singular form, however, has two consistencies that are essential to understanding a noun:
  □ the genitive singular will provide the base for the noun
  □ the genitive singular will identify the declension of a noun
- As you learn more nouns and noun endings, you will find that some nominative endings overlap, i.e. a noun of the second declension can have the same nominative singular as a noun of the third declension. The genitive singular ending, which will be unique for each declension, will identify to which declension these nouns with like nominative endings belong.

10. Gender

1. How many genders are there and what are they?
2. What is the gender of most first declension nouns?
3. What are the four most common masculine nouns of the first declension?

   _____

   • other masculine nouns of the first declension:
     aurīga, -ae = *charioteer*
     pīrāta, -ae = *pirate*

   _____

4. What are the three most common non-masculine -*us* nouns of the second declension (include their genders in your answer)?
5. What does the -*um* ending in the nominative of a second declension noun indicate?

11. Dictionary Entry

1. What forms does the dictionary entry for a noun include?
2. Why is the genitive singular form important?

Dictionary Entry Exercise

Using the following ten nouns from the vocabulary list on page 20 of the textbook, identify the declension, base, and gender of each noun.

1. amīcus, -ī
2. animus, -ī
3. bellum, -ī
4. dominus, -ī
5. littera, -ae

6. nātūra, -ae
7. puer, puerī
8. puella, -ae
9. regnum, -ī
10. vir, virī

12. First Declension

1. Using the forms of the first declension noun *fēmina* that appear on page 15 of your textbook, identify the vowel common to most first declension endings.

   _____

   • The horizontal line that distinguishes the ablative singular from the nominative singular, and appears over some other vowels as well, is called a macron (pl. = macra). The macron renders a vowel long.
   • Not all texts will use macra, so it is important to know naturally long endings (the ablative singular, and dative and ablative plural

being common examples), but it is also important to learn to recognize these forms from context.

- ☐ The *-ā* of the ablative singular will not only overlap with the *-a* of the nominative singular, but also with the *-a* of the neuter nominative and accusative plural (of the second declension in this chapter); the *-īs* of the dative and ablative plural will overlap with the *-is* of the third declension genitive singular (which you will learn in a later chapter). In texts that do not use macra, these forms will be more difficult to distinguish.

- ☐ Recognizing the forms of endings that overlap is dependent on a comination of vocabulary, i.e. knowing the declension of a given noun, and context, i.e. recognizing what case might better fit the meaning of a given clause.

13. Second Declension

1. What are the three possible nominative singular endings for second declension nouns?
2. What is the "neuter rule?" Or, what do all neuter nominative and accusative forms have in common?

- The "neuter rule" will apply not just to second declension neuters but to all neuter nouns that you will learn.

First and Second Declension Nouns Text

Vergil, *Aeneid* **1.1.** These are the iconic first words of Vergil's *Aeneid*, memorized (in addition to subsequent lines) by countless students, and recalling the epic convention of Homer that states at the outset both the hero and the theme of the poem.

Arma virumque canō,

Vocabulary

arma, -ōrum. arms, weapons, war
canō, -ere. to sing, to recite (poetry)

1. What is the gender of each accusative noun?
2. Using the vocabulary above, translate the excerpt.

First and Second Declension Nouns Text

Catullus 23.7-11. In this poem Catullus is addressing one Furius who, according to Catullus, has everything going for him: his father takes care of everything he needs. In this excerpt, Catullus is reinforcing what Furius need not be afraid of (*timetis nihil*).

...bene nam valētis omnēs,	...bene nam valētis omnēs,
pulcre concoquitis, nihil timētis,	pulcre concoquitis, nihil timētis,
nōn <u>incendia</u>, nōn gravēs <u>ruīnās</u>,	nōn incendia, nōn gravēs ruīnās,
nōn <u>facta</u> impia, nōn <u>dolos</u> venēnī,	nōn facta impia, nōn dolos venēnī,
nōn cāsūs aliōs perīculōrum.	nōn cāsūs aliōs perīculōrum.

1. All of the nouns underlined above are in the accusative case. Identify the gender, number, and declension of all of the underlined nouns. An unannotated text is next to the underlined text for reference.

First and Second Declension Nouns Text

Martial 2.48. Martial here draws a distinction between the simpler life of the country and the hectic life of the city.

Cōpōnem laniumque <u>balneumque</u>,	Cōpōnem laniumque balneumque,
tonsōrem tabulamque <u>calculōsque</u>	tonsōrem tabulamque calculōsque
et <u>paucōs</u>, sed ut ēligam, <u>libellōs</u>:	et paucōs, sed ut ēligam, libellōs:
<u>ūnum</u> nōn nimium *<u>rudem sodālem</u>*	ūnum nōn nimium rudem sodālem
et *<u>grandem</u>* <u>puerum</u> diuque *<u>levem</u>*	et grandem puerum diuque levem 5
et <u>cāram</u> puerō meō <u>puellam</u>:	et cāram puerō meō puellam:
haec praestā mihi, Rufe, vel Butuntīs,	haec praestā mihi, Rufe, vel Butuntīs,
et <u>thermās</u> tibi habē <u>Nerōniānās</u>.	et thermās tibi habē Nerōniānās.

1. All underlined nouns are in the accusative case.
2. Identify the gender, number and declension of these nouns (the italicized, underlined nouns are not first or second declension; you will be introduced to those endings later).
3. The double-underlined words are adjectives, which will use the same endings as first and second declension nouns (the italicized, double-underlined adjectives do not use these endings; you will be introduced to their endings later.)

First and Second Declension Nouns Text

Plautus, *Miles Gloriosus* 189-189a. The scene is the same as is described in the *Miles Gloriosus* excerpt of Chapter 1: the old man Periplectomenus and the slave Palaestrio plot to illicitly bring together a young man and a young woman. In this excerpt Palaestrio gives Periplectomenus instructions to pass on to the young woman: use her feminine wiles to her advantage and deny under every circumstance that she was in the same house as the man she wants to be with.

Ōs habet, linguam, perfidiam, malitiam atque audāciam,
confidentiam, confirmitātem, fraudulentiam.   189a

---

1. How many first declension accusatives are in the above excerpt?
2. Translate *habet* in line 188. Who is its subject? Explain your answer.
3. Choose two of the direct objects of *habet* and translate them with it based on English words derived from the Latin words.

First and Second Declension Nouns Text

Peter Damian, *On the Paradise of God* 1-3, 13-21. A description of what Heaven might look like.

Ad perennis <u>vītae</u> fontem mens sītivit *ārida*,
<u>claustra</u> carnis praestō frangī *clausa* quaerit <u>anima</u>,
gliscit, ambit, ēluctatur exul fruī <u>patriā</u>...

Hiems horrens, aestus torrens, illīc numquam saeviunt,
flōs *perpetuus* <u>rosārum</u> vēr agit *perpetuum*,   5
candent <u>līlia</u>, rubescit <u>crocus</u>, sūdat <u>balsamum</u>.

Virent <u>prāta</u>, vernant <u>sata</u>, <u>rīvī</u> mellis influunt;
<u>pigmentōrum</u> spīrat odor, liquor et arōmatum;
pendent <u>pōma</u> *flōridōrum* nōn *lapsūra* nemorum.

Nōn alternat <u>lūna</u> vicēs, sōl vel cursus sīderum;   10
<u>agnus</u> est fēlīcis urbis lūmen *inocciduum*;
nox et tempus dēsunt <u>ei</u>, diem fert *continuum*...

In the annotated text above, the underlined words are first or second declension nouns; the italicized words are first and second declension adjectives which will use first and second declension endings.

1. Identify all possible cases, numbers, and genders, along with the corresponding declension, for all underlined nouns.

2. Of the words that are neither underlined nor italicized, i.e. they are not first or second declension nouns, identify ten that have endings that overlap with first and second declension nouns.

3. Identify five verbs and, using their endings, identify their subjects.

First and Second Declension Nouns Text

Vergil, *Aeneid* **4.50.** Anna, the sister of Dido, who encourages her to forsake her vow to her dead husband Sychaeus and pursue a relationship with Aeneas, here advises her to pray to the gods.

Tū modo posce deōs veniam,

---

1. The above excerpt illustrates a double accusative.

2. What are the two accusatives of the double accusative?

3. Finish the translation below by supplying the two accusatives.

> Now, demand _____ [*veniam; venia, -ae* = forgiveness] _____ [*deōs*].

14. The Conjunction

- Conjunctions create parallel structure, i.e. grammatical structures that have the same functions.

  - The sailor <u>helps</u>
        and
        <u>works</u>.

  - <u>The woman</u>
    and
    <u>the man</u> teach.

  - The boy <u>shouts</u>
        but
    the man <u>is silent</u>.

- The use of the Latin conjunction *-que* can be confusing because it is attached to the second word of the joined pair.
  - Thus, "peanut butter and jelly" could be rewritten as:
    peanut butter *et* jelly
    peanut butter jelly*que*

- Conjunctions are perhaps the most important words for understanding the structure of complex Latin sentences. They often serve as markers for such structure.

15. Reading Latin: Using Expectations

- You realize the importance of context when faced with very technical language in your own language, e.g. reading an instructional manual for a very advanced or specific piece of technology, or reading an article about a technical scientific topic.[1]

- Even though something is written in English, a language you speak easily and freely, that is no guarantee that you will understand the meaning of it. This disparity between knowledge and understanding illustrates the importance of context.

- When you read Latin, you will require two types of context:
  - **cultural:** it will be difficult to read Latin if you don't have some idea of what you're reading and the necessary background information to understand it; your teacher and /or books should provide this for you in the form of introduction, notes, etc.

  - **grammatical:** more important, perhaps, is developing a sense of expectation as you read Latin; as certain parts of the sentence become clear, they will dictate the grammar of subsequent parts of the sentence.

  - As you become familiar with more grammatical constructions, your sense of grammatical context will become more developed.

---

1   See Ken Kitchell, "Latin III's Dirty Little Secret: Why Johnny Can't Read," *New England Classical Journal* 27 (2000) 205-226 for a compelling discussion of the impact of expectations on comprehension.

CHAPTER 3

Chapter 3 introduces two additional cases, the genitive and the dative, equivalent to the English possessive and objective cases. Further discussion of using expectations, and another sentence pattern is also included.

Terms to Know

genitive
possession
partitive
dative
indirect object
reference

16. Genitive Case

1. With what English preposition is the genitive often translated?
2. What are the two most common uses of the genitive case?
3. Define what is meant by the Partitive Genitive (Part of a Whole).

- It is important to understand that the genitive case can be thought of as the adjective case. (The ablative, a case not yet learned, will function as the adverb case.)

- Two practical considerations emerge from the genitive as the adjective case:

  □ When confronted with a genitive noun, you should consider with which other noun in a sentence the genitive should be read.

    – In the examples on page 21 of your book, the *puellae* of *liber puellae* is read with *liber* as is the *virī* of *animus virī* with *animus*.

  □ The genitive in English will be used to define a Latin adjective when there is no corresponding English adjective.

    – The Latin adjective *patrius, -a, -um* means "of or belonging to the fatherland or homeland."

    – English does not have a corresponding adjective; we could create something like "fatherlandly."

    – To compensate for the lack of an English adjective, the English genitive "of the fatherland" is used.

    – Thus *imperium patrium* means "the fatherlandly power" or, more appropriate, "the power of the fatherland," even though the Latin *patrium* is an adjective and not a genitive noun.

Genitive Case Text

Archipoeta, *Aestuans intrinsecus* **73-76.** The Archpoet in this poem forsakes his profligate life for one more reflective and spiritual. The final stanza of the poem, excerpted below, recalls the innate confidence of the lion, the *rex ferārum*, which the Archpoet asks the leaders of men to emulate.

Parcit enim subditīs leō, rex ferārum,
et est ergā subditōs immemor īrārum;
et vōs idem facite, principēs terrārum!
Quod caret dulcēdine nimis est amārum.

Vocabulary

leō, leōnis. lion	**īra, -ae.** anger
rex, rēgis. king	**princeps, principis.** prince,
fera, -ae. wild beast	leader
immemor, -oris. unmindful (of)	**terra, -ae.** land

1. There are three genitives in the passage. What are they (*amārum* in line 4 is not a genitive, although it looks like one)?
2. If the *leō* is described as the *rex ferārum*, what/who is he? How is he described?
3. What does the phrase *immemor īrārum* indicate that the *leō* has put aside or is unmindful of?
4. What do the *principēs* have power over, as indicated by the phrase *principēs terrārum*?

Genitive Case Text

Catullus 4.1-4. Catullus dedicates his fourth poem to a *phaselus*, a small boat, that has safely conveyed him, according to the rest of the poem, throughout the ancient world.

Phasēlus ille, quem vidētis, hospitēs,
ait fuisse nāvium celerrimus,
neque ūllius natantis impetum trabis
nequīsse praeterīre...

1. *Nāvium* is genitive (even though it does not use an ending from this chapter; this is the third declension genitive which you will learn later). If *celerrimus* means "fastest" and describes the *phasēlus*, how is Catullus describing the *phasēlus* with the phrase *celerrimus nāvium*?

2. *Trabis* is also a third declension genitive. If *impetum* means "power" and *trabis* means "boat," what does *impetum trabis* mean?

Genitive Case Text

Horace, *Carmina* 1.10.5-8. Horace devotes this poem to the god Mercury. In this excerpt, Horace identifies Mercury in his messenger role and credits him with inventing the lyre.

> Tē canam, magnī Iovis et deōrum   5
> nuntium curvaeque lyrae parentem,
> callidum quidquid placuit iocōsō
>   condere furtō.

Vocabulary

magnus, -a, -um. great	**deus, -ī.** god
Iovis = "of Jupiter"	**curvus, -a, -um.** curved, bent
[a third declension genitive]	**lyra, -ae.** lyre, ancient harp

1. What are the four first and second declension genitives in lines 5-6?

2. Using the vocabulary above, complete the following translation by translating the bracketed words.

   I will sing of you, messenger _____ [*magnī Iovis et deōrum*] and inventor _____ [*curvae lyrae*],

3. Both *magnī* (*magnus*) and *curvae* (*curvus*) are adjectives that use the same endings as first and second declension nouns.

17. Dative Case

1. What are the two English prepositions often used to translate the dative?

2. Define an indirect object.

3. Define what is meant by the Dative of Reference.

Dative Case Text

Martial 2.44.7-9. Martial here half-jokes that the man from whom he borrows money now sees him coming and tries to dissuade Martial from asking for another loan. In this excerpt, Martial quotes the money-lender as he murmurs to himself, though loud enough that Martial can hear, how much he owes other people, and so how little he has for Martial.

"Septem mīlia dēbeō Secundō,
Phoebō quattuor, ūndecim Philētō,
et quadrans mihi nullus est in arcā."

Vocabulary

septem. seven	**Philētus, -ī.** Philetus
mīlia. thousand	**quadrans.** money, coin
Secundus, -ī. Secundus	**mihi** = "my"
Phoebus, -ī. Phoebus	**nullus, -a. -um.** no, none
quattuor. four	**est.** is
ūndecim. eleven	**arca, -ae.** coffer

1. Answer the following questions, based on the excerpt; vocabulary is provided above.
   a. To whom does Sextus owe seven thousand?
   b. To whom does Sextus owe four thousand?
   c. To whom does Sextus owe eleven thousand?
   d. How much does Sextus have for himself?
2. Translate the excerpt.

Dative Case Text

Martial 6.87. A prayer whose precise tone is ambiguous. Martial hopes that the gods and Caesar give to Caesar what he wants, and that Martial himself receives the same treatment if he deserves it. Martial, of course, never specifies whether Caesar should receive what Caesar wants if he deserves it. Is Martial then praising Caesar by acknowledging that he should get whatever he wants without earning it, or is he implictly criticizing the divine cult of the emperor that leads to such indulgence?

Dī tibi dent et tū, Caesar, quaecumque merēris:
   dī mihi dent et tū quae volō, sī meruī.

1. The forms *mihi* and *tibi* are the dative forms of the first and second person singular pronoun.

2. Translate the poem above by translating the dative forms in brackets.

> May the gods and you, Caesar, give whatever you deserve _____ [*tibi* = you]: may the gods and you give _____ [*mihi* = me] what I want if I deserve it.

Dative Case Text

Martial 7.3. Pontilianus asks Martial why he won't send any of his poetry to him. Martial responds curtly: so that Pontilianus won't send any of *his* poetry to Martial.

> Cūr nōn mittō meōs tibi, Pontiliāne, libellōs?
> Nē mihi tū mittās, Pontiliāne, tuōs.

1. Translate the poem above by translating the dative forms in brackets.

> Why do I not send my books ____ [*tibi*], Pontilianus?
> So you don't send your books ____ [*mihi*].

2. The forms *mihi* and *tibi* are the dative forms of the first and second person singular pronoun.

Dative Case Text

Ovid, *Metamorphoses* 1.481-482. Ovid establishes Daphne as a Diana-figure, i.e. a woman who eschews the traditional life of marriage that was expected of a woman for a life of natural existence in the woods. In this excerpt, her father is pressuring her to accept the role expected of her.

> Saepe pater dīxit "Generum mihi, fīlia, dēbēs;"
> Saepe pater dīxit "Dēbēs mihi, nāta, nepōtēs."

Vocabulary

gener, generī. son-in-law
filia, -ae. daughter
    [*here, the addressee of* debes]

nāta, -ae. daughter
nepōtēs. grandchildren
    [*a third declension accusative plural*]

1. Translate the two quotes. The verb form *dēbēs* should be recognizable from the vocabulary of your textbook.

18. Expectations

1. What are the three case-number combinations that the -*ae* ending indicates?

2. What are the two case-number combinations that the -*ī* ending indicates?

Expectations Exercise

Use expectations, in addition to your knowledge of endings, to identify whether each underlined noun is accusative or dative. Some forms will use accusative and dative endings from the other declensions to force you to use expectations, but each sentence adheres to a fairly standard sentence structure.

1. Deus <u>templum</u> aedificat.
2. Puerī litterās <u>puellae</u> dant.
3. Agricola rosam <u>amīcīs</u> monstrat.
4. Dominus <u>aquam</u> portat.
5. Nēmō <u>consilium</u> dubitat.
6. Turba <u>mīlitem</u> pugnat.
7. Dī fābulam <u>cīvibus</u> narrant.
8. Fābulae imperium <u>sorōribus</u> narrant.
9. Arma <u>turbīs</u> nocent.
10. Deus <u>virtūtem</u> <u>rēgī</u> dat.

19. Sentence Pattern: Special Intransitive

1. What are the two sentence patterns you have already seen?

2. In what case does the Special Intransitive sentence pattern take its object?

- Some other Latin verbs that follow the Special Instransitive pattern:

confīdō, -ere: *to trust*	parcō, -ere: *to spare*
crēdō, -ere: *to believe*	persuādeō, -ēre: *to persuade*
displiceō, -ēre: *to displease*	resistō, -ere: *to resist*
faveō, -ēre: *to favor*	serviō, -īre: *to serve*
ignoscō, -ere: *to forgive*	studeō, -ēre: *to be eager*
imperō, -āre: *to command*	

- The dative is also used as the object of compound verbs.

Sentence Pattern: Special Intransitive Text

Vergil, *Aeneid* **2.533-534.** During the sack of Troy, Achilles' son Pyrrhus mercilessly kills Priam's son Polites before the eyes of his father and mother. Priam, in this excerpt, prepares to address Pyrrhus.

Hīc Priamus, quamquam in mediā iam morte tenētur, nōn tamen abstinuit nec vōcī īraeque pepercit:

1. Complete the translation below by translating the datives in brackets.

   Here Priam, although he is already in the throes of death, does not yet give in and does not spare _____ [*vōcī; vox, vōcis* is a third declension dative meaning "voice"] or his _____ [*īrae; īra, -a*e = anger].

2. The combination of the nouns *vōcī īraeque* is a rhetorical figure called hendiadys, when two nouns are joined by a conjunction, in this instance *-que*, that could be read as a noun-adjective, or a noun-genitive pair. The hendiadys here then takes the place of the noun-adjective expression "angry voice."

Sentence Pattern: Special Intransitive (Dative with a Compound) Text

Petronius, *Satyricon* **111.** The husband of a woman in Ephesus has just died. His wife is known for her virtue, dedication, and faithfulness; as a demonstration of these qualities, she follows her husband to his tomb and attends his corpse. Her maidservant (*ancilla*) accompanies her.

Assidēbat aegrae fidissima ancilla....

1. What is the dative in the above excerpt?
2. What is the compound verb in the above excerpt?
3. What case is *fidissima ancilla*?

Sentence Pattern: Special Intransitive
(Dative with a Compound) Text

Ovid, *Metamorphoses* 4.73. Pyramus and Thisbe directly address the wall that separates their houses and them.

"Invide" dīcēbant "pariēs, quid amantibus obstās?"

Vocabulary

quid = why
amantibus. lover [a third declension dative plural]
obstō, -āre. to obstruct, to get in the way of

---

1. What is the compound verb in the above excerpt?
2. Using the vocabulary above, translate *quid amantibus obstās?*

Chapter 4 introduces the concept of the adverb: both adverbs themselves and adverbial expressions. The adverb becomes an important element of the sentence because it, in general, brings expansion and nuance of meaning to the action of a sentence.

Terms to Know

adverb
ablative
means/instrument
   (ablative of)
preposition
place where
place from which
place to which
chunks

20. The Adverb

1. About what four things do adverbs give information?
2. What questions do adverbs answer?
3. What four things can adverbs modify?
4. What are the two most common endings for adverbs?

- The English ending *-ly* is commonly used for adverbs, e.g. quick = adjective while quickly = adverb. But some English adverbs use the same form as the adjective:

   The <u>fast</u> runner won the race.
   The woman ran <u>fast</u>.
   She took a <u>hard</u> test.
   She hit the ball <u>hard</u>.

   The first and third examples are adjectives; they modify the nouns "runner" and "test."

   The second and fourth examples are adverbs: *how* did she run? *fast*; *how* did she hit the ball? *hard*.

   Even though the English form stays the same, the grammatical function differs.

Adverb Text

Martial 2.7. Martial lauds his friend Atticus for all the things he does well.

Dēclāmās <u>bellē</u>, causās agis, Attice, <u>bellē</u>,
   historiās <u>bellās</u>, carmina <u>bella</u> facis,
compōnis <u>bellē</u> mīmōs, epigrammata <u>bellē</u>,
   <u>bellus</u> grammaticus, <u>bellus</u> es astrologus,
et <u>bellē</u> cantas et saltās, Attice, <u>belle</u>,   5
   <u>bellus</u> es arte lyrae, <u>bellus</u> es arte pilae.
Nīl bene cum faciās, faciās tamen omnia <u>bellē</u>,
   vīs dīcam quid sīs? Magnus es ardaliō.

Vocabulary

dēclāmō, -āre. to declaim, to speak
causās agō, -ere. to plead a case
historia, -ae. history
faciō, -ere. to create, to write
carmen, -inis. poem

The underlined words are all forms of the word *bellus, -a, -um*, an adjective meaning "beautiful" or "wonderful." The adjective endings used on these forms are the same as the noun endings you have already learned.

1. Using the adverb endings from the chapter, identify how many times *bellus* is used as an adverb.
2. How many times is *bellus* used as an adjective?
3. Using the vocabulary above, translate the first two lines of the poem, keeping in mind the difference between adjectives and adverbs.

Adverb Text

Martial 2.27. Selius is a mooch who is always looking for a free dinner. Martial advises the reader to oblige, but only after Selius has earned his dinner by publically praising whoever will feed him.

Laudantem Selium cēnae cum rētia tendit
   accipe, sīve legās sīve patrōnus agās:
"Effectē! graviter! citō! nēquiter! euge! beātē!
   Hoc voluī!" "Facta est iam tibi cēna, tacē."

Line 3 is comprised entirely of adverbs.

1. List each adverb according to its ending. Remember that there are two common adverb endings.
2. What is the one irregular adverb in line 3 that does not have one of these two common endings?

Adverb Text

Pliny, *Epistulae* 5.19.3. Pliny writes to his friend about about how he treats his servants. In this excerpt, Pliny praises the various skills of Zosimus, one of his slaves.

Nam prōnūntiat ācriter, sapienter, aptē, decenter etiam; ūtitur et cithara perite, ultrā quam comoedō necesse est. Īdem tam commodē ōrātiōnēs et historiās et carmina legit, ut hoc sōlum didicisse videātur.

Vocabulary

nam (*adv.*). for
prōnūntiō, -āre. to speak, to announce
ācer, -cris, -cre. sharp, clear

sapiens, -ntis. wise, knowledgable
aptus, -a, -um. appropriate
decens, -ntis. decent

1. Identify the four adverbs in the first sentence.
2. Identify to which declension each belongs.
3. Using the vocabulary above, translate the first sentence.
4. Identify the one adverb in the last sentence.

21. Ablative Case

1. In what kind of letter does the ablative singular always end?
2. What is the difference between the first declension nominative singular and the first declension ablative singular endings?
3. What does the ablative of means/instrument show?
4. What are the two English prepositions with which the ablative of means/instrument can be translated?

- The ablative case has a variety of functions, but most of them are adverbial in nature; as the genitive case often functions as the adjective case, so the ablative case often functions as the adverb case.

- It is important then to consider what an ablative will describe.

- With an adverbial function, ablatives will modify the same things that adverbs modify: verbs, adjectives, and other adverbs, though verbs will by far be the most common.

- When an ablative is encountered then, it must be considered not in isolation, but rather in terms of what other word or expression it expands the meaning of.

- The ablative case will sometimes be used with a Latin preposition, but sometimes will be used without a Latin preposition.

  - Even when Latin ablatives do not have a preposition, they will likely require a preposition when translated into English to link them to their clause.

Ablative Case Text

Ovid, *Metamorphoses* **4.63.** Here, Ovid describes how the forbidden lovers, Pyramus and Thisbe, communicate.

…nūtū signīsque loquuntur,

Vocabulary

nūtus, -ūs. wink, nod	**loquuntur** = "they speak"
signum, -ī. hand gesture	

---

1. Using the vocabulary above, translate the sentence.
2. What kind of ablative is *nūtū signīsque*?

Ablative Case Text

Catullus 63.1-11. Attis was a Phrygian youth who, driven mad, castrated himself with a sharp stone as part of the cult initiation of Cybele, the mother goddess. In this excerpt, the opening of the poem, Attis and his castration are described.

Super alta vectus Attis <u>celerī</u> **rate** maria,
Phrygium ut nemus <u>citātō</u> cupide **pede** tetigit
adiitque opāca **silvīs** redimīta loca deae,
stimulātus ibi <u>furentī</u> **rabiē**, vagus **animīs**,
dēvolvit īlī <u>acūtō</u> sibi pondera **silice**,   5
Itaque ut relicta sensit sibi membra sine <u>virō</u>,

etiam <u>recente</u> terrae sola **<u>sanguine</u>** maculans,
<u>niveīs</u> citāta cēpit **<u>manibus</u>** leve typanum,
typanum tuum, Cybēbē, tua, mater, initia,
quatiensque terga taurī <u>tenerīs</u> cava **<u>digitīs</u>**   10
canere haec suīs adorta est tremebunda comitibus.

Vocabulary

celer, celeris. quick, swift
ratis, -is. boat
citātus, -a, -um. swiftly moving
pēs, pedis. foot
silva, -ae. forest
furens, -ntis. raging, out of
  control
rabiēs, -ēī. madness

acūtus, -a, -um. sharp
silex, -icis. stone, flint
recens, -ntis. fresh
sanguen, -inis. blood
niveus, -a, -um. white, pale
manus, -ūs. hand
tener, -era, -erum. soft, tender
digitus, -ī. finger

The underlined words are all ablative; the bold underlined words are the nouns (the non-bold being adjectives).

1. Using the ablative endings on page 27 of your book, identify the declension of each of the nouns. For those declensions whose endings are not listed on page 27, write *nesciō* (Latin for "I don't know").

2. All of the phrases below contain ablatives of means/ instrument. Using the vocabulary above and the context provided by the translated Latin (the English in parentheses), translate the ablatives of means.

   a. vectus (*having been conveyed*) celerī rate:

       _____

   b. tetigit nemus (*he arrived in the clearing*) citāto pede:

       _____

   c. stimulātus (*goaded on*) furentī rabiē:

       _____

   d. dēvolsit sibi (*he castrated himself*) acūtō silice:

       _____

   e. maculans sola (*spraying the ground*) recente sanguine:

       _____

   f. cēpit typanum (*he picked up a drum*) niveīs manibus:

       _____

   g. quatiens terga taurī (*shaking the bull hide* [*drum*]) tenerīs digitīs: _____

Ablative Case Text

Martial 9.75. Martial criticizes a certain Tucca for misappropriating the materials with which he built a bath complex; Tucca uses too much marble in an attempt to aggrandize himself and his bath complex. Now he doesn't have any wood with which to heat the baths sufficiently.

Nōn silice dūrō structilīve caementō,
nec latere coctō, quō Samīramis longam
Babylōna cinxit, Tucca balneum fēcit:
sed strāge nemorum pīneāque conpāge,
ut nāvigāre Tucca balneō possit.   5
Īdem beātās lautus extruit thermās
dē marmore omnī, quod Carystos invēnit,
quod Phrygia Synnās, Afra quod Nomas mīsit
et quod virentī fonte lavit Eurōtās.
Sed ligna dēsunt: sūbice balneum thermīs.   10

Vocabulary

silex, silicis. stone   **caemuntum, -ī.** cement
dūrus, -a, -um. hard   **later, lateris.** brick, tile
structilis, -e. used for building   **coctus, -a, -um.** baked, fired

---

1. Complete the following translation of lines 1-3 by translating the ablatives in brackets.

    Not _____ [*silice durō*] or _____ [*structilī caemento*] nor _____ [*latere coctō*], with which Semiramis encircled sprawling Babylon, did Tucca build his bath.

2. The nouns *silex* and *later* are third declension nouns, whose nominatives and genitives are included in the vocabulary list and whose ablative forms appear in Martial's poem. The adjectives *dūrus* and *coctus* use the same endings as the nouns you have already learned, and will be formally introduced in Chapter 5. The adjective *structilis, -e* is a third declension adjective.

22. The Preposition

1. With what two kinds of words must a preposition appear?
2. In what two cases does the Latin object of a preposition appear?

3. Where is a Latin preposition often placed in relationship to its object?

4. What grammatical expectation should seeing a Latin preposition create?

23. Expressions of Place

1. What Latin case indicates motion away from?

2. What Latin case indicates motion towards?

3. Identify two Latin prepositions that indicate place where.

4. Identify two Latin prepositions that indicate place from which.

5. Identify two Latin prepositions that indicate place to which.

6. What type of verb should be expected with an expression of place to which or place from which?

Expressions of Place Text

Plautus, *Miles Gloriosus* **126-128.** Latin comic plays tended to open with an extended prologue, delivered by a character in the play, that sets the scene and narrates the backstory. This excerpt is from the prologue of Plautus' *Miles Gloriosus*, spoken by the crafty slave Palaestrio. He describes here how, when coincidentally reunited with the girlfriend of his former master, she told him how unhappy she was with her new master, the Miles Gloriosus of the title, and how she wants to be reunited with her old master. This will become the central conflict of the play.

Palaestrio. Āit sēsē Athēnās fugere cupere ex hāc domū,
sēsē illum amāre, meum erum, Athēnīs quī fuit,
neque pēius quemquam ōdisse quam istum mīlitem.

Vocabulary

Athēnae, -ārum. Athens   **domus, -ūs.** house
hāc = "this"

1. Complete the following translation by translating the place expressions in brackets.

    She says that she wants to flee _____ [*Athēnās*] _____ [*ex hāc domū*], that she wants to love that master of mine, who was _____ [*Athēnīs*], and that she hated no one worse than that soldier.

2. *Domū* is a fourth declension noun. What case is it? Explain your answer.

Expressions of Place Text

Vergil, *Aeneid* **2.203-205.** Aeneas, as he describes the fall of Troy to Dido, has just described the Trojan priest Laocoön's reaction to the Trojan horse; Laocoön utters that famous phrase, *timeō Danaōs et dōna ferentīs*, as he advocates that the Trojans reject the Greeks' gift. If the Trojans considered heeding Laocoön's advice, they did not after what happens here: two huge snakes appear out of the sea to devour Laocoön and his two sons. This dramatic scene was immortalized in a Hellenistic sculpture that is now in the Vatican Museum.

Ecce autem geminī ā Tenedō tranquilla per alta—
(horrēscō referēns)—immēnsīs orbibus anguēs
incumbunt pelagō pariterque ad lītora tendunt;   205

1. Identify the three place constructions in the above excerpt.

Expressions of Place Text

Catullus 55.3-5. Catullus looks for Camerius, who has been keeping himself from Catullus. Here, Catullus lists some of the places in which he's looked for Camerius.

Tē [in] Campō quaesīvimus minore,
tē in Circō, tē in omnibus libellīs,
tē in templō summī Iovis sacrātō.

Vocabulary

Campus, -ī. Campus, field
Circus, -ī. Circus, racetrack
omnis, -e. all, every

libellus, -ī. bookstore
templum, -ī. temple
Iūpiter, Iovis. Jupiter [king of the gods]

Catullus 101.1-2. In one of Catullus' most poignant poetic moments, he describes his heartwrenching journey to visit the grave of his brother, who died suddenly in Bithynia, an ancient region in the northeast corner of modern-day Turkey.

Multās per gentēs et multa per aequora vectus
  adveni hās miserās, frāter, ad īnferiās,...

Vocabulary

per (*prep.* + *acc.*). through
gens, gentis. people, tribe
aequor, -oris. sea, water

miser, -era, -erum. miserable, awful
īnferiae, -ārum. ghost, grave

Catullus 63.58-60. Attis has castrated himself out of devotion to the goddess Cybele and spent the night in pain-inspired ecstasy before he fell asleep. He has now awakened and, understanding what he has done, reflects on what he had and what he no longer will have.

Egone ā meā remōta haec ferar in nemora domō?
[ā] patriā, [ā] bonīs, [ab] amīcīs, [ā] genitōribus aberō?
aberō [ā] forō, [ā] palaestrā, [ā] stadiō et gymnasiis?

Vocabulary

meus, -a, -um. my
nemus, -oris. meadow, grove
domus, -ī. home
patria, -ae. homeland
bonum, -ī. possession

genitor, -ōris. parent
forum, -ī. forum, marketplace
palaestra, -ae. gym
stadium, -ī. stadium
gymnasium, -ī. training ground

Bracketed words are not in Catullus' original. Often in poetry, prepositions that would otherwise be included are omitted.

1. Make three columns on a page, one for **place where**, one for **place from which**, one for **place to which**. Fill each column with the appropriate Expressions of Place from all three texts. (There are four "place where," four "place to which," and eight "place from which.")

2. Fill in the blanks below to complete the English
translation with the correct translation of each ablative.

Text A

I have sought you (*quaesīvimus*)

([*in*] *Campō*) _____

(*in Circō*) _____

(*in omnibus libellīs*) _____

(*in templō Iovis*) _____

Text B

Having been carried (*vectus*)

(*per gentēs*) _____.

(*per aequora*) _____.

I arrive, brother, (*adveniō, frāter*)

(*ad miserās inferiās*) _____.

Text C

Will I be brought (*ferar*)

(*ā meā domō*) _____ ?

(*in nemora*) _____ ?

Will I be away (*aberō*)

([*ā*] *patriā*) _____ ?

([*ā*] *bonīs*) _____ ?

([*ab*] *amicīs*) _____ ?

([*ā*] *genitōribus*) _____ ?

Will I be away (*aberō*)

([*ā*] *forō*) _____ ?

([*ā*] *palaestrā*) _____ ?

([*ā*] *stadiō et gymnasiīs*) _____ ?

Ablative Consolidation Text

Vergil, *Eclogues* **8.69-71.** Vergil here describes the power of poetry.

Carmina vel [ā] <u>caelō</u> possunt dēdūcere lūnam,
<u>carminibus</u> Circē sociōs mūtāvit Ulixī,
frigidus in <u>prātīs</u> cantandō rumpitur anguis.

Vocabulary

caelum, -ī. sky, heaven   **prātum, -ī.** meadow, grass
carmen, -inis. poem, song

All of the underlined words are ablative. Each, however, is a different use of the ablative, all of which are covered in this chapter.

1. Identify the uses of each ablative. Remember that your choices are ablative of means or instrument, ablative of place where, and ablative of place from which. You should be able to do this without knowing the vocabulary information. Use context and prepositions as your clues.

2. Each sentence is translated below. Fill in the blank with the translation of each ablative.

line 69: Poetry is able to pull the moon (*ā caelō*)

_____.

line 70: Circe changed the companions of Ulysses (*carminibus*)

_____.

line 71: With poetry, the cold snake (*in prātīs*)

_____

is broken apart.

24. Word Order

1. Explain the difference between word order in Latin and word order in English.

2. Which words will usually appear first and last in a Latin sentence?

3. Explain what is meant by the term "chunk."

CHAPTER 5

As Chapter 4 introduced the concept of the adverb, so Chapter 5 introduces the adjective. With adjectives comes perhaps one of Latin's most problematic grammatical feature: noun-adjective agreement. It is imperative that this concept is understood to be able to read Latin. The irregular verb "to be" (*sum*) is introduced, as are two new ablatives.

25. The Adjective

1. What is the primary difference between adjectives and nouns in terms of their endings?

2. What are the endings that each type of adjective uses?

26. Agreement

1. What are the three categories in which adjectives agree with their nouns?

2. When an adjective modifies more than one noun, with which one does it agree?

3. Why might an adjective not appear next to the noun that it modifies?

The Adjective and Agreement Text

Catullus 49.4-7. Catullus here thanks the famous Roman orator Cicero. But Catullus is perhaps being disingenuous. Cicero criticized Catullus and his literary circle for the poetry that they wrote, and some read this poem as a bitingly sarcastic retort: Catullus fills this excerpt with superlatives that can be read as either exceedingly generous or exceedingly excessive.

... gratiās tibi <u>maximās</u> Catullus
agit <u>pessimus</u> omnium poēta,
tantō <u>pessimus</u> omnium poēta,
quantō tū <u>optimus</u> omnium patrōnus.

Each of the underlined words above is an adjective.

1. Identify the gender, number, and case of the three different adjectives.
2. Identify which noun each adjective modifies. (Hint: *pessimus* will agree with a noun that has a different ending, but of course still has the same gender, number, and case.)

The Adjective and Agreement Text

Martial 1.9. Martial chides Cotta for wanting to be more attractive, because being attractive alone won't make him great.

Bellus homō et magnus vīs idem, Cotta, vidērī:
   sed quī bellus homō est, Cotta, pusillus homō est.

Horace, *Carmina* 1.24.5-8. Horace mourns the death of a certain Quintilius, likely Quintilius Varus, about whom little else is known except his friendship with both Horace and Vergil. Here, Horace equates Quintilius with those abstract values that the Romans most prized: honor, justice, trust, truth.

Ergō Quintilium perpetuus sopor   5
urget? Cui Pudor et Iustitiae soror,
incorrupta Fidēs, nūdaque Vēritās
   quandō ullum inveniet parem?

Martial 7.71. An entire family bears warts that resemble protrusions on the stems of mushrooms. (The technical term for these warts is "tubers," which is a mushroom-related word.) How ironic then that the family can grow not a single mushroom!

Ficōsa est uxor, ficōsus et ipse marītus,
   fīlia ficōsa est et gener atque nepōs,
nec dispensātor nec vīlicus ulcere turpī
   nec rigidus fossor, sed nec arātor eget.
Cum sint ficōsī pariter iuvenēsque senēsque,   5
   rēs mīra est, fīcōs nōn habet ūnus ager.

---

1. The table below includes all of the nouns from the three

poems/excerpts. Identify which adjective agrees with each noun. Since some nouns will have the same gender, number, and case, you will have to use elements of sentence structure to help assign adjectives with their nouns. Some nouns may not have adjectives that agree with them; in these instances, write "none". And some adjectives may be used to agree with more than one noun.

Text & Ln. #	Noun	Gender	Number	Case	Adjective
Mart 1.9.1	homō	*masc.*	*sing.*	*nom.*	
Mart 1.9.2	homō	*masc.*	*sing.*	*nom.*	
Mart 1.9.2	homō	*masc.*	*sing.*	*nom.*	
Horace 1.24.5	Quintilium	*masc.*	*sing.*	*acc.*	
Horace 1.24.5	sopor	*masc.*	*sing.*	*nom.*	
Horace 1.24.6	Pudor	*fem.*	*sing.*	*nom.*	
Horace 1.24.6	soror	*fem.*	*sing.*	*nom.*	
Horace 1.24.7	Fidēs	*fem.*	*sing.*	*nom.*	
Horace 1.24.7	Vēritās	*fem.*	*sing.*	*nom.*	
Horace 1.24.8	ullum	*masc.*	*sing.*	*acc.*	parem [*a third decl. adj.*]
Mart 7.71.1	uxor	*fem.*	*sing.*	*nom.*	
Mart 7.71.1	marītus	*masc.*	*sing.*	*nom.*	
Mart 7.71.2	fīlia	*fem.*	*sing.*	*nom.*	
Mart 7.71.2	gener	*masc.*	*sing.*	*nom.*	
Mart 7.71.2	nepōs	*masc.*	*sing.*	*nom.*	
Mart 7.71.3	dispensātor	*masc.*	*sing.*	*nom.*	
Mart 7.71.3	vīlicus	*masc.*	*sing.*	*nom.*	
Mart 7.71.3	ulcere	*neut.*	*sing.*	*abl.*	turpī [*a third decl. adj.*]
Mart 7.71.4	fossor	*masc.*	*sing.*	*nom.*	
Mart 7.71.4	arātor	*masc.*	*sing.*	*nom.*	
Mart 7.71.5	iuvenēs	*masc.*	*pl.*	*nom.*	
Mart 7.71.5	senēs	*masc.*	*pl.*	*nom.*	
Mart 7.71.6	rēs	*fem.*	*nom.*	*sing.*	
Mart 7.71.6	fīcōs	*masc.*	*acc.*	*pl.*	
Mart 7.71.6	ager	*masc.*	*nom.*	*sing.*	

The Adjective and Agreement Text

Catullus 43.1-4. Can any woman be as beautiful as Catullus' love Lesbia? Not according to Catullus. But nonetheless he provides here this description of a woman considered beautiful by most, despite physical features that seem less than attractive. The poem then raises the question of whether Catullus views this *puella* as unattractive only because he is comparing her to his Lesbia, or whether she is truly unattractive and he is criticizing those who are unable to see this.

Salvē, nec minimō puella nāsō
nec bellō pede, nec nigrīs ocellīs,
nec longīs digitīs nec ōre siccō
nec sānē nimis ēlegante linguā, …

Vocabulary

nec. not [*here used to create the opposite of the adjective next to which it is placed, i.e. the* minimo naso *is "the smallest nose" the* nec minimo naso *is "not the smallest nose"*]
minimus, -a, -um. smallest
nāsum, -ī. nose
bellus, -a, -um. beautiful, pretty
pēs, pedis. foot [*gender = masc.;* pede = *abl. sing.*]
niger, nigra, nigrum. black

ocellus, -ī. eye
longus, -a, -um. long
digitus, -ī. finger
ōs, ōris. mouth [*gender = neut.;* ore = *abl. sing.*]
siccus, -a, -um. *neut.*; dry
lingua, -ae. *neut.*; tongue, language, way of speaking
ēlegante. elegant [*this is a feminine, singular, ablative third declension adjective*]

In the above passage, there are six noun-adjective pairs.

1. Identify each of the pairs (two will include a third declension noun, whose endings you have not learned yet; use the vocabulary above for assistance with these nouns).

2. The passage addresses the *puella* in line 1. Each of the noun-adjective pairs, which are in the ablative case, describe the girl. The passage begins "Hello, girl with…" The noun-adjective pairs follow the "with." Identify the six ways Catullus describes the *puella*.

3. The poem provides an extended example of a rhetorical figure known as litotes whereby something is described by emphasizing its opposite. So the nose of the *puella* is *nec minimō*, not the smallest; her feet are *nec bellō*, not attractive, etc.

27. The Gap

1. Which term, other than "the gap," is used to describe when "an adjective can be used without an accompanying noun?"
2. How do you know what noun is missing in English?
3. What additional grammatical information helps you identify the noun in Latin?
4. What is another example of words that Latin can leave out (or "gap")?

- Some substantive adjectives are used so commonly without an expressed noun that they are included in glossaries and dictionaries as separate nouns.
  - The adjective *malus, -a, -um* means "evil" or "bad," but its neuter substantive, *malum, -i*, "evil" (the noun) is so common that it has become a separate word.
- The term "parallel structure" becomes important when verbs are left out or "gapped." The gapping effect will create grammatical parallels between the two clauses. Identifying and understanding these parallels will help illuminate what word(s) is being gapped.
  - These examples from Ovid's "Apollo and Daphne" illustrate both gapping and parallel structure. In the second iteration of each example, the underlined words are the gapped words from the original.

    Prīmus amor Phoebī Daphnē Pēnēia, quem nōn fors ignāra dedit, sed saeva Cupīdinis īra. …

    The first love of Apollo was Daphne, daughter of Peneus, a love which ignorant chance did not give, but the harsh anger of Cupid did. …

    Prīmus amor Phoebī Daphnē Pēnēia, quem nōn fors ignāra dedit, sed <u>quem</u> saeva Cupīdinis īra <u>dedit</u>,…

    The first love of Apollo was Daphne, daughter of Peneus, a love which ignorant chance did not give, but <u>which</u> the harsh anger of Cupid <u>did give</u>,…

    Ista decent umerōs gestāmina nostrōs, quī dare certa ferae, dare vulnera possumus hostī, …

    Those weapons are appropriate for my shoulders, which can give certain wounds to a wild beast, can give wounds to an enemy, …

> Ista decent umerōs gestāmina nostrōs,
> quī dare certa vulnera ferae <u>possumus</u>, <u>quī</u> dare <u>certa</u>
> vulnera possumus hostī…
>
> *Those weapons are appropriate for my shoulders,*
> *which <u>can</u> give certain wounds to a wild beast, <u>which</u> can*
> *give <u>certain</u> wounds to an enemy…*

- In Latin, the gap will often occur in the first clause, with the word to be understood expressed in the second clause: in the fourth example above, *possumus* is gapped (left out of) in the first clause, and included in the second. English gaps words in the opposite order: "I like basketball, he soccer."

The Gap Text

Martial 5.43. Ancient dentures? According to Martial, yes. In this epigram, he discusses the teeth of two women.

> Thāis habet nigrōs, niveōs Laecania dentēs.
>   Quae ratiō est? Emptōs haec habet, illa suōs.

---

1. In the first line, what is the noun that is gapped?
2. Rewrite the first line, including the gapped noun written out.

The Gap Text

Martial 9.1.1-2. Martial jokingly catalogs the imperial and divine origins of the names of the months as a satirical commentary on the reach of influence of the emperor.

> Dum Iānus hiemēs, Domitiānus autumnōs,
> Augustus annīs commodābit aestātēs,

---

1. If these lines are three clauses, what kind of word is gapped in the first two clauses, i.e. what important kind of word is missing from these two clauses?
2. Rewrite the clauses with the gapped word included.

28. *Sum*: Present Indicative and Infinitive

1. Why must all the forms of *sum* be memorized?

29. Sentence Pattern: Linking

1. What are the three sentence patterns you have learned so far?
2. Why is the new pattern called the "linking" pattern?
3. What are the two terms for the word to which the linking verb links the subject?
4. What are the three elements to the linking sentence pattern?
5. What is a clue that *sum* is functioning in an intransitive role?

- A list of the most common Latin linking verbs:
  sum, esse   *fiō, fierī*   *videor, vidērī*
- A list of English linking verbs (the starred [*] verbs at the end can function as either linking verbs or transitive verbs):

appear	remain	taste	prove*
be	seem	become	run*
feel	smell	get*	turn*
lie	sound	grow*	
look	stay	fall*	

- When *sum* is used in an intransitive pattern, it is also sometimes referred to as the existential *sum* because it expresses that something exists or exists as something.
- A linking verb can link either a noun or an adjective to the subject.

Linking Text

Aulus Gellius, *Noctes Atticae* **18.2.9.** Gellius here is describing how he and friends passed the time at a dinner party. In this excerpt, Gellius quotes one of the philosophical conundra posed to the guests.

"Quod ego sum, id tū nōn es; homō ego sum: homō igitur tū nōn es."

1. Complete the translation below by translating the linking verbs and their subjects in brackets.

   That which _____ [*ego sum*], _____ [*tū nōn es*]; ____ [*ego sum*] a man: therefore, _____ [*tū nōn es*] a man.

The word *homō* is a third declension noun, nominative singular, whose endings you will learn in a later chapter, but you might recognize it from expressions like *homō sapiens*.

Linking Text

Ovid, *Amores* **1.8.1-2.** Ovid describes at length a procuress, a woman who brought men and women together for her gain, financial or otherwise. This excerpt is Ovid's introduction to her.

Est quaedam—quīcumque volet cognoscere lēnam,
audiat!—est quaedam nōmine Dipsas anus.

1. If *quaedam* means "a certain woman," what does the *est quaedam* of line 1 mean?

Linking Text

Martial 2.33. Martial asks, and then answers a question: Why do I not kiss you, Philaenius?

Cūr nōn basiō tē, Philaenī? Calva es.
Cūr nōn basiō tē, Philaenī? Rūfa es.
Cūr nōn basiō tē, Philaenī? Lusca es.
Haec quī bāsiat, ō Philaenī, fellat.

Vocabulary

calvus, -a, -um. bald
rūfus, -a, -um. red-faced
luscus, -a, -um. one-eyed

1. What are the three reasons why Martial does not kiss Philaenius? Translate the three answers.

Linking Text

Anonymous, *Miraculum Sancti Nicholai* **50-58.** In this dialogue, the validity of Apollo as a god is debated by the king and the boy.

Rex:
Deus meus Apollō deus est   50
quī mē fēcit; vērax et bonus est;
regit terrās, regnat in aethere;
Illī sōlī dēbēmus crēdere.

Puer:

Deus tuus mendax et malus est;   55
stultus, caecus, surdus et mūtus est;
tālem deum nōn dēbēs colere,
quī nōn potest seipsum regere.

Vocabulary

Apollō, Apollonis. the Roman god of light, music, and poetry.

verāx, verācis. trustworthy

mendax, mendācis. untrustworthy

stultus, -a, -um. stupid

caecus, -a, -um. blind

surdus, -a, -um. corrupt

mūtus, -a, -um. silent, mute

1. Identify the four clauses that follow the linking pattern.
2. Identify whether the word(s) linked to the subject are nouns or adjectives.
3. Identify the Latin words that are linked to each of the subjects listed below, and then using the vocabulary above, translate those Latin words into English. (Line numbers for each subject are included in parentheses.)
   a. Deus meus (50)
   b. [Deus meus (*as subject of* est)] (51)
   c. Deus tuus (55)
   d. [Deus tuus (as subject of est)] (56)

30. More Uses of the Ablative

1. What are the three uses of the ablative that you learned in Chapter 4?
2. What Latin preposition is used with the ablative of accompaniment and the ablative of manner?
3. What criterion for nouns distinguishes the ablative of accompaniment and the ablative of manner?
4. What information does the ablative of accompaniment express?
5. What information does the ablative of manner express?
6. What are the two effects that the inclusion of an adjective in an ablative of manner can have?

More Uses of the Ablative Text

Beloit College (WI) Motto

Scientia vēra cum fidē pūrā.

University of Waterloo (Ontario) Motto

Concordia cum vēritate.

Vocabulary

scientia, -ae. knowledge
vērus, -a, -um. true
fidēs, -ēī. faith

pūrus, -a, -um. pure
concordia, -ae. harmony, peace
vēritās, -atis. truth

1. What type of ablative is *fidē pūrā* and *vēritate*? Explain your answer.
2. What are the two things that Beloit College and the University of Waterloo advocate its students learn (each of course advocates two different things)?
3. Translate the mottoes.
4. How can you tell the difference between the cases of *vēra* and *pūrā* in the Beloit motto?

More Uses of the Ablative Text

Vergil, *Aeneid* **2.531-532.** During the sack of Troy, Achilles' son Pyrrhus mercilessly kills Priam's son Polites before the eyes of his father and mother. This excerpt is the description of Pyrrhus' death.

Ut tandem ante oculōs ēvāsit et ōra parentum,
concidit, ac multō vītam cum sanguine fūdit.

Vergil, *Aeneid* **2.687-688.** Aeneas' wife Creusa begs Aeneas not to leave her and their family alone in the house. An omen of bright light suddenly appears on his son's head, convincing Aeneas of his destiny to flee Troy and travel to Italy. In this excerpt, his father Anchises is about to pray to the gods to ask them for help in their journey.

At pater Anchīsēs oculōs ad sīdera laetus
extulit, et caelō palmās cum vōce tetendit:

1. Identify the ablatives in the above excerpts.
2. Are the ablatives used in an ablative of accompaniment or an ablative of manner? Explain your answer.

More Uses of the Ablative Text

Vergil, *Aeneid* **4.215-217.** When Dido founded Carthage, she had fled from her murderous brother who had killed her husband. In honor of her husband's memory, she foreswore men (a pledge she will later break with Aeneas). One of Dido's suitors was a local ruler named Iarbas. When he heard of Dido's relationship with Aeneas, he angrily prayed to Jupiter for justice. In this excerpt, Iarbas describes Aeneas as a "Paris" and his companions as *semiviri*, the former a reference to the Trojan warrior who was often characterized as fearful and hesitant to join battle.

Et nunc ille Paris cum sēmivirō comitātū,   215
Maeoniā mentum mitrā crīnemque madentem
subnexus, raptō potitur:

Vocabulary

sēmivir, -ī (*adj.*). half-man
comitātūs, -ūs. retinue, group of companions [*a fourth declension ablative singular*]

1. Complete the translation below by translating the ablative phrase in brackets.

    And now that Paris _____ [*cum sēmivirō comitātū*]

More Uses of the Ablative Text

Livy, *Ab urbe condita* **1.16.1.** Apotheosis is the deification of a human and was a relatively common phenomenon for Roman emperors. Livy here describes the miraculous circumstances under which Romulus, Rome's first king, disappeared before the eyes of his soldiers: a cloud surrounded him amidst thunder and lightning, and he was never seen again. Immediately, his divinity was proclaimed after such a portentious demise. The dome of the United States Capitol Building is decorated with a fresco entitled "The Apotheosis of George Washington."

Hīs immortālibus ēditīs operibus, cum ad exercitum recensendum contiōnem in campō ad Caprae palūdem habēret, subitō coörta tempestās cum magnō fragōre tonitribusque tam densō rēgem operuit nimbō ut conspectum eius contiōnī abstulerit;

1. Identify the ablative that uses *cum* in the above excerpt; write the entire ablative expression.
2. Is the ablative an ablative of accompaniment or an ablative of manner? Explain your answer.
3. How do you know that the *cum* in line 1 is not used in an ablative expression?

More Uses of the Ablative Text

Anonymous, *In Praise of Wine* **1-4.**

Vīnum bonum et suave
bibit abbas cum priore;
conventus dē pēiore
bibit cum tristitiā.

1. There is both an ablative of accompaniment and an ablative of manner in the above passage.
2. Identify both prepositional phrases that use *cum*.
3. Identify each as the ablative of accompaniment or the ablative of manner. Explain your answer.

CHAPTER 6

Chapter 6 expands upon your knowledge of verbs, introducing two new tenses of first and second conjugation verbs: the imperfect and the future. The imperative mood, which issues commands, is also introduced, as is the vocative case, which signifies direct address and is often used with the imperative.

31. Imperfect Active Indicative (First and Second Conjugation)

1. How many past tenses does Latin have?
2. What is the tense sign for the imperfect tense?
3. What is the one person and number where the imperfect personal endings and the present personal endings differ?
4. What are the three endings before which the long -*ā* shortens?
5. What kind of action does the Latin imperfect indicate?
6. List the four categories of action and their corresponding translations.

- The term "imperfect" comes from the Latin verb *perficiō*, which means "to complete." Thus the "imperfect" tense refers to a past action that is incomplete. (You will later learn the perfect tense, which refers to a past action that has been completed.)

First and Second Conjugation Imperfect Active Indicative Text

Petronius, *Satyricon* 111. The story of the Matron of Ephesus takes satirical aim at the virtue of women and their supposed loyalty to their husbands. This excerpt is from the beginning of the story when the scene is being set. The final sentence introduces the one, singular act that will set in motion the forces that drive the narrative.

…complōrātaque singulāris exemplī fēmina ab
omnibus quintum iam diem sine alimentō trahēbat.
Assidēbat aegrae fidissima ancilla, simulque et lacrimās
commodābat lūgentī et quotienscumque dēfēcerat
positum in monumentō lūmen renovābat. Ūna igitur   5
in tōtā cīvitāte fābula erat, sōlum illud affulsisse vērum
pudīcitiae amōrisque exemplum omnis ordinis hominēs
 confitēbantur, cum interim imperātor prōvinciae latrōnēs
iussit crucibus affīgī secundum illam casulam, in quā
recens cadāver mātrōna dēflēbat.   10

1. There are six imperfect verbs in the above excerpt. Identify them.

   a. Five of them are first or second conjugation verbs.

   b. One of the second conjugation verbs uses a passive ending. Although you have not yet learned these, you should still be able to identify the imperfect. This verb is included in the number of verbs to be found.

   c. The form *erat* in line 6 is the irregular imperfect of *sum*. This verb is not included in the number of verbs to be found.

2. Complete the following translation (from *sōlum illud* to *dēflēbat*) by translating the verb forms in brackets. The second form, *iussit*, is the perfect tense, which you have not yet learned. But you should still be able to translate it by context: it is a past tense that is not the imperfect.

   Men of every type _____ [*confitēbantur; confiteor, -ērī* = to confess, to say] how this alone shone as a true example of dedication and love, when meanwhile the governor of the province _____ [*iussit; iubeō, -ēre* = to order] thieves to be hanged on crosses right next to that little domicile in which the Matron _____ [*dēflēbat; dēfleō, -ēre* = to weep, to mourn] the recently dead body.

First and Second Conjugation Imperfect Active Indicative Text

Martial 1.90. Martial here compares his observations of a certain Bassa, who appears to be virtuous beyond reproach, to her reality, that she is a virago whose sexual appetite rivals that of men.

Quod numquam maribus iunctam tē, Bassa, vidēbam
　　quodque tibi moechum fābula nulla dābat,
omne sed officium circā tē semper obibat
　　turba tuī sexūs, nōn adeunte virō,
esse vidēbāris, fateor, Lucrētia nōbīs:　　　　　　　5
　　at tū, prō facinus, Bassa, futūtor erās.
Inter sē geminōs audēs committere cunnōs
　　mentīturque virum prōdigiōsa Venus.
Commenta es dignum Thēbānō aenigmate monstrum,
　　hic ubi vir nōn est, ut sit adulterium.　　　　　10

1. Identify the four imperfect verbs in the above poem (one will have a passive ending, which you have not yet learned, but focus on the tense sign to identify the form).

2. The form *erās* in line 6 is a fifth imperfect form, but it is an irregular imperfect of the irregular verb *sum, esse,* "to be."

3. Identify the one second conjugation present form (Hint: its subject is "you.")

The Lucretia of line 5 refers to the Roman aristocrat who killed herself to preserve her honor after being raped by the son of the king. Her husband and his friends, the son of the king among them, had decided to test their wives while they were away on campaign. They stole back to the city to see which of their wives was being the most virtuous in their absence. Lucretia won: she was sitting up at night, weaving. Sextus, the son of the king, returned to Lucretia's house and threatened her with dishonor if she did not yield to him: he would kill a slave and her, strip them naked, and put them in bed, saying he found them this way and killed them for their crime. Lucretia, after the rape, summoned her father and husband and told them what had happened. Although they comforted her that there was nothing she could have done, she nonetheless killed herself out of shame. Her suicide and her rape inspired her husband, her father and allies to overthrow the king, and thus ended in 509 BCE the period of Roman history known as the monarchy.

First and Second Conjugation Imperfect Active Indicative Text

Vergil, *Aeneid* **2.730-734.** Aeneas is fleeing Troy with his family. His father Anchises here encourages him to hurry because Greek soldiers are coming near.

Iamque propinquābam portīs omnemque vidēbar   730
ēvāsisse viam, subitō cum crēber ad aurīs
vīsus adesse pedum sonitus, genitorque per umbram
prōspiciēns "Nāte," exclāmat, "fuge, nāte; propinquant.
ārdentes clipeōs atque aera micantia cernō."

1. Identify the two imperfect first and second conjugation verbs in the above excerpt (one will have a passive ending, which you have not yet learned, but focus on the tense sign to identify the form).
2. How do you know that *crēber* in line 731 is not the imperfect form of a verb?
3. What are the two first conjugation present verbs in the excerpt?

First and Second Conjugation Imperfect Active Indicative Text

Ovid, *Metamorphoses* **1.527-530.** Apollo, after he propositions the nymph Daphne and she rejects him, pursues her through the woods. In this excerpt, Ovid describes the physical effect of her flight on her body.

Nūdābant corpora ventī,
obviaque adversās vibrābant flāmina vestēs,
et levis impulsōs retrō dabat aura capillōs;
aucta fōrma fugā est.

1. What are the three first and second conjugation imperfect verbs in the above excerpt?

2. Each of the underlined words below corresponds to an underlined Latin imperfect verb in the excerpt. But each verb has been translated with the perfect rather than the imperfect tense. Change the translation of the underlined verbs from the perfect to the imperfect.

> The wind <u>made bare</u> her body,
> and the breezes in her face <u>shook</u> her clothes that struck them,
> and a slight breeze <u>sent</u> her hair, that had been set in motion,
>   behind her,
> and her beauty was increased by her flight.

Note: The form *aucta est* in line 530 is a perfect form, and so its translation has not been underlined above.

32. Future Active Indicative (First and Second Conjugation)

1. What is the tense sign for the future tense of the first and second conjugations?
2. What are the two vowel changes that occur when the *-bi-* is combined with certain personal endings?

First and Second Conjugation Future Active Indicative Text

Columbia University Motto

In lūmine tuō vidēbimus lūmen.

Johns Hopkins University Motto

Vēritās vōs līberābit.

Vocabulary

lūmen, -inis. light, brilliance	**vōs.** you (*pl.*)
tuus, -a, -um. your	[in the accusative case]
vēritās, -ātis. truth	**līberō, -āre.** to free, to set free

---

1. Identify the future verb in each motto.
2. Translate the mottoes.

First and Second Conjugation Future Active Indicative Text

Martial 5.42. Martial here muses on the fickleness of Fortune to control especially a person's financial situation.

Callidus effractā nummōs fūr auferet arcā,
    prosternet patriōs impia flamma larēs:
dēbitor ūsūram pariter sortemque negābit,
    nōn reddet sterilis sēmina iacta seges:
dispensātōrem fallax spoliābit amīca,   5
    mercibus extructās obruet unda ratēs.
Extrā fortūnam est si quid dōnātur amīcīs:
    quās dederis sōlās semper habēbis opes.

1. What are the three first and second conjugation future tense verbs in the above poem?
2. What are their subjects? (Use verb endings to identify the subject.)

First and Second Conjugation Future Active Indicative Text

Vergil, *Aeneid* **4.333-336.** Dido has confronted Aeneas about his leaving Carthage and her. Aeneas here opens his response to her, in which he explains that, while he does indeed love her, his first duty must be to the gods and his destiny to reach Italy.

    Ego tē, quae plūrima fandō
ēnumerāre valēs, numquam, Rēgīna, negābō
prōmeritam, nec mē meminisse pigēbit Elissae   335
dum memor ipse meī, dum spīritus hōs regit artūs.

1. In the above excerpt, identify the two first and second conjugation future verbs.
2. Identify their conjugations.
3. Identify their subjects. (Use verb endings to identify the subject.)

First and Second Conjugation Future Active Indicative Text

Martial 1.49. Dedicated to a certain Licinianus, this lengthy (for Martial) poem celebrates not only the pleasures of the rural, non-urban life, but also the ability of Licinianus to choose such a life over the more glamorous and popularly esteemed rewards that the hustle and bustle of city life bring.

Vir *celtibēris* nōn tacende gentibus
    nostraeque laus Hispāniae,
vidēbis altam, Liciniāne, Bilbilin,
    equīs et armīs nōbilem,
senemque Caium nivibus, et fractīs sacrum   5
    Vadaverōnem montibus,
et delicātī dulce Boterdī nemus,
    Pōmōna quod fēlix amat.
Tepidī natābis lēne Congēdī vadum
    mollēsque Nymphārum lacūs,   10
quibus remissum corpus *adstringēs* brevī
    Salōne, quī ferrum gelat.
Praestābit illīc ipsa figendās prope
    Voberca prandentī ferās.
Aestūs serenōs aureō *frangēs* Tagō   15
    obscūrus umbrīs arborum;
avidam rigens Dercenna placābit sitim
    et Nutha, quae vincit nivēs.
At cum December cānus et brūma impotens
    Aquilōne raucō *mūgiet,*   20
aprīca *repetēs* Tarracōnis lītora
    tuamque Lālētāniam.
Ibi inligātātas mollibus dammās plāgīs
    mactābis et vernās aprōs
lepōremque fortī callidum *rumpēs* equō,   25
    cervōs *relinquēs* vīlicō.
Vīcīna in ipsum silva *descendet* focum
    infante cinctum sordidō;
vocābitur vēnātor et *veniet* tibi
    convīva clāmātus prope;   30

lūnāta nusquam pellis et nusquam togā
    olidaeque vestēs mūrice;
procul horridus Liburnus et querulus cliens,
    imperia viduārum procul;
nōn *rumpet* altum pallidus somnum reus,   35
    sed mane tōtum *dormiēs*.
Mereātur alius grande et insānum sophōs:
    miserēre tū fēlicium
vērōque fruere nōn superbus gaudiō,
    dum Sura laudātur tuus.   40
Nōn inpudenter vīta quod relicum est petit,
    cum fāma quod satis est habet.

The underlined verbs are future tense verbs. Those that are italicized too are future tense forms that you have not yet learned.

1. Fill in the chart using the passage above.
    a. Vocabulary is provided for the translation column (except for those verbs that have already been included in the vocabulary lists of the textbook).
    b. Remember that the conjugation will be indicated by the vowel that precedes the tense sign.
    c. Use the subject contained in the personal ending for both the "Subject" column and the translation.
2. Choose five of the non-first and second conjugation future tense verbs, write them in the far left column of the chart, and fill in the "subject" and "translation" columns for them.
    a. These verbs are included in a separate section of vocabulary below.
    b. Only choose from the verbs in the second group of the vocabulary section; some verbs whose forms you cannot yet translate are left out of the list.

Verb	Vocabulary	Conjugation	Subject	Translation
vidēbis				
natābis	natō, -āre = to swim			
praestābit	praestō, -āre = to surpass			
placābit	placō, -āre = to soothe			
mactābis	mactō, -āre = to kill			

adstringō, -ere. to draw together, to bind
rumpō, -ere. to break
mūgiō, -īre. to moan, to low
repetō, -ere. to seek again

relinquō, -ere. to leave behind
descendō, -ere. to go down, to descend
vēniō, -īre. to come
dormiō, -īre. to sleep

33. Commands: The Imperative

1. What mood does Latin use to express simple statements and simple questions?
2. What does the imperative mood indicate?
3. What form of the verb also functions as the singular imperative?
4. What is the ending used for the plural imperative?

The Imperative Text

Roberts Wesleyan University (NY) Motto

Ōrā et labōrā.

1. Translate the motto.

34. Vocative Case

1. For what is the vocative case used?
2. To what case's forms is the vocative identical?
3. What are the two exceptions to #2?
4. Which is the correct vocative form of *Cornēlius: Cornēlī* or *Cornēliī*?

5. What Latin word often precedes, and so signals, the vocative case?

6. In what type of sentence is the vocative case most common?

-   Students often associate the vocative case exclusively with the imperative mood. While it is true that vocatives and imperatives often go hand-in-hand, vocatives can and do appear regularly in non-imperative sentences, e.g. "Do your homework, class" vs. "Did you do your homework, class?" vs. "Everybody did their homework, class." All three sentences contain a vocative, but only one is an imperative.

Vocative Case Text

Alcuin's *Farewell to his Cell* ll.1-2. Alcuin addresses his personified monastic cell in the opening couplet to this poem dedicated to it.

Ō mea cella, mihi habitātiō dulcis, amāta,
    semper in aeternum, ō mea cella, valē.

---

1. In the above excerpt, what is the first declension vocative noun?

2. What two adjectives agree with this noun?

3. Use the translation below to determine which other Latin noun is vocative. (It is a third declension noun, whose forms you do not yet know, but yields an English derivative in the translation.)

    My cell, my sweet habitation, loved
        always and forever, my cell, farewell.

Vocative Case Text

Anonymous, *Miraculum Sancti Nicholai* ll.80-83. Getron's queen Eufrosina will not be consoled for the loss of her son, here addressing him directly and mourning his absence.

Fīlī cāre, fīlī cārissime,
fīlī, meae magna pars animae,
nunc es nōbīs causa tristitiae,
quibus erās causa laetitiae.

---

1. If *fīlī* is a vocative singular form, what declension is it? How do you know? What would its nominative singular be? Explain your answer.

2. If *cāre* is also a vocative singular form, what would its nominative be? How do you know? Explain your answer.

3. Explain the difference in the vocative endings of both words.

Vocative Case Text

Martial 5.2.1-2. Martial here dedicates his fifth book of epigrams and says, immediately following this excerpt, that it will be more suitable than the previous four for the more prudish among his readers. It is unclear, however, whether Martial is serious or is further mocking the prudishness of such readers.

Mātrōnae puerīque virginēsque,
vōbīs pāgina nostra dēdicātur.

Vocabulary

mātrōna, -ae. matron, married woman
virgō, virginis. unmarried girl, virgin
vōbīs = to you
pāgina, -ae. page
dēdicō, -āre. to dedicate [*here in the passive, i.e.* "the *pāgina* is dedicated *vōbīs*"]

All three nouns in line 1 are in the vocative case (the third word, *virginēs*, is a third declension vocative plural).

1. Using the vocabulary above, translate the two lines.

Vocative Case Text

Martial 2.90.1-4. Martial here criticizes the expectation that he should sacrifice his enjoyment of life for more supposedly worthy and lofty pursuits. The Quintilian of line 1 is a famous Roman teacher and scholar whom Martial uses to represent the life that he himself eschews.

Quintiliāne, vagae moderātor summe iuventae,
    glōria Rōmānae, Quintiliāne, togae,
vīvere quod properō pauper nec inūtilis annīs,
    dā veniam: properat vīvere nēmō satis.

1. What are the three second declension vocatives in lines 1-2?

2. The word *moderātor* in line 1 is also a vocative; it is a third declension noun, whose endings you don't yet know. You can, however, still determine the nominative of this noun based on its vocative form. What is its nominative (remember the rule for forming vocatives)?

3. What is the imperative verb in line 4, that directly addresses the vocative expression in lines 1-2?

CHAPTER 7

Nouns of the first two declensions followed a fairly regular pattern. Chapter 7 introduces nouns of the third declension, which will prove the most numerous of Latin nouns and, in many ways, the most difficult. Nouns of the third declension do not have a fixed nominative form and a stem that often changes from the nominative singular to the genitive singular. This makes mastery of third declension noun vocabulary information both more important and more difficult. Additional forms of *sum* are also introduced, as is the dative of possession.

> **Terms to Know**
>
> i-stem
> dative of possession

35. Third Declension Nouns

1. How many general categories of third declension nouns are there and what are they?
2. What are the two groups for consonant stem nouns?
3. How do you identify the stem of a third declension noun?
4. What two pairs of cases have identical endings in the third declension plural?
5. What is the only case and number in which i-stem third declension nouns look different?
6. What are the differences between third declension masculine/feminine endings and third declension neuter endings?
7. What two cases always have the same endings in neuter nouns?
8. In what four instances do neuter i-stems show the "i"?

Third Declension Nouns Text

MGM Motto

Ars grātiā artis.

---

1. Identify the cases of the two third declension nouns in the motto.

2. If *grātiā* means "for the sake of," translate the motto.

3. How does the motto reflect MGM's values and principles?

Third Declension Nouns Text

University of Michigan Motto

Artēs, scientia, vēritās.

---

1. What is the case and declension of each of the above nouns? Explain your answer.

Third Declension Nouns Text

Albertson College of Idaho Motto

Lux, lex, dux, rex.

---

1. Two of these nouns appear in the vocabulary of this chapter. Form the genitive singular forms of each of the above nouns, using the patterns of the nouns from this chapter to determine the genitives of the nouns not included in this chapter.

Third Declension Nouns Text

Plautus, *Menaechmi* 75-76. This excerpt concludes the Prologue to the *Menaechmi*, an ancient equivalent to modern printed programs that would be spoken prior to the play itself. It is unclear to what extent these prologues were products of Plautus himself or producers of Plautus' plays (much as each production of a modern play has a different printed program). These last two lines, which detail the sort of characters to be found in any comic play, are omitted from some editions of the *Menaechmi*.

modo hīc habitat <u>lēnō</u>, modo <u>adulescens</u>, modo <u>senex</u>,   75
<u>pauper</u>, <u>mendīcus</u>, <u>rex</u>, <u>parasītus</u>, <u>hariolus</u>.

The underlined words in the above excerpt are all nominative.

1. Identify the declension of each.

Third Declension Nouns Text

Catullus 64.19-21. Catullus 64 is an epyllion, a mini-epic whereby non-epic poets like Catullus experiment with both epic meter and, to a lesser extent, epic content. Catullus' epic centers on the wedding of Peleus and Thetis, who will later become the parents of Achilles. In this excerpt, Thetis' growing love for Peleus is described. But almost a third of Catullus 64 is devoted not to the wedding itself but rather to an extended ecphrasis, a literary description of something visual, often nature or art. Peleus and Thetis have received as a wedding gift a tapestry or bedsheet on which is woven the lament of Ariadne, the Cretan maiden who helped the Athenian hero Theseus defeat the Minotaur and who was then abandoned by him as they fled Crete.

tum <u>Thetidis</u> Pēleus incensus fertur amōre,
tum <u>Thetis</u> hūmānōs nōn despexit hymenaeōs,
tum <u>Thetidī</u> pater ipse iugandum Pelēa sensit.

The underlined word above is a proper name, that of the goddess Thetis, perhaps best known as the mother of Achilles.

Thetis' name in Latin is a third declension noun: *Thetis, Thetidis.*

1. Identify the cases of each of the three forms of her name.
2. Decline her name in the other seven cases (even though her name wouldn't really appear in the plural).

Third Declension Nouns Text

Cicero, *In Catilinam* 3.16. Cicero has described the power that Catiline wielded while in Rome. In this short excerpt, he describes Catiline's willingness to sacrifice even his personal comfort to achieve his goals.

frīgus, sitim, famem ferre poterat.

---

1. There are three third declension accusatives in the above excerpt. What are they?
2. One has an irregular accusative ending; which one?
3. One is neuter; which one? Explain your answer.

Third Declension Nouns Text

Catullus 34.9-12. The goddess Diana is invoked in her different incarnations, as goddess of nature, of fertility, and of the moon, to ultimately protect Rome. The prayer is sung by a chorus of boys and girls and is written in the formulaic style of a Roman hymn. In this excerpt, Catullus focuses on Diana's role as hunter-goddess.

…montium domina ut forēs
silvārumque virentium
saltuumque reconditōrum
    amniumque sonantum:

1. There are six genitives in the above selection. Write each genitive in the column on the left and identify whether it is singular or plural. Using the genitive ending, identify the delension, and then for the third declension nouns only, identify whether the noun is an i-stem or not. (There is a seventh genitive noun, *saltuum*, but it is a fourth declension noun.)

Genitive	Number	Declension	i-stem? (third decl. only)

Third Declension Nouns Text

Anonymous, The Alleluiatic Sequence 23-28. The author celebrates the meteorological wonders of God.

Fluctūs et undae,
imber et procellae,
tempestās et serēnitās,
cauma, gelū, nix, pruīnae,
saltūs, nemora pangant
Alleluia.

1. Complete the chart below with the requested information about the underlined nominative nouns in the above excerpt.

2. In the "Change of Number" column, change the number of each noun: if it is singular, make it plural and vice versa.

   (The non-underlined nouns are also nominatives, but do not fit into this exercise because of declension. *Nemora* is a third declension neuter plural noun.)

3. Finally, below the chart analogies have been drawn between third declension nouns in the vocabulary list of your textbook on page 57 and third declension nouns in the passage above. Use the pattern of the nouns in your vocabulary list to determine the genitive singular forms of the nouns here. (*Nix* has been left out because it does not have an analogous noun in the list.)

Noun	Number	Declension	Change of Number
undae			
imber			
procellae			
tempestās			
serēnitās			
cauma			
nix			
pruīnae			

Third Declension Nouns from page 57   **Analogous Nouns from above Passage**

(*Write the genitive of each noun in the blank based on the pattern of the noun on the left.*)

frāter, frātris   imber, _____

civitās, civitātis   tempestās, _____

                           serēnitās, _____

Third Declension Text

Cicero, *In Catilinam* 2.21. Cicero has been elaborating on the different types of men who are loyal to Catiline. These types are largely delineated on economic lines, specifically having to do with each type's debt vs. their desire to appear wealthy. In this excerpt, Cicero introduces the fourth type, which exists farther down the economic ladder.

Quārtum genus est sānē varium et mixtum et
　　turbulentum;

---

1. The word *genus* is a third declension neuter noun. How many adjectives agree with it?
2. Why is it difficult to recognize which adjectives agree with *genus*?

Third Declension Text

Seneca, *Phaedra* 1211-1212. Phaedra has just killed herself and now lies dying atop the body of Hippolytus. This excerpt is from her husband and Hippolytus' father, Theseus' lament in response. Here he takes responsibility, if melodramatically, for his role in their tragedy.

S̲ī̲d̲e̲r̲a̲ et m̲ā̲n̲ē̲s̲ et undās *scelere* complēvī meō:
amplius *sors* nulla restat; regna mē nōrunt tria.

---

1. The third declension nouns in the above excerpt are underlined. Identify all possible cases and numbers of them.
2. The third declension nouns that are also italicized have adjectives agreeing with them. Identify which adjectives agree with these nouns.

Third Declension Text

Catullus 64.205-206. Ariadne has just finished her lament with a curse of Theseus and his family for abandoning her: "by means of the same mindset with which he abandoned me, let him and his family perish." Jupiter assents, and signals his assent with an earthquake.

...quō mōtū tellūs atque horrida contremuērunt
aequora concussitque micantia sīdera mundus.

Vocabulary

quō mōtū = "By this motion"	**concussit** = "shook"
tellūs, tellūris. earth, land	**-que.** and
atque. and	**micantia** = "shining"
horridus, -a, -um. horrid, choppy	**sīdus, sīderis.** star
contremuērunt = "trembled"	**mundus, -ī.** heaven, universe
aequor, aequoris. sea, ocean	

1. Identify the three third declension nouns in the passage above.
2. Identify which two of these nouns are neuter (you can tell by their forms in the passage).
3. Using the vocabulary provided, translate the excerpt.

36. Imperfect and Future of *sum*

1. What is the "stem" of the imperfect of *sum*?
2. What is the "stem" of the future of *sum*?
3. What are the two exceptions to the use of the "stem" of the future of *sum*?
4. What are the four ways to translate the imperfect of *sum*?

Future of *sum* Text

Martial 8.55.21-24. Martial has outlined an epigrammatic tribute to Vergil, in which he details both Vergil's poetic accomplishments and the patron, Maecenas, under whom such output was possible. Martial, however, concludes the poem in the four lines excerpted here by restating his allegiance to the less glamorous, less serious genre of epigram that he prefers to write. (The Marsus of line 24 is another epigrammatic poet.)

Quid Variōs Marsōsque loquar dītātaque vātum
    nōmina, magnus erit quōs numerāre labor?
Ergō erō Vergilius, sī mūnera Maecēnātis
    dēs mihi? Vergilius nōn erō, Marsus erō.

1. What are the two different forms of the future of *sum* in the above excerpt?

2. What are the two different subjects (based on the endings, rather than any nouns in the excerpt) of these forms?

3. Complete the following translation of lines 23-24 by translating the forms of *sum* in brackets. (Note that the first sentence is a question; translate the verb accordingly.)

> Therefore, _____ [*erō*] a Vergil, if you give me the patronage of a Maecenas? _____ [*nōn erō*] a Vergil, but _____ [*erō*] a Marsus.

Future of *sum* Text

Catullus 49.1-3. Catullus here thanks the famous Roman orator Cicero, showering him with the praise of the first line: "Most eloquent of the descendants of Romulus." But Catullus is perhaps being disingenuous. Cicero criticized Catullus and his literary circle for the poetry that they wrote, and some read this poem as a bitingly sarcastic retort.

Disertissime Rōmulī nepōtum,
quot <u>sunt</u> quotque <u>fuēre</u>, Mārce Tullī,
quotque post aliīs <u>erunt</u> in annīs,…

1. Each underlined verb in the text is a different tense of *sum*. Which is the future form?

2. Which is the present form?

The other form is a form of the perfect of *sum*, which you will learn later.

3. Fill in the blanks in the English below with the appropriate translation of the form of *sum*. The blanks in the Latin indicate the corresponding form of *sum* for the English.

> O most honored of the descendants of Romulus, however many _____ [*sunt*] and however many <u>there were</u> [*fuēre*], Marcus Tullius, and however many _____ [*erunt*] that follow for years afterward,…

37. Dative of Possession

1. What are the two uses of the dative that have already been learned?

2. What does the dative of possession express?

- A form of *sum* is an indicator for the dative of possession; if you encounter a dative whose meaning or use is not immediately clear and there is a form of *sum* in the same clause, there is a good chance that it will be a dative of possession.

- The dative of possession can sometimes be used in a way similar to possessive adjectives, i.e. the English "my" is usually expressed with the Latin adjective *meus, -a, -um*, but can also be expressed with the dative *mihi*. This use of the dative of possession will not necessarily be used with a form of *sum*, and should be identified by context.

Dative of Possession Text

Plautus, *Menaechmi* 1107-1108. The climax to Plautus' *Menaechmi* is of course the recognition scene, when Menaechmus and his twin brother Sosicles are introduced to each other. The slave Messenio is the one who determines that both twins are in the same town and the one who brokers the recognition, part of which is described in this excerpt. The price Messenio exacts for introducing the brothers to each other is his freedom.

Messenio. Est tibi nōmen Menaechmō?
Menaechmus. Fateor.
Messenio. Est itidem tibi?
Sosciles. Est.
Messenio. Patrem fuisse Moschum tibi ais?
Menaechmus. Ita vērō.
Sosciles. Et mihi.

1. Complete the following literal translation of the dative of possession by translating the datives in parentheses.

> **Messenio.** Is the name _____ [*tibi*] _____ [*Menaechmō*]?
>
> **Menaechmus.** Yes.
>
> **Messenio.** Is it _____ [*tibi*] too?
>
> **Sosciles.** It is.
>
> **Messenio.** Do you say that there was the father Moschus _____ [*tibi*]?

Menaechmus. Yes.

Sosciles. Me too.

2. Complete the following more idiomatic translation of the dative of possession by translating the datives in parentheses.

Messenio. Is _____ [*tibi*] name _____ [*Menaechmō*]?

Menaechmus. Yes.

Messenio. Is it _____ [*tibi*] too?

Sosciles. It is.

Messenio. Do you say that Moschus was _____ [*tibi*] father?

Menaechmus. Yes.

Sosciles. Me too.

Dative of Possession Text

Ovid, *Amores* 1.1.5, .13, .19, .27. Ovid's *Amores* is a collection of love poetry from his early career. Even this early in Ovid's literary output, however, his interest in testing and expanding the limits of genre are already apparent. Ovid, instead of opening his love poetry with an introduction to his love, as many other love poets before him had, instead opens by saying how much he really wanted to write epic instead of love poetry. There are four separate lines excerpted here from *Amores* 1.1.

'Quis <u>tibi</u>, saeve puer, dedit hoc in carmina iūris?

Sunt <u>tibi</u> magna, puer, nimiumque potentia rēgna:

Nec <u>mihi</u> māteria est numerīs leviōribus apta,

Sex <u>mihi</u> surgat opus numerīs, in quīnque resīdat;

Each line has a dative pronoun that is underlined.

1. Of the four, which two are most likely to be datives of possession? Why?

2. Of the four, which one is most likely to be an indirect object? Why?

3. Of the four, which one is most likely to be a dative of reference? Why?

CHAPTER 8

The introduction of the perfect tense also introduces the third principal part, from which all perfect actives will be formed. The basic formula for the perfect will be very different from that of the second principal part tenses. Every verb will form its perfect tense in the same way, with the same endings, even irregular verbs. The difficulty of the perfect tense lies not in its formation but rather the fact that many verbs undergo stem changes from the second to the third principal part. So while the perfect itself is relatively easy to form, it requires a more detailed knowledge of vocabulary information to recognize from which verb a perfect form comes. A compound of *sum* and the use of the infinitive as a noun are also introduced.

> **Terms to Know**
>
> perfect (tense)
> imperfect (tense)
> historical perfect
> present perfect
> perfect active infinitive
> complementary
>   infinitive
> infinitive as noun

38. Perfect Active Indicative

1. Which principal part has been used for the present, imperfect, and future tenses?
2. Which principal part does the perfect active use?
3. How do you form the perfect stem?
4. What is an alternate ending for the third person plural, found most often in poetry?

- There are two clues to help distinguish this alternate third person plural from the present active infinitive of second and third conjugation verbs, which use the same -*ere* ending (albeit the former with a long -*ēre* and the latter with a short -*ere*):

  □ If in poetry, where the alternate third person plural form is more commonly used, the first -*e* is a long -*ē* ; scansion will help identify it, especially because the present active infinitive that uses the long -*ē*, the second conjugation infinitive, is less common that that of the third conjugation, whose infinitive uses a short -*e*.

  □ When used in the perfect tense, the -*ēre* ending will be attached to the third principal part. Differences between the third and second principal parts then will identify whether it is the perfect indicative or the infinitive, e.g. *docēre* vs. *docuēre*. The -*u*- in *docuere* is the only difference between the syncopated perfect and the present infinitive. (There are some verbs whose present and perfect stem are the same, e.g. *defendō, defendere, defendī, defensus*. In these instances, context will be your clue; the English verb "read" presents a similar ambiguity: "read" can be either the present or the perfect form.

- It is important to note that the formation of the perfect tense works the same way for every verb, even irregular verbs: form the perfect stem by dropping the *-ī* ending and add the endings. There are no exceptions to this rule. The irregularity of the perfect stem comes not from its formation but rather from the stem changes that often occur between the second and third principal parts.

5. How is the historical perfect translated?
6. What is the difference between the perfect and the imperfect?

- The term "perfect" comes from the Latin verb *perficio, perficere*, which means "to complete" or "to finish."
- Thus, the perfect tense is the "completed" tense or the tense that indicates completed action, and the imperfect, with the *im-* as a negating prefix, is the "incomplete" tense or the tense of action that has not yet been completed.

7. What is meant by the term "historical present?"
8. What kind of action does the present perfect indicate?

Perfect Active Indicative Text

Rockhurst University (MO) Motto

Sapientia aedificāvit sibi domum.

1. If *aedificō, -āre* means "to build," translate the form *aedificāvit* in three different ways.
2. Which of the three translations from #1 makes the most sense to complete the following translation of the motto?

   Wisdom _____ its own house.

39. Perfect Active Infinitive

1. What is the ending for the perfect active infinitive?
2. How is the perfect active infinitive formed?

Perfect Active Indicative and Infinitive Text

Plautus, *Menaechmi* 398-400. The humor of the *Menaechmi* is derived from the mishaps that occur when the two twins are, unbeknownst to each other, in the same city. One is repeatedly mistaken for the other and accused of doing things that the other has done. In this excerpt, Menaechmus' mistress Erotium asks Sosicles (thinking of course that she is asking Menaechmus) why he took his wife's cloak from her. Sosicles of course vehemently denies it; he was never married and has never been to this town before. How could he have taken any cloak from or to his non-existent wife?

Erotium. Pallam tē hodiē mihi dedisse uxōris. **Sosicles.** Etiam nunc negō. Ego quidem neque umquam uxōrem habuī neque habeō neque hūc umquam postquam nātus sum, intrā portam penetrāvī pedem.   400

1. What is the perfect active infinitive in the excerpt?
2. What is the difference in tense between *habuī* and *habeō* in line 399?
3. What is the perfect active indicative verb in line 400?
4. Complete the translation below of lines 399-400 by translating the verb forms in brackets.

    Indeed I never _____ [*habuī*] a wife nor _____ [*habeō*] a wife, nor ever up to this point, since I was born, _____ [*penetrāvī* = *penetrō, -āre*, "to enter"] your door.

40. Forms of *possum*

1. Is *possum* a regular or irregular verb?
2. What two words are combined to form *possum*?
3. What kind of word will follow *possum* to complete its meaning?

- Since this chapter introduces the perfect tense, it is illustrative to note that, although *possum* is an irregular verb, its perfect tense will be formed no differently from any other verb: the perfect endings will be added to its perfect stem.

Forms of *possum* Text

Martial 1.21.5-6. The last Roman king, the Etruscan Tarquinius Superbus, was expelled from Rome in 509 BCE after his son raped the Roman matron Lucretia. The Etruscans, however, continued to battle the Romans. One of the heroes of the Roman Republic, whose courage epitomized the values of early Rome, is described in the excerpt below. A Roman soldier, Mucius, offered to steal into the Etruscan camp to kill their king Lars Porsena. Not knowing what Porsena looked like, however, Mucius killed the wrong man. Once captured, Mucius was surrounded by a ring of fire and compelled by the king to reveal the Roman plan. Rather than capitulate, Mucius thrust his right hand into the nearest fire, declaring that this was the courage the Etruscans were facing and that there were many more like him. As a reward for his bravery, Mucius was set free and, because of his burnt right hand, became known as Mucius Scaevola, or "Lefty."

ūrere quam potuit contemptō Mūcius igne,
    hanc spectāre manum Porsena nōn potuit.

Vocabulary

ūrō, -ere. to burn   Mūcius, Porsena. [*names*]
spectō, -āre. to look at, to see

1. Identify the two forms of *possum* in the couplet, and their tenses.
2. Identify the infinitive that will go with each form of *possum*.
3. Complete the translations below, using the words in parentheses to fill in each blank.
    a. Mucius _____ (*potuit*) _____ (*ūrere*).
    b. Porsena _____ (*potuit*) _____ (*spectāre*).

Forms of *possum* Text

Catullus 29.1-4. Catullus in this poem inveighs against Caesar, Pompey, and a certain Mamurra for their rapacious abuse of the Roman provincial system that has allowed them to profit immeasurably from conquest and plunder. In this excerpt, Catullus opens the poem with a rhetorical question that establishes his shock at and distaste for such men.

Quis hoc potest vidēre, quis potest patī,
nisi impudīcus et vorax et āleō,
Mamurram habēre quod Comāta Gallia
habēbat unctī et ultima Britannia?

Vocabulary

Quis. who
hoc. this

patī = to endure

1. Identify the tense of the two forms of *possum* in line 1 of the excerpt.
2. What are the two infinitives in the line? (One will be recognizable from your vocabulary, while one you will need to determine from the vocabulary above.)
3. Using the vocabulary above, translate the line. What word of the first clause is gapped in the second?

Forms of *possum* Text

Ovid, *Metamorphoses* 4.152-153. After Pyramus tragically kills himself, Thisbe finds his body and kills herself in grief. Before she dies, she delivers a speech, from which the excerpt below is taken, in which she pledges her devotion to the now dead Pyramus.

> ...quīque ā mē morte revellī
> heu sōlā poterās, poteris nec morte revellī.

1. What is the difference between *poterās* and *poteris* in line 153?

Forms of *possum* Text

Martial 6.14. Martial encourages Laberius, perhaps mockingly, to do more than just talk about writing poetry; he should actually write it.

Versūs scrībere posse tē disertōs
affirmās, Laberī: quid ergō nōn vīs?
Versūs scrībere quī potest disertōs,
conscrībat, Laberī: virum putābo.

1. What form is *posse* in line 1?
2. What form is *potest* in line 3?
3. Complete the following translation of lines 3-4 by filling in the blanks with the correct translation of the verb in brackets.

> He who _____ [*potest*] to write refined verses, let him write them, Laberius: _____ [*putābo; putō, -āre* = "to think"] him a man.

Forms of *possum* Text

Vergil, *Aeneid* **4.419-420.** Dido's sister Anna was instrumental in convincing her to pursue her feelings for Aeneas, despite Dido's pledge of fidelity to her dead husband Sychaeus. At this point in Book 4, Dido knows that Aeneas is leaving, and is distraught. In this excerpt, she asks Anna (the *soror* of line 420) to try to convince Aeneas to stay.

Hunc ego sī potuī tantum spērāre dolōrem,
et perferre, soror, poterō.　　　　　　　420

1. Identify the tense of the form of *possum* in line 419.
2. Identify the infinitive that depends on it.
3. Identify the infinitive that depends on *possum* in line 420. (This infinitive is irregular and has not yet been learned, but should look enough like an infinitive to be identifiable.)

41. Infinitive as a Noun

1. What is the previous use of the infinitive that you have learned?
2. What is the gender and number of the infinitive as a noun?
3. With what verb and what types of verbs is the infinitive as noun most commonly used?

- Impersonal verbs will often use the formula "It is... to...," e.g. *Licetne mihi īre ad lātrīnam?* = "Is it permitted to me to go to the bathroom?"

- Looking at the example above, answer the following: What is permitted? By this formulation, despite English's somewhat convoluted word order, it is clear that the infinitive "to go" (*īre*) is the subject of the verb.

- English tends to prefer the "It is…" formulation because English prefers to avoid complex subjects.

Infinitive as a Noun Text

Tottenham Hotspur (English Soccer Club) Motto

Audēre est facere.

1. If *facere* means "to do," translate the motto.
2. How does the motto reflect the values and principles of Tottenham Hotspur?

Infinitive as a Noun Text

Anonymous, *Conflictus veris et hiemis* 32-33. In this allegorical dialogue between winter and spring, here winter concludes his argument as he prepares to hunker down for another chilly season.

Haec inimīca mihi sunt, quae tibi laeta videntur,
sed placet optātas gāzās numerāre per arcās
et gaudēre cibīs simul et requiescere semper.

Vocabulary

numerō, -āre. to count   **requiescō, -ere.** to rest
gaudeō, -ēre. to rejoice

1. What are the three infinitives in these three lines?
2. What is the impersonal verb upon which they depend?
3. Using the vocabulary above, translate the impersonal verb with its three infinitives, i.e. *Placet numerāre, gaudēre, et requiescere.*

Infinitive as a Noun Text

Vergil, *Aeneid* 2.27-30. Aeneas begins his extended recounting to Dido and her guests of the fall of Troy and his journey to Carthage, the former comprising Book 2 of the *Aeneid* and the latter Book 3. Here, at the beginning of his story, the Trojans rush out of the city to behold the land so recently held by the Greeks as part of the siege that now apparently has so abruptly ended.

Panduntur portae, iuvat īre et Dōrica castra
dēsertōsque vidēre locōs lītusque relictum:
hīc Dolopum manus, hīc saevus tendēbat Achillēs;
classibus hīc locus, hīc aciē certāre solēbant.   30

---

1. Identify each infinitive in lines 27, 28, and 30.
2. Identify the impersonal verb on which each depends.
3. Vergil uses a rhetorical figure called anaphora to emphasize the excitement of the Trojans. Anaphora is the unnecessary repetition of a word or phrase for emphasis. In lines 29-30, *hic*, "here," is repeated four times, repeatedly emphasizing how the Trojans looked in different places for evidence of the Greeks' presence, and now absence. Anaphora is very commonly used in political speeches and TV/movie courtroom speeches, among other rhetorical places.

Infinitive as a Noun Text

Martial 7.85. Martial compliments Sabellus for writing some witty poems, but cautions him that maintaining that output to write entire books is difficult. This of course becomes a subtle compliment to Martial himself, who, at this point, has written seven books of epigrams, and will write fourteen.

Quod nōn insulsē scrībis tetrasticha quaedam,
    disticha quod bellē pauca, Sabelle, facis,
laudō nec admīror. Facile est epigrammata bellē
    scrībere, sed librum scrībere difficile est.

Vocabulary

facile = easy   **scrībō, -ere.** to write
epigrammata = epigrams   **liber, -brī.** book
    [*acc. pl.*]   **difficile** = difficult
bellē (*adv.*). well

---

1. Using the vocabulary above, translate lines 3-4, *Facile est...difficile est.*

Infinitive as a Noun Text

Horace, *Carmina* **3.2.13.** Horace is best known for *carpe diem*, the iconic phrase that comes from poem 1.11. Perhaps his second-best known *sententia* is this, one that has proven inspirational and even controversial because of its bald, and some would say blind, patriotism.

Dulce et decōrum est prō patriā morī:

Vocabulary

dulce = *neuter nominative singular of* **dulcis, -e.** sweet, satisfying
decōrus, -a, -um. fitting, appropriate
prō (*prep. + abl.*). for, on behalf of
morī = "to die"

1. Using the vocabulary above, translate the line. It is rewritten below in a more Anglicized word order for your assistance.

    Est dulce et decōrum morī prō patriā.

2. The poem below, written in 1917 by the World War I poet Wilfred Owen, takes its title and its closing lines from Horace's *sententia*.

    Bent double, like old beggars under sacks,
    Knock-kneed, coughing like hags, we cursed through
       sludge,
    Till on the haunting flares we turned our backs
    And towards our distant rest began to trudge.
    Men marched asleep. Many had lost their boots
    But limped on, blood-shod. All went lame; all blind;
    Drunk with fatigue; deaf even to the hoots
    Of tired, outstripped Five-Nines that dropped behind.

    Gas! Gas! Quick, boys! –An ecstasy of fumbling,
    Fitting the clumsy helmets just in time;
    But someone still was yelling out and stumbling
    And flound'ring like a man in fire or lime...
    Dim, through the misty panes and thick green light,
    As under a green sea, I saw him drowning.

    In all my dreams, before my helpless sight,
    He plunges at me, guttering, choking, drowning.

If in some smothering dreams you too could pace
Behind the wagon that we flung him in,
And watch the white eyes writhing in his face,
His hanging face, like a devil's sick of sin;
If you could hear, at every jolt, the blood
Come gargling from the froth-corrupted lungs,
Obscene as cancer, bitter as the cud
Of vile, incurable sores on innocent tongues,-
My friend, you would not tell with such high zest
To children ardent for some desperate glory,
The old Lie: *Dulce et decorum est*
Pro patria mori.

CHAPTER 9

As third declension nouns are both the most common and perhaps the most difficult of nouns, so are third conjugation verbs the most common and the most difficult of verbs. The difficulties that third conjugation verbs present are not introduced in this chapter; they are confined to the future and the perfect tenses. Nonetheless, you will notice that, unlike the first two conjugations, especially the first, there is no set pattern for third conjugation principal parts; third conjugation verbs will usually undergo a significant stem change between the second and third principal parts, a change which must be memorized as part of learning your vocabulary. The first and second person pronouns are also introduced.

> **Terms to Know**
>
> third conjugation
> pronoun
> personal pronoun

42. Third Conjugation

1. In which vowel does the third conjugation stem end?
2. What are the two forms in the present tense where third *-iō* verbs differ from regular third conjugation verbs?

- With the introduction of third and third *-iō* verbs, three types of verbs will use *-ere* as the present active infinitive ending; it becomes imperative then to be able to distinguish among these three types of verbs (less so between third and third *-iō* but more so between third and second).

  - While the second conjugation *-ēre* uses a long *-ē-* and the third conjugation *-ere* uses a short *-e-*, not every text will include these long marks; you will need another way to tell them apart.

  - When the present active infinitive does not conclusively determine conjugation (and the *-ere* is the only ending that will introduce such ambiguity), the first principal part will make the final determination of conjugation; use the chart below as a guide.

    -eō, -ēre = *second conjugation, e.g.* sedeō, sedēre
    -ō, -ere = *third conjugation, e.g.* agō, agere
    -iō, -ere = *third conjugation* -io, *e.g.* capiō, capere

▫ The distinction between third conjugation and third conjugation -*iō* becomes more important for other tenses and when the fourth conjugation is introduced.

3. What are the four common verbs whose imperatives are irregular because they do not use the stem vowel as part of their imperative?

Third Conjugation Present Active Indicative Text

Anonymous, *Carmina Burana: The Return of Spring* 11-20. As winter yields to spring, those who cannot enjoy it will be unhappy.

> Iam liquescit
> et decrescit
> grandō, nix et cetera,
> brūma fugit,
> et iam sūgit   15
> vēr estātis ūbera;
> illī mens est misera,
> quī nec vīvit,
> nec lascīvit
> sub estātis dextera.   20

1. Identify all of the third conjugation verbs in the above passage.
2. The verb *lascīvit* in line 19 looks like a 3rd conjugation verb, but in reality is a 4th conjugation verb, which you have not yet learned.

Third Conjugation Present Active Indicative Text

Eugenius of Toledo, *Carmen Philomelaicum* 1-10. In the opening to this poem dedicated to the nightingale's song, the power of the nightingale's voice and the sylvan environment in which the nightingale lives are described.

> Vox, Philomēla, tua cantūs ēdīcere cōgit,
>   inde tuī laudem rustica lingua canit.
> Vox, Philomēla, tua citharās in carmine vincit
>   et superāt mīrīs mūsica flabra modīs.
> Vox, Philomēla, tua cūrārum sēmina pellit,   5

recreat et blandīs anxia corda sonīs.
Flōrea rūra cōlis, herbōsō caespite gaudēs,
　　frondibus arboreīs pignera parva fovēs.
Cantibus ecce tuīs recrepant arbusta canōris,
　　consonat ipsa suīs frondea silva comīs.　　　　10

1. In the above passage, identify the one third conjugation infinitive.

2. In the above passage, identify the four third conjugation present indicative forms.

   Note: *cōlis* in line 7 is a third conjugation verb, but because of the *-s* ending and its overlap with noun endings, it is difficult to identify; it is not counted as one of the four.

3. In the above passage, identify the four first conjugation verbs.

4. In lines 7-8, identify the two second conjugation verbs.

Third Conjugation Present Imperative Text

Plautus, *Menaechmi* **1162.** This is the final line in Plautus' play. Messenio, the slave of Sosicles, who has just (re)introduced the twin brothers to each other and in the process has won his freedom, now closes the play.

Nunc, spectātōrēs, valēte et nōbīs clārē plaudite.

Vocabulary

spectātōr, -ōris (*m.*). spectator; audience (*in pl.*)
plaudō, -ere. to applaud, to cheer, to make noise

1. What are the two imperatives?
2. What are their conjugations?
3. Using the vocabulary above, translate the line.
4. What case is *spectātōrēs*?

Third Conjugation Present Imperative Text

Ovid, *Metamorphoses* **1.1-4.** Ovid's *Metamorphoses* states its theme in its title: change. In his prologue, excerpted here, Ovid describes what he envisions both for the theme and content of the poem, and its long-term literary significance.

> In nova fert animus mūtātās dīcere formās
> corpora. Dī, coeptīs (nam vōs mūtāstis et illās)
> aspīrāte meīs: prīmāque ab orīgine mundī
> ad mea perpetuum dēdūcite tempora carmen.

1. In the above passage, identify the one present active infinitive.
2. In the above passage, identify the one present indicative verb. (*Mūtāstis* in the second line is a perfect indicative verb, but is a poetic form that has not been learned yet.)
3. In the above passage, identify the two present imperatives. To what conjugation does each belong?

Third Conjugation Present Imperative Text

Plautus, *Miles Gloriosus* **1394-5.** Palaestrio, the crafty slave, and Periplectomenus, the kindly old man, have conspired to trap Pyrgopolynices, the Miles Gloriosus. They lure him into the house of Periplectomenus, where a woman playing the part of Periplectomenus' wife throws herself at him. Periplectomenus of course discovers them and, in this excerpt, is dragging Pyrgopolynices out of the house to have him flogged and killed. Those threats are all part of the plan.

Periplectomenus. Dūcite istum; sī nōn sequitur, rapite sublīmem forās.
Facite inter terram atque caelum acivium sit: discindite.

1. In the above passage, identify the four imperatives.
2. What do the endings tell you about the audience for these commands?

The form *siet* in line 1395 is an archaic form of the present subjunctive of *sum*.

Third Conjugation Present Imperative Text

Seneca, *Phaedra* **1-8.** Seneca, as does Euripides, opens his *Phaedra* with an extended preface in which Hippolytus proclaims his allegiance to the huntress goddess Diana, and to the natural realm over which she holds sway. This allegiance recalls Hippolytus' mother, Hippolyta the Amazon, and establishes Hippolytus as one who will shun the societal trappings of love and marriage, as Diana herself did.

Hippolytus. Īte, umbrōsās cingite silvās
summaque montis iuga Cecropiī!
Celerī plantā lustrāte vagī
quae saxōsō loca Parnēthō
subiecta iacent, quae Thrīasiīs   5
vallibus amnis rapidā currens
verberat undā; scandite collēs
semper cānōs nive Rīphaeā.

1. There are four imperatives in the above excerpt.
2. What are the two third conjugation imperatives?
3. What is the one first conjugation imperative?
4. What is the irregular imperative? (Although you have not yet learned this verb, you should be able to determine both that it is an imperative form and that is irregular.)

Third Conjugation Present Imperative Text

Seneca, *Phaedra* **448-451.** The Nurse here encourages Hippolytus to embrace the pleasure of life and not be so burdened by life's seriousness. The Nurse is trying to make Hioppolytus amenable to the advances of his stepmother, Phaedra.

Nutrix. Cūr torō viduō iacēs?
Tristem iuventam solve; nunc cursūs rape,
effunde habēnās, optimōs vītae diēs   450
effluere prohibe.

1. What are the four third conjugation imperatives in the excerpt?

2. Although it ends in an -e, why is *effluere* in line 451 not an imperative? Give two reasons for your answer, one grammatical and one contextual.

3. What is the tense and conjugation of *iacēs* in line 448?

Third Conjugation Present Imperative Text

Anonymous, *Ave maris stella* **9-12.** Mary's power to change for the better people's lives is described.

Solve vincla reīs,
prōfer lūmen caecīs,
mala nostra pelle,
bona cuncta posce.

Vocabulary

solvō, -ere. to loosen, to break	**malum, -ī.** evil
vinclum, -ī. chain	**pellō, -ere.** to banish, to eliminate
reus, -ī. prisoner	
prōferō, prōferre. to offer	**bonum, -ī.** good
lūmen, lūminis. light	**cunctus, -a, -um.** all
caecus, -ī. blind person	**poscō, -ere.** to demand

1. In the above passage, identify the four imperatives.

2. Translate the passage.

Third Conjugation Present Imperative Text

Plautus, *Menaechmi* **1009-1019.** The father of Menaechmus' wife has returned with men to punish Menaechmus for the shame he has dealt to her. Messenio, Sosicles' slave, sees these men roughing up Menaechmus and, thinking Menaechmus is his master Sosicles, intervenes. Menaechmus, grateful for the assistance, thinks a stranger has come to help. In this excerpt, Menaechmus and Messenio collaborate to fend off the men. Once they are successful, they will have a confusing exchange in which Menaechmus professes never to have seen Messenio (which he hasn't) and Messenio wonders why his master refuses to recognize him. This exchange will lead to the recognition scene between the two brothers.

Messenio. Immō et operam <u>dabō</u> et dēfendam et <u>subvenībō</u> sēdulō.

Numquam tē <u>patiar</u> perīre, mē perīrest aequius.   1010

<u>Ēripe</u> oculum istī, ab umerō quī <u>tenet</u>, ere, tē <u>obsecrō</u>.

Hīsce ego iam sēmentem in ōre <u>faciam</u> pugnōsque <u>obseram</u>.

Maximō hodiē malō hercle vostrō istunc <u>fertis</u>: <u>mittite</u>.

Menaechmus. <u>Teneō</u> ego huic oculum. **Messenio.** <u>Face</u> ut oculī

locus in capite <u>appāreat</u>.

Vōs scelestī, vōs rapācēs, vōs praedōnēs. **Lorarii.** <u>Periimus</u>.   1015

<u>Obsecrō</u> hercle! **Messenio.** <u>Mittite</u> ergō. **Menaechmus.** Quid mē

vōbīs tactiōst?

<u>Pecte</u> pugnīs. **Messenio.** <u>Agite</u>, <u>abīte</u>, <u>fugite</u> hinc in malam crucem.

Em tibi etiam! Quia postrēmus <u>cēdis</u>, hoc praemī <u>ferēs</u>.

Nimis bene ōra <u>commētāvī</u> atque ex meā sententiā.

---

1. Complete the table below with the requested information about the underlined verbs in the above excerpt.

   Some forms that have not yet been learned have been done for you. Those that are partially done have left blank that information which you should still be able to determine.

Line #	Verb Form	Prin. Parts	Conj.	Mood	Tense	Subj.
1009	dābō	dō, dare				
1009	subvenībō	subveniō, -īre	4	*Indicative*	*Future*	
1010	patiar	patior, patī	3	*Indicative*	*Future*	*I*
1011	ēripe	eripiō, -ere				
1011	tenet	teneō, -ēre				
1011	obsecrō	obsecrō, -āre				
1012	faciam	faciō, -ere	3	*Indicative*	*Future*	*I*
1012	obseram	obserō, -ere	3	*Indicative*	*Future*	*I*
1013	fertis	ferō, ferre	Irreg.	*Indicative*	*Present*	*You* (pl.)
1013	mittite	mittō, -ere				
1014	teneō	teneō, -ēre				
1014	face	faciō, -ere				
1014	appāreat	appareō, -ēre	2	*Subjunctive*	*Present*	
1015	periimus	pereō, -īre	*Irreg.*	*Indicative*	*Perfect*	
1016	obsecrō	obsecrō, -āre				
1016	mittite	mittō, -ere				
1017	pecte	pectō, -ere				
1017	agite	agō, -ere				
1017	abīte	abeō, -īre	*Irreg.*			

Line #	Verb Form	Prin. Parts	Conj.	Mood	Tense	Subj.
1017	fugite	fugiō, -ere				
1018	cēdis	cedō, -ere				
1018	ferēs	ferō, ferre	*Irreg.*	*Indicative*	*Future*	
1019	commētāvī	commētō, -āre, -āvī				

The form *face* in line 1014 is an archaic form, but should still be recognizable given the rules for forming the imperative.

Third Conjugation Present Imperative Text

Plautus, *Menaechmi* 143-159. Peniculus, the mooch, has just run into Menaechmus, who promises good news for Peniculus. First, however, Peniculus must pay the price: Peniculus flatters Menaechmus, which he is happy to do if it will lead to a free meal.

Menaechmus. Dīc mī, ēnumquam tū vīdistī tabulam pictam in *pariete,*
ubi aquila Catameitum raperet aut ubi Venus Adōneum?
Peniculus. *Saepe.* Sed quid istae pictūrae ad mē adtinent?
   Menaechmus. <u>Age</u> mē <u>aspice.</u>   145
ecquid adsimulō *similiter*? **Peniculus.** Quī istīc ornātus tuos?
Menaechmus. Dīc hominem lepidissimum *esse* mē. **Peniculus.** Ubi essurī
   sumus?
Menaechmus. Dīc modo hoc quod ego tē iubeō. **Peniculus.** Dīcō: homō
   lepidissime.
Menaechmus. Ecquid audēs dē tuō istuc addere? **Peniculus.** Atque
   hilarissime.
Menaechmus. <u>Perge</u> <perge>. **Peniculus.** Nōn pergō *hercle*, nisi sciō
   quā gratiā.   150
lītigium tibist cum uxōre, eō mī abs tē caveō cautius.
Menaechmus. Clam uxōrem ubi sepulchrum habeāmus atque hunc
   combūrāmus diem.   152-153
Peniculus. <u>Age</u> sānē igitur, quandō aequom ōrās, quam mox
   incendō rogum?
   diēs quidem iam ad umbilīcum dīmidiātus mortuōs.
Menaechmus. Tē <u>morāre</u>, mihi quom <u>obloquere.</u> **Peniculus.** Oculum
   <u>ecfoditō</u> per solum   156
mihi, Menaechme, sī ullum verbum faxō, nisi quod iusseris.
Menaechmus. <u>Concēde</u> hūc ā foribus. **Peniculus.** Fiat. **Menaechmus.**
   Etiam <u>concēde</u> hūc. **Peniculus.** Licet.
Menaechmus. Etiam nunc <u>concēde</u> audacter ab leōnīnō cavō.

1. How many times is the imperative of *dīcō, -ere* used in the above excerpt? Identify each use by line number.

2. Complete the table below with the requested information about the underlined imperative forms. Some of the underlined forms are imperatives that you have not yet learned. They are not included in the table and will be explained below the table.

Line #	Imperative	Conjugation	First 2 Principal Parts
145, 154	age		
145	aspice		
150	perge		
158, 159	concēde		

morāre, obloquere (156): passive imperatives, whose endings you have not yet learned

ecfoditō (156): future imperative, a rare form often used in verse.

3. The italicized forms are words that might look imperative but are not. Explain what aspects of the words themselves or their context might indicate that they are not imperative.

43. The Pronoun

1. What is a noun?

2. What is a pronoun?

- A pronoun can also be defined as a word that takes the place of a noun.

3. How are Latin pronouns similar to Latin nouns? How are they different?

4. What does Latin use instead of a third person personal pronoun?

5. For what three purposes is the nominative of the Latin personal pronoun generally used?

Pronoun Text

Catullus 63.63-73. Attis has castrated himself out of devotion to the goddess Cybele and spent the night in pain-inspired ecstasy before he fell asleep. He has now awakened and, understanding what he has done, reflects on what he had and what he no longer will have.

Ego mulier, ego adulescens, ego ephēbus, ego puer,
ego gymnasī fuī flōs, ego eram decus oleī:
mihi ianuae frequentēs, mihi limina tepida,   65
mihi flōridīs corollīs redimīta domus erat,
linquendum ubi esset ortō mihi sōle cubiculum.
Egone et deum ministra et Cybelēs famula ferar?
Ego Maenās, ego mei pars, ego vir sterilis erō?
Ego viridis algida Īdae nive amicta loca cōlam?   70
Ego vītam agam sub altīs Phrygiae columinibus,
ubi cerva silvicultrix, ubi aper nemorivagus?
Iam iam dolet, quod egī, iam iamque paenitet.

---

1. In the above excerpt, how many times does the nominative of the first person singular pronoun appear?
2. Two other cases of the first person singular pronoun appear. What are they? How many times does each appear? What are the forms and line numbers of each?

Pronoun Text

Catullus 68.20-24. Catullus responds to the request of a certain Manius for Catullus' poetry. Catullus explains, however, that by not honoring Manius' request he does not mean to be insulting but rather has lost his joy for writing because of the death of his brother (the poignant subject of Catullus' Poem 101). In this excerpt, Catullus address his brother directly as he describes the effect of his brother's death on his life.

Ō miserō frāter adempte mihi,   20
tu mea tu moriens fregistī commoda, frāter,
    tēcum ūnā tōta est nostra sepulta domus,
omnia tēcum ūnā periērunt gaudia nostra,
    quae tuus in vītā dulcis alēbat amor.

1. In the above excerpt, what case of the first person singular pronoun appears?

2. In the above excerpt, what cases of the second person singular pronoun appear?

3. *Mea* (line 21), *nostra* (line 23), and *tuus* (line 24) are words that are related to the pronouns learned in this chapter, but are not actually pronouns. What do you think they mean?

4. The addressing of someone or something not present, as Catullus above addresses his brother, is called apostrophe.

Pronoun Text

Miraculum Sancti Nicholai **66-73.** Eufrosina, whose son has been taken, prays to St. Nicholas and laments her situation.

> Heu! Heu! Heu! Mihi miserae!
> Quid agam? Quid queam dicere?
> Quō peccātō meruī perdere
> nātum meum et ultrā vīvere?
>
> Cūr mē pater infēlix genuit?   70
> Cūr mē māter infēlix abluit?
> Cūr mē nūtrix lactāre dēbuit?
> Mortem mihi quārē nōn praebuit?

Vocabulary

cūr. why
infēlix. unhappy
gignō, -ere. to give birth to
abluō, -ere. to baptize

nūtrix, -icis. wet-nurse, female caretaker
lactō, -āre. to feed milk to
quārē. why
praebeō, -ēre. to offer, to give

1. In the above passage, what are the two different forms of the first person personal pronoun? What case are they?

2. One word in the above passage means "my." What word is it? (Hint: it looks like a form of *ego*, but it does not appear in the list of forms in your textbook.)

3. Using the vocabulary above, translate the second stanza (lines 70-73).

4. Why is *mihi* in line 73 in the dative case?

Pronoun Text

Catullus 92. Catullus, as he does elsewhere (e.g. poem 83), reveals the often contradictory nature of his relationship with Lesbia. On the one hand, he says that he needs Lesbia's love to survive. On the other hand, he says that he needs to love Lesbia to survive. Such an emotional quandary in many ways epitomizes the poetic position of the elegiac poet.

Lesbia mī dicit semper malē nec tacet umquam
    dē mē: Lesbia mē dispeream nisi amat.
Quō signō? Quia sunt totidem mea: dēprecor illam
    assiduē, vērum dispeream nisi amō.

Vocabulary

Lesbia, -ae. [*name*]
mī = **mihi**
malē. badly
nec. and…not [*a conjunction that negates the verb*]
taceō, -ēre. to be quiet

umqaum. ever [*with* **nec** = "never"]
dispeream = "May I perish"
nisi. if…not [*the negative form of* **si**, "if"]

1. What is the clue that the two appearances of *mē* in line 2 are different cases?
2. Using the vocabulary above, translate lines 1-2. (The second part of line 2 has been rewritten below in a more understandable word order.)

    Dispeream nisi Lesbia mē amat.

Pronoun Text

Martial 1.5. Martial criticizes the writings of a certain Marcus.

Dō tibi naumachiam, tū dās epigrammata nōbīs:
    vīs, putō, cum librō, Marce, natāre tuō.

Vocabulary

naumachia, -ae. sea-battle [*staged in a stadium*]; **naumachia** [*perhaps best to simply use the Latin term since there really is no good English equivalent*]

epigramma, -atos (**epigrammata** = *acc. sing.*). epigram, short poem
vīs = "you want"
putō, -āre. to think
Marcus, -ī. [*name*]
natō, -āre. to swim

1. Using the vocabulary, translate the couplet.
2. What case is *Marce* in line 2?

Pronoun Text

Plautus, *Menaechmi* **639-648.** Menaechmus' mistress gave Sosicles a dress to be tailored that Menaechmus had given to her. Sosicles, of course, not knowing Menaechmus' mistress, gladly accepted what he saw as a free gift. Sosicles had also encountered Peniculus, Menaechmus' mooch, and declined to feed him after Menaechmus had promised him a sumptuous meal (and Peniculus, of course, mistakes Sosicles for Menaechmus). Peniculus, feeling slighted, told Menaechmus' wife about the dress and, in this excerpt, Menaechmus unexpectedly finds himself under attack by both Peniculus and his wife, and tries to defend himself.

      Matrona. Quasi tū nesciās:
[palla mi est domō surrepta. **Menaechmus.** Palla surrepta est tibi?]   639b
Matrona. Mē rogās? **Menaechmus.** Pol haud rogem tē, sī sciam.
      Peniculus. Ō hominem malum,
ut dissimulat. Nōn potes cēlāre: rem nōvit probē:
Omnia hercle ego ēdictāvī. **Menaechmus.** Quid id est? **Matrona.**
      Quandō nīl pudet
neque vīs tuā voluntāte ipse profitērī, audī atque ades.
Et quid tristis <sim> et quid hic mihi dīxerit, faxō sciās.
Palla mihist domō surrupta. **Menaechmus.** Palla surruptast mihi?   645
Peniculus. Vidēn ut <tē> scelestus captat? Huic surruptast, nōn tibi:
nam profectō tibi surrupta sī esset—salva non foret.
Menaechmus. Nīl mihi tēcumst.

---

1. Complete the following translation by translating the forms of the personal pronoun in brackets (Some of the dative forms will have unexpected translations).

    My dress has been stolen _____ [*mī* = *mihi*; 639b] from my house.
    Menaechmus. Your dress has been stolen _____ [*tibi*; 639b]?
    Matrona. You're asking _____ [*mē*; 640]? ... **Matrona.** I will make you understand why I am sad and what this man said _____ [*mihi*; 644].
    My dress has been stolen _____ [*mī* = *mihi*; 645].
    Menaechmus. My dress has been stolen _____ [*mihi*; 645]?
    Peniculus. Don't you see how that hated man fools _____ [*tē*; 646]? Your dress has been stolen from this man, not _____ [*tibi*; 646]. For indeed if it had been stolen _____ [*tibi*; 647] - it would not be right.
    Menaechmus. I want nothing to do _____ [*tēcum*; 648].

CHAPTER 10

Demonstratives are perhaps Latin's most commonly used words. In their most basic meaning, they mean "this" or "that," but they can also be used in a number of different ways: as simple adjectives, "this book," "that dog;" as a substantive, "this man," "that woman;" or as a personal pronoun, "he," "she," "it." It is important then not only to know the forms of the demonstratives but also to be aware of the different contexts within which they can be used.

A type of irregular adjective is also introduced, whose irregularity mimics some of the forms of the demonstratives, and a new sentence pattern, the factitive, is added to the sentence patterns already learned.

44. Demonstrative Pronouns

1. What are demonstrative pronouns used for?

2. What parts of the demonstratives in this chapter are regular? irregular?

3. What is the difference between *hic* and *ille*, and *is, ea, id*?

4. To what does *hic* refer? *ille*?

- All three of these demonstratives can be used as adjectives or pronouns, i.e. the examples of *is, ea, id* at the top of page 72 of your textbook can use *hic* and *ille* as well:

Hic / Ille est amicus.	He is a friend. (*This* / *That* man is a friend.)
Amo hanc / illam.	I love her. (I love *this* / *that* woman.)
Videmus haec / illa.	We see *these* / *those* things.
Hic / Ille amicus est bonus.	*This* / *That* friend is good.
Amo hanc / illam feminam.	I love *this* / *that* woman.
Videmus haec / illa loca.	We see *these* / *those* places.

- All three of these demonstratives are used by Latin authors as the third person pronoun.

Terms to Know

demonstrative
   pronouns
adjectives in *-ius*
factitive (sentence
   pattern)
intransitive
transitive
special intransitive
linking (verb/sentence
   pattern)
object complement

- It is important when reading Latin to recognize when these demonstratives are being used as adjectives, i.e. when they agree with a noun in the sentence, or when they do not agree with a noun in the sentence.

- When they are used by themselves, their gender will determine how they will be translated, i.e. *hic / ille* = "this man / that man," *haec / illa* = "this woman / that woman," *hoc / illud* = "this thing / that thing."

- The neuter nominative and accusative plural of *hic, haec, hoc* tends to prove particularly confusing because of its overlap with the feminine singular. Be especially careful when faced with the *haec* form to use context to determine whether it is the feminine or the neuter form.

Demonstrative Pronouns Text

Cicero, *In Catilinam* 1.2. Cicero has just opened the first of his orations against Catiline with a series of rhetorical questions designed to expose Catiline's arrogance. The famous exclamation excerpted here maintains Cicero's focus on Catiline's arrogance but also wonders how such a man can be allowed to remain free.

Ō tempora, ō mōrēs! Senātus haec intellegit, cōnsul videt; hic tamen vīvit.

1. Identify the case, number, and gender of both demonstratives in the above excerpt.
2. What is the clue that *haec* is not feminine?

Demonstrative Pronouns Text

Martial 6.40. Martial draws a comparison between Glycera, Martial's current love interest, and Lycoris, the poetic lover of the first century BCE elegiac poet Cornelius Gallus. Gallus, little of whose poetry survived, but whom ancient poets generally considered the best of the elegiac poets, memorialized Lycoris in his poetry, which Martial now does for Glycera.

Fēmina praeferrī potuit <u>tibi</u> nulla, Lycori:
    praeferrī Glycērae fēmina nulla potest.
<u>Haec</u> erit <u>hoc</u> quod <u>tū</u>: <u>tū</u> nōn potes esse quod <u>haec</u> est.
    Tempora quid faciunt! <u>Hanc</u> volō, <u>tē</u> voluī.

1. Complete the chart below with the requested information about both the demonstratives and the personal pronouns in the above poem.

Line #	Form	Gender	Number	Case
1	tibi			
3	haec			
3	hoc			
3	tū [*both*]			
3	haec			
4	hanc			
4	tē			

The gender of the personal pronouns might be difficult, but should still be accessible.

Demonstrative Pronouns Text

Martial 8.81. A certain Gallia is excessively attached to her pearls, more than to religion or to her family. The poem closes with an unknown reference; it is unclear what the effect of the hand of Annaeus Serenus will be. The poem is certainly an invective against materialism but it is unclear, because he is otherwise unknown, whether it is also a slight of Annaeus Serenus.

Nōn per mystica sacra Dindymēnēs
nec per Niliacae bovem iuvencae,
nullōs dēnique per deōs deāsque
iūrat Gellia, sed per uniōnēs.
Hōs amplectitur, hōs perosculātur,   5
hōs frātrēs vocat, hōs vocat sorōrēs,
hōs nātis amat ācrius duōbus.
Hīs sī quō careāt misella cāsū,
victūram negat esse sē nec hōram.
Ēheu, quam bene nunc, Papiriāne,   10
Annaeī faceret manus Serēnī!

1. Complete the following translation of lines 5-9 by translating the demonstratives in brackets. Translate each demonstrative in two different ways.

She embraces _____ [*hōs*], she kisses _____ [*hōs*] all over,
she calls _____ [*hōs*] brothers, she calls _____ [*hōs*] sisters,
she loves _____ [*hōs*] more deeply than her two children.

Demonstrative Pronouns Text

Plautus, *Miles Gloriosus* **55-67.** The Miles Gloriosus Pyrgopolynices and his servant Artotrogus have been discussing the military prowess of the Pyrgopolynices in bombastic and exaggerated terms. In this excerpt, the discussion turns to the irresistible appeal of the Miles Gloriosus to women.

Artotrogus. Quid tibi ego dicam, quod omnēs mortālēs sciunt,	55
Pyrgopolynīcem tē ūnum in terrā vīvere	
virtūte et forma et factīs invictissumum?	
Amant ted [= tē] omnēs mulierēs neque iniūriā,	
quī sīs tam pulcher. Vel illae quae here palliō	
mē reprehendērunt... **Pyrgopolynices.** Quid eae dīxērunt tibi?	60
Artotrogus. Rogitābant: "Hicine Āchillēs est?" inquit mihi;	
"Immō eius frāter" inquam "est." Ibi illārum altera	
"Ergō mecastor pulcher est" inquit mihi	
"et liberālis. Vidē caesariēs quam decet:	
nē illae sunt fortunātae quae cum istō cubant."	65
Pyrgopolynices. Itane āibant tandem? **Artotrogus.** Quae mē ambae	
obsecrāverint,	
ut tē hōdiē quasi pompam illa praeterdūcerem.	

---

1. Translate the excerpts below; vocabulary is in brackets.

    58: Amant tē omnēs mulierēs. [omnēs = *"every"*; mulier, -eris. *woman*]

    60: Quid eae dīxērunt tibi? [quid = *"what"*]

    > Is the subject of *dixerunt* masculine or feminine? Explain your answer.

    61: Hicine Āchillēs est? [hicine = hicne = hic + -ne]

2. In the above passage, there are seventeen pronoun forms, some from this chapter, some from the previous. Complete the chart below with the appropriate information. The left hand "pronoun" column is for the forms as they appear in the passage.

pronoun	line #	case	number	gender

Demonstrative Pronouns Text

Ovid, *Amores* 1.9.17-20. In *Amores* 1.9, Ovid draws an extended analogy between love and war, or the lover and the soldier.

Mittitur īnfestōs alter speculātor in hostēs;
　　in rīvāle oculōs alter, ut hoste, tenet.
Ille gravēs urbēs, hic dūrae līmen amīcae
　　obsidet. Hic portās frangit, at ille forēs.　　20

---

1. Use the translation of lines 17-18 below as a reference for the following exercise.

   One man is sent as a spy among the hated enemy, the other keeps his eyes on his rival as if he were his enemy.

2. Complete the translation below by translating the forms of *hic* and *ille* in brackets.

   _____ [*ille*] destroys weighty cities, _____ [*hic*] destroys the doorstep of his unyielding girlfriend; _____ [*hic*] breaks down gates, while _____ [*ille*] breaks down doorways.

3. Identify which demonstrative refers to the "one" or "the other" referred to in lines 17-18.

Demonstrative Pronouns Text

Ovid, *Metamorphoses* **1.468-473.** Apollo has just bragged to Cupid that his arrows are more powerful than Cupid's. Cupid then decides to teach Apollo a lesson. In this excerpt, the two arrows that Cupid will use to make Apollo love Daphne and to ensure that Daphne does not love Apollo are described, as is the actual shooting of Apollo with his arrow.

...ēque sagittiferā prōmpsit duo tēla pharetrā
dīversōrum operum; fugat hoc, facit illud amōrem.
Quod facit aurātum est et cuspide fulget acūtā,   470
quod fugat obtūsum est et habet sub harundine
    plumbum.
Hoc deus in nymphā Pēnēide fīxit, at illō
laesit Apollineās trāiecta per ossa medullās.

-----

1. From *ēque...operum*, lines 468-469 = "And Cupid took from his arrow-bearing quiver two arrows for different purposes:"
   a. What are the different purposes of the two arrows? Translate the end of line 469, *fugat...amōrem*. [*fugō, -āre* = to make something (*acc.*) flee, instead of the more common *fugiō, -ere*, "to flee"]

   Line 470 describes the arrow that *facit amōrem*; line 471 describes the arrow that *fugat* (*amōrem*).
   b. In lines 472-473, Ovid describes how Cupid shot the god Apollo with one of the arrows and the unsuspecting nymph Daphne with the other. If line 472 (up to the *at illō* at the end) refers to Daphne, and lines 472-3 (*at illō...medullās*) refers to Apollo, who received which arrow?

Demonstrative Pronouns Text

Plautus, *Menaechmi* **17-50.** This lengthy excerpt describes the backstory to the *Menaechmi*, how Menaechmus was kidnapped in Tarentum and how Menaechmus' twin brother Sosicles was renamed Menaechmus in his missing twin's honor.

Mercātor quīdam fuit Syrācūsīs senex,
eī sunt nātī fīliī geminī duo,
ita formā similī puerī, ut māter sua
nōn internōsse posset quae mammam dabat,   20
neque adeō māter ipsa quae illōs pepererat,
ut quidem ille dīxit mihi, quī puerōs vīderat:
ego illōs nōn vīdī, nē quis vostrum censeat.
Postquam iam puerī septuennēs sunt, pater
onerāvit nāvem magnam multīs mercibus.   25
Inpōnit geminum alterum in nāvem pater,
Tarentum āvexit sēcum ad mercātum simul:
illum relīquit alterum apud mātrem domī.
Tarentī lūdī forte erant, quom illūc venit.
Mortālēs multī, ut ad lūdōs, convēnerant: 30
puer aberrāvit inter hominēs ā patre.
Epidamniensis quīdam ibi mercātor fuit:
is puerum tollit āvehitque Epidamnium eum.
Pater eius autem postquam puerum perdidit,
animum despondit: eāque is aegritūdine   35
paucīs diēbus post Tarentī ēmortuost.
Postquam Syrācūsās dē eā rē rediit nuntius
ad avom puerōrum, puerum surruptum alterum
patremque puerī Tarentī esse ēmortuom,
immūtat nōmen avos huic geminō alterī   40
ita illum dīlexit quī subruptust alterum
illīus nōmen indit illī quī domīst,
Menaechmō, idem quod alterī nōmen fuit.
Et ipsus eōdemst avos vocātus nōmine.
(Proptereā illīus nōmen meminī facilius,   45
quia illum clāmōre vīdī flāgitārier.)
Nē mox errētis, iam nunc praedicō prius:
idemst ambōbus nōmen geminīs frātribus.
Nunc in Epidamnum pedibus redeundumst mihi,
ut hanc rem vōbīs examussim disputem.   50

1. The underlined words are all forms of one of the three demonstratives from this chapter. Choose the correct form of each of the other two demonstratives that corresponds to the form from the text.

   Some of the corresponding forms will be relatively easy to identify: the endings will be the same or it is clear that the demonstrative modifies a word whose case, number, and gender is obvious.

   Some of the corresponding forms, however, will prove difficult because you will need to rely on context to identify with certainty the gender, number, and/or case of the original form. In these instances, make certain to explain how you arrived at your answer; even if the answer itself is not correct, the process and the decision-making therein become as important.

eī (18)	huic / hī / huius	illī / illa / illīus
illōs (21,23)	hōs / hī / hunc	eōs / eī / eum
ille (22)	hic / haec / hoc	is / ea / id
illum (28,40,46)	hōrum / hunc / hoc	eōrum / eum / id
is (33)	hic / hunc / hoc	ille / illum / illud
eius (34)	hic / huius / huic	ille / illīus / illī
eā (35)	hic / haec / hāc	ille / illā / illa
is (35)	hic / haec / hōc	ille / illa / illo
eā (37)	hic / haec / hāc	ille / illa / illā
huic (40)	illō / illī / illīus	eō / eī / eius
illīus (42,45)	huic / huius / hic	eī / eius / is
illī (42)	huic / huius / hic	eī / eius / is
hanc (50)	illum / illam / illud	eum / eam / id

2. Identify whether each form is used as an adjective or a pronoun.

45. Special Adjectives in *-īus*

1. How many adjectives follow the *-īus, -ī* pattern?

2. In what two cases do the *-īus, -ī* endings appear?

• Of these two endings, the *-ī* ending is perhaps the more confusing because of its overlap with the regular *-ī* ending that is used for the genitive singular. The *-īus* is different enough that it signals the irregularity more clearly, but the *-ī* ending, because of its rarity as a dative ending for *-us, -a, -um* adjectives, is often confused for the genitive singular or nominative plural.

Special Adjectives in *-īus* Text

CIL IX 2128. Roman epitaphs tended to be formulaic: the tomb was often personified and would often address the passerby, asking him to stop and hear the story of the tomb. On the other hand, the personified tomb, after communicating its story to the passerby, often abruptly ends the "conversation" by telling the passerby that it is finished speaking and that the passerby should continue on his way.

Homō es: resiste et tumulum contemplā meum:
iuvenis tetendī ut habērem quod ūterer;
iniūriam fēcī nullī, officia fēcī plūribus.
Bene vīve, properā, hoc est veniundum tibi.

1. What is the special adjective in the above epitaph?
2. What case is it?

Special Adjectives in *-īus* Text

Seneca, *Phaedra* 665-669. Phaedra has just described how she sees the young Theseus in his son Hippolytus, and loves him. In this excerpt, she laments how the same family has destroyed two sisters; Theseus her sister Ariadne, and Hippolytus Phaedra herself.

Domus sorōrēs ūna corripuit duās: 665
tē genitor, at mē nātus.
    En supplex iacet
adlapsa genibus rēgiae prōlēs domūs.
Respersa nullā lābe et intacta, innocens
tibi mūtor ūnī.

1. There are two forms of one of the special adjective in *-īus* in the above excerpt.
2. Identify their line number.
3. Identify their case and number.

46. Sentence Pattern: Factitive

1. What four regular sentence patterns have been learned thus far?
2. What three types of verbs are often involved in the factitive sentence pattern?
3. What is the second accusative in the factitive sentence pattern commonly called? Why?
4. What are the four elements of the factitive sentence pattern?

Sentence Pattern: Factitive Text

Martial 8.73. The poetry of the elegiac poets often focused on their perhaps fictional love affairs with married or otherwise unattainable women. Their poetry cataloged the spectrum of emotions involved in such affairs: joy, sorrow, despair, resentment, intrigue, hope; Martial provides a list of the most famous of these poets and their corresponding elegiac women. Martial here is looking for his own elegiac lover, perhaps as a way to satirize the melodrama of the genre, and turns to a certain Instantius for assistance.

> Instantī, quō nec sincērior alter habētur
>   pectore nec niveā simplicitāte prior,
> sī dare vīs nostrae vires animōsque Thaliae
>   et victūra petis carmina, dā quod amem.
> Cynthia tē vātem fēcit, lascīve Propertī;   5
>   ingenium Gallī pulchra Lycōris erat;
> fāma est argūtī Nemesis formōsa Tibullī;
>   Lesbia dictāvit, docte Catulle, tibi:
> nōn mē Paelignī nec spernet Mantua vātem,
>   sī qua Corinna mihi, sī quis Alexis erit.   10

---

1. The factitive sentence pattern occurs in line 5. What is the factitive verb?
2. What are the two objects of the factitive verb?

Sentence Pattern: Factitive Text

> **Ovid, *Metamorphoses* 10.267-269.** The sculptor Pygmalion treats his sculpture as if it were his girlfriend. In this excerpt, he dresses it in nice clothes and puts it to bed.

Collocat hanc strātīs conchā Sīdōnide tīnctīs
appellatque [hanc] torī sociam acclīnātaque colla
mollibus in plūmīs, tamquam sēnsūra, repōnit.

The *hanc* in brackets in line 268 is not in Ovid's original text but is included for clarity's sake.

1. Complete the following translation by translating the words in brackets.

   He lay _____ [*hanc*] on sheets dyed with Sidonian purple and he called _____ [*hanc*] _____ [*sociam; socia, -ae* = "companion"] of his bed and he lay her neck back, after it had been positioned, onto soft pillows as if she could feel them.

2. What is the factitive verb?

3. What are the two Latin objects of the factitive verb?

CHAPTER 11

Third conjugation verbs maintain the same formation as the other conjugations for the imperfect, but use a very different formation for the future. The introduction of this new future tense will introduce the potential for an overlap in forms that did not previously exist: the "e" in a form like *pōnet* can now signal either a second conjugation present or a third conjugation future; only knowing a verb's vocabulary information can distinguish between those forms. Numerals and different ways to express cause are also introduced.

> **Terms to Know**
>
> cardinal (numerals)
> ordinal (numerals)
> indeclinable
> cause

47. Imperfect Active Indicative (Third Conjugation)

1. What is the tense sign for the imperfect?
2. What is the difference between the characteristic vowels of the third conjugation and the third -*iō* conjugation?

Imperfect Active Indicative (Third Conjugation) Text

Vergil, *Aeneid* 4.331-332. Dido has just finished ripping into Aeneas for leaving her defenseless and heartbroken. In the excerpt below, Aeneas prepares to respond.

Dīxerat. Ille Iovis monitīs immōta tenēbat
lūmina et obnīxus cūram sub corde premēbat.

1. Identify the conjugations of *tenēbat* and *premēbat*. Explain your answer.

Imperfect Active Indicative (Third Conjugation) Text

Anonymous, *Dē lupō ossa corrodente* 1-4. A wolf has a bone stuck in his throat. Promising rewards, he convinces the crane to extract it. When the crane asks for his reward, the wolf laughs and chides the crane for wanting more than being allowed to put his head in the wolf's mouth and remove it unharmed.

Quondam Lupus improbus ossa corrōdēbat;
ūnum suīs dentibus transversum fīgēbat.
Dē gnārīs sollicitē medēlam quaerēbat,
sed quī sōlāmen ferret non inveniēbat.

1. Identify the three third conjugation imperfect tense verbs. (Do not include any that look like third *-iō* verbs.)

2. Translate just those verbs. (A dictionary may be required.)

3. *Inveniēbat* in line 4 looks like a third *-iō* verb, but in reality is a fourth conjugation verb; you will learn that third *-iō* and fourth conjugation verbs look alike in most forms.

48. Future Active Indicative (Third Conjugation)

1. What vowel does the future of the third conjugation use?

2. What is the one person and number when this vowel is not used? What vowel is used instead?

3. What is the difference between the characteristic vowels of the third conjugation and the third *-iō* conjugation?

- "Ham and Five Eggs" or "h**A**m and five **E**ggs" is a saying used to remember that third and third *-iō* verbs use an "a" in the first person singular and "e" throughout the five other forms of the future tense.

- The use of the "e" in the future tense of third and third *-iō* verbs introduces a potential confusion with second conjugation verbs, and serves as a reminder that it is imperative to know full vocabulary information rather than just the meaning of a word.

- Compare the following verb forms: *docet* and *reget*. They both use the same characteristic vowel, but are they same tense? What tense is each form? How do you know? The overlap of characteristic vowels will make knowing the conjugation of a verb of primary importance.

Future Active Indicative (Third Conjugation) Text

The College of the Holy Cross (MA) Motto. This motto is taken from an episode of Roman history involving the emperor Constantine. Before a battle against his rival for control of the Empire, Constantine prayed to the Christian God for assistance, and saw a vision of angels holding a banner on which this motto was written. He won the battle the next day and proclaimed Christianity to be the official religion of the Empire.

In hōc signō vincēs.

1. Translate the motto (*signum, -ī* = sign, signal)

Future Active Indicative (Third Conjugaton) Text

Catullus 9.6-9. Catullus' good friend Veranius has been on a long journey and has just returned home. In the excerpt below, Catullus rejoices at being able to see Veranius again.

Vīsam tē incolumem audiamque Hibērum
narrantem loca, facta, nātiōnēs,
ut mōs est tuus; applicansque collum
iucundum ōs, oculōsque suāviābor.

1. There is one first person third conjugation verb, and one first person fourth conjugation verb, which will look just like a third *-iō* verb. Use your knowledge of characteristic vowels and personal endings to identify them.
2. There is also one first conjugation future tense verb. What is it?

Future Active Indicative (Third Conjugation) Text

Martial 6.75. A poem directed at a certain Pontia, who according to Martial in other poems, poisoned her children. Martial then says that he will neither eat nor pass along any food that Pontia sends him.

Cum mittis turdumve mihi quadramve placentae,
    sive femur leporis, sīve quid hīs simile est,
bucellās mīsisse tuās tē, Pontia, dīcis.
    Hās ego nōn mittam, Pontia, sed nec edam.

1. What are the two third conjugation future verbs in the second couplet?
2. With what noun form might they be confused? Identify at least two contextual clues that they are not noun forms.
3. What is the tense of *mittis* in line 1?

Future Active Indicative (Third Conjugation) Text

Catullus 8.13-18. Catullus 8 is perhaps his most despondent and resentful poem toward Lesbia. He steels himself (though we are given the impression that he will be unsuccessful) against a life without Lesbia and here in this excerpt imagines for Lesbia, perhaps optimistically, what her life will be without him.

…nec tē requīret nec rogābit invītam.
At tū dolēbis, cum rogāberis nulla.
Scelesta, vae tē, quae tibi manet vīta?
Quis nunc tē adībit? Cui vidēberis bella?
Quem nunc amābis? Cuius esse dīcēris?
Quem bāsiābis? Cui labella mordēbis?

1. In the above excerpt, there are ten future tense verbs of the first, second, and third conjugations. What are they?
2. Identify the conjugation of each.
3. There is one present tense verb. What is it?
4. *Invītam* in line 13 looks like a first person, third conjugation future verb. How does *rogābit* signal that *invītam* is most likely not a verb at all? What form is *invītam*, if it is not a verb?

Future Active Indicative (Third Conjugation) Text

Seneca, *Phaedra* **568-573.** The nurse has been trying to convince Hippolytus not to foreswear women. Hippolytus here responds to the Nurse, reiterating his position that he wants nothing to do with women or love.

Hippolytus. Ignibus iungēs aquās
et amīca ratibus ante prōmittet vada
incerta Syrtis, ante ab extrēmō sinū   570
Hesperia Tēthys lūcidum attollet diem
et ōra dammīs blanda praebēbunt lupī,
quam victus animum fēminae mītem geram.

1. Complete the following table with the requested information about the verbs in the above passage.

Line #	Form	Principal Parts	Conjugation	Tense	Subject
568	iungēs	iungō, -ere			
569	prōmittet				
571	attollet	attollō, -ere			
572	praebēbunt	praebeō, -ēre			
573	geram	gerō, -ere			

2. How do you distinguish between the present active infinitives of second and third conjugation verbs?

Future Active Indicative (Third Conjugation) Text

Catullus 65.10-12. Catullus laments the death of his brother (as he also does most poignantly in poem 101).

Numquam ego tē, vītā frāter amābilior,
aspiciam posthāc? At certē semper amābō,
semper maesta tuā carmina morte canam,…

Vocabulary

numquam. never
vītā = "than my life"
amābilior = "more pleasing"
aspiciō, -ere. to see
posthāc. afterwards, ever again

at. but
certē. certainly, of course
maestus, -a, -um. sad
canō, -ere. to sing

1. There are three first person singular, future tense verbs. One is a first conjugation verb, one is a third conjugation verb. One is a third -*iō* conjugation verb. What are they?

2. Translate the passage.

49. Numerals

1. What is the difference between cardinal and ordinal numbers?
2. How are ordinal numerals declined?
3. How are cardinal numerals declined?
4. Which prepositions will Latin often use for partitive expressions that use numerals?

- Because the cardinal numbers, except for one, two, and three (*ūnus, duo* and *trēs*) are indeclinable, you cannot determine agreement by the customary gender, number, case; you have to use context to determine what noun a cardinal number (other than one, two, or three) modifies. Don't forget, however, that cardinal numbers other than *ūnus* will modify plural nouns; forms like *septem* and *novem*, whose endings look like accusative singular third declension, can be misleading.

- As you will see below, Latin will also use *ūnus, -a, -um* as the indefinite article (*a / an*).

Numerals Text

Martial 1.71. Martial is putting himself to sleep by counting down the letters of women's names: for each letter he pours some wine, and hopes that he will sleep, since the women themselves are not present.

Laevia sex cyathīs, septem Iustīna bibātur,
    quinque Lycas, Lydē quattuor, Īda tribus.
Omnis ab infusō numerētur amīca Falernō,
    et quia nulla venit, tū mihi, Somne, venī.

---

1. The first couplet is about how much wine Martial pours for each woman. Complete the table below with information from the first couplet.

Name	Glasses of wine
Laevia	
Iustīna	
Lycas	
Lydē	
Īda	

2. What case are *sex, septem, quīnque, quattuor,* and *tribus*? How do you know?

    Hint: *cyathīs* comes from *cyathus, -ī.*

Numerals Text

Martial 2.44.7-12. Martial here half-jokes that the man from whom he borrows money now sees him coming and tries to dissuade Martial from asking for another loan. In this excerpt, Martial quotes the money-lender as he murmurs to himself, though loud enough that Martial can hear, how much he owes other people, and so how little he has for Martial.

"Septem mīlia dēbeō Secundō,
Phoebō quattuor, ūndecim Philētō,
et quadrans mihi nullus est in arcā."
Ō grande ingenium meī sodālis!   10
Dūrum est, Sexte, negāre, cum rogāris:
quantō dūrius, antequam rogēris!

1. The words *Secundō, Phoebō,* and *Philētō* are second
   declension names (and so of course not here in the
   nominative case). What case are they with a word like
   dēbeō?

2. Fill in the chart below with how much Martial's money-
   lender owes each.

Name	How much owed
Secundus	
Phoebus	
Philētus	

Numerals Text

Plautus, *Miles Gloriosus* 42-46. The Miles Gloriosus and his slave
are discussing the (false) statistics of how many men he has killed
in various places.

Pyrgopolynices. Ecquid meministī? **Artotrogus.** Meminī: centum in Ciliciā
et quīnquāgintā, centum in Scytholatrōniā,
trīgintā Sardeiss, sexāgintā Macedonēs
sunt, omnes quōs tu occidistī ūnō diē.   45
Pyrgopolynices. Quanta istaec hominum summast? **Artotrogus.** Septem
   mīlia.

Answer the following questions about these statistics.

1. How many men did he kill in Cilicia?
2. How many men did he kill in Scytholatronia?
3. How many men from Sardis did he kill?
4. How many Macedonians did he kill?
5. How many men did he kill in total (line 46)?

Numerals Text

Martial 1.19. A certain Aelia only has four teeth, but her strenuous coughing has expelled even those four. She can now cough with impunity: there are no more teeth left to expel.

Sī meminī, fuerant tibi quattuor, Aelia, dentēs:
    expulit ūna duōs tussis et ūna duōs.
Iam secūra potes tōtīs tussīre diēbus:
    nīl istīc quod agat tertia tussis habet.

Vocabulary

sī. if	**dens, -ntis.** tooth
meminī = "I remember"	**expellō, -ere, -uī, -ultus.** to remove, to eject, to throw out
fuerant tibi = "You had"	
Aelia, -ae. [name]	**tussis, -is.** cough, cold

1. Translate the first couplet, lines 1-2.
2. What case is *tibi* in line 1 and what use of this case is it? (*Fuerant* is a form of *sum, esse*, which should be a clue.)

Numerals Text

Catullus 5. Catullus is excited about his relationship with Lesbia; he pledges fidelity and imagines their passionate nights together.

Vīvāmus, mea Lesbia, atque amēmus,
rūmōrēsque senum sevēriōrum
omnēs ūnius aestimēmus assis!
Sōlēs occīdere et redīre possunt:
nōbīs cum semel occīdit brevis lux,   5
nox est perpetua ūna dormienda.
Dā mī bāsia mille, deinde centum,
dein mille altera, dein secunda centum,
deinde usque altera mille, deinde centum.
Dein, cum mīlia multa fēcerimus,   10
conturbābimus illa, ne sciāmus,
aut nē quis malus invidere possit,
cum tantum sciat esse bāsiōrum.

1. What is the form of *ūnus* in line 3? In what case is it?
2. In lines 7-9, Catullus lists how many kisses he wants Lesbia to give him. What is the total number?

50. Expressions of Cause

1. What are the three different ways to express cause?
2. What is a good way to try to distinguish among the ablatives of cause, means, and manner?
3. What Latin prepositions can be used to express cause (include what case each takes)?
4. What case goes with *causā* and *grātiā*?

Expressions of Cause Text

Vergil, *Aeneid* **2.108-109.** Aeneas, at the beginning of his description of the fall of Troy to the Carthaginian queen Dido and her banquet guests, explains how the Greeks set up the ruse of the Trojan horse. A Greek named Sinon is captured by the Trojans and in this excerpt explains to them how tired the Greeks were of fighting and how much they wanted to return home. Sinon's information, of course, is intentionally false; he was sent by the Greeks to be captured and to convince the Trojans that the Trojan Horse was not in fact the treacherous trick that it was.

Saepe fugam Danaī Trōiā cupiēre relictā
mōlīrī et longō fessī discēdere bellō;

---

1. Complete the following translation by translating the ablative of cause in parentheses.

   Often the Greeks wanted to feign flight by leaving Troy behind and to leave, tired, _____ [*longō bellō*].

Expressions of Cause Text

Ovid, *Metamorphoses* **1.533-539.** Ovid compares Apollo's pursuit of Daphne to a hound chasing a hare in the epic simile that comprises the first six lines of the excerpt below. An epic simile is an extended simile, characterized by its narrative development, its details, and the multiple levels of comparison that can be drawn to the narrative proper. In Latin, *ut*, or a related word (e.g. *velut, veluti*) will often introduce an epic simile, and then *sic* (in line 539) will often signal the end of the epic simile and the return to the narrative. Thus, in line 539, *sīc, deus* and *virgō*, signifying Apollo and Daphne, signal the end of the simile of the hound and the hare.

Ut canis in vacuō leporem cum Gallicus arvō
vīdit, et hic praedam pedibus petit, ille salūtem,
alter inhaesūrō similis iam iamque tenēre   535
spērat et extentō stringit vēstīgia rōstrō,
alter in ambiguō est, an sit comprēnsus, et ipsīs
morsibus ēripitur tangentiaque ōra relinquit:
sīc deus et virgō est, hic spē celer, illa timōre.

Vocabulary

spēs, -eī. hope [*a fifth declension noun*]
timor, -ōris. fear

1. Ovid identifies both Apollo and Daphne as *celer*, "quick." Why is Apollo (*hic*) *celer*? Why is Daphne (*illa*) *celer*?
2. What word is gapped in line 539?

Expressions of Cause Text

Ovid, *Metamorphoses* **8.686.** Ovid's touching story of Baucis and Philemon, an old couple who invited Jupiter and Mercury into their modest home for dinner when no one else would, includes a wonderfully amusing "goose-chase." When Baucis and Philemon realize that they are hosting gods, they move to slay their only livestock, a goose, whom Ovid jokingly describes as "the guard of the house." The goose, however, sensing his demise, refuses to be caught; the result is described in the excerpt below.

Ille celer pennā tardōs aetāte fatīgat…

1. Finish the translation below with the correct translation of the ablatives of cause in parentheses.

    That goose, quick _____ [*pennā; penna, -ae* = feather, wing], tires Baucis and Philemon, slow _____ [*aetāte; aetās, -ātis* = age].

Expressions of Cause Text

Horace, *Carmina* **1.7.1-4.** This poem focuses on a theme common to Horace's poetry: the celebration of spring and the simple country life. In the opening two couplets to this poem, Horace catalogs famous Greek places and why they are famous.

Laudābunt aliī clāram Rhodon aut Mytilēnen
        aut Epheson bimarisve Corinthī
moenia vel Bacchō Thēbās vel Apolline Delphōs
        insignīs aut Thessala Tempē:

1. Who are the two gods mentioned in line 3?
2. Why then is Thebes famous? Delphi?
3. What is the case of *Bacchō* and *Apolline*?

CHAPTER 12

Third declension nouns complicated your knowledge of nouns because they introduced variable nominatives, changing stems, and unpredictable genders. Third declension adjectives will likewise complicate adjectives. Third declension adjectives use essentially the same endings as third declension nouns, but some important, and potentially confusing, changes occur. Third declension adjectives also further complicate noun-adjective agreement. You should already be familiar with the difficulty of *-us*, *-a*, *-um* adjectives modifying third declension nouns, but now you will be faced with the opposite: third declension adjectives modifying first and second declension nouns. Properly understanding which adjectives agree with which nouns is now based as much on knowing full vocabulary information for words as on knowing endings, i.e. if you don't know the declension of a noun or adjective, it will become very difficult with certain endings to identify case, number, and gender. The different ways Latin expresses time are also introduced.

> **Terms to Know**
>
> three-ending adjectives
> two-ending adjectives
> one-ending adjectives
> time when (ablative of)
> time within which
> (ablative of)
> length of time
> (accusative of)

51. Third Declension Adjectives

1. How are third declension adjectives characterized or organized?
2. What are the names for these three categories?
3. What adjective is the one exception to the 3-ending pattern?
4. Why is this adjective exceptional?

- Third declension adjectives complicate an already difficult aspect to Latin. Agreement is determined by the same gender, number, and case of adjectives and nouns. The introduction of third declension adjectives increases the chances that nouns and adjectives that agree will have different endings. You must always be vigilant against assuming that words with the same endings agree.

- Third declension adjective endings are largely identical to third declension noun endings. There is one difference between these endings, however, that proves especially difficult and should be kept in mind.

- The ablative singular ending of third declension adjectives is -ī. This proves difficult because the -ī ending is a much more common ending, for both nouns and verbs, than the ablative singular -e ending of third declension nouns. This means that knowing that a word is a third declension adjective as part of your vocabulary study is especially important.

- An additional difficulty is presented by 2-ending adjectives because the nominative singular of the neuter form ends in -e, which is often confused with the ablative singular of third declension nouns. The latter form is much more common.

Third Declension Adjectives Text

Martial 7.72.1-6. Martial wishes well to a certain Paulus so that Paulus, apparently a patron of Martial, might defend him if someone should ascribe falsely to Martial particularly virulent or nasty poetry. Since Martial writes exactly this kind of poetry, one questions the sincerity of the poem. This excerpt introduces Martial's good wishes toward Paulus in terms of financial and career success.

Grātus sīc tibi, Paule, sit December
nec vānī triplicēs brevēsque mappae
nec tūris veniant levēs selībrae,
sed lancēs ferat et scyphōs avōrum
aut grandis reus aut potens amīcus: 5
seu quod tē potius iuvat capitque;

The third declension adjectives in the above passage are listed in the left hand column of the table below.

1. Complete the chart based on each third declension adjective. You should include all possible genders, numbers, and cases.

2. In the last column, write in the noun in the passage that the adjective modifies (all nouns that the adjectives modify are first or second declension nouns).

3. Finally, for those adjectives where multiple genders or cases were possible, circle the correct gender and case based on the noun that the adjective modifies.

	Gender	Number	Case	Modifies?
triplicēs				
brevēs				
levēs				
grandis				
potens				

Third Declension Adjectives Text

Seneca, *Phaedra* 640 - 644. Phaedra is preparing to confess to Hippolytus her love for him. In this excerpt, she describes the madness of her love. Immediately following this excerpt, Hippolytus, thinking still that Phaedra's love is for his father Theseus, wonders how that can be madness. In response, Phaedra finally admits to her illicit love for her stepson.

Phaedra. Pectus insānum vapor   640
amorque torret. Intimīs saevit ferus
penitus medullas atque per vēnās meat
visceribus ignis mersus et vēnās latens
ut agilis altās flamma percurrit trabēs.

Vocabulary

640. **pectus, pectoris** (*n.*); **insānus, -a, -um; vapor, vaporis**
641. **amor, amoris** (*m.*); **intimus, -a, -um; ferus, -a, -um**
642. **medulla, -ae; vēna, -ae**
643. **viscus, visceris** (*n.*) [*often only in the plural:* **viscera, viscerum** (*n.*)]; **ignis, ignis** (*m.*); **mersus, -a, -um; vēna, -ae; latens, latentis** (*adj.*)
644. **agilis, agile; altus, -a, -um; flamma, -ae; trabs, trabis** (*f.*)

1. Identify all noun-adjective pairs (not every noun will have an adjective that modifies it).

2. Identify the gender, number, and case of each noun-adjective pair.

3. *Pectus* in line 1 is a neuter noun, which means that it can be either nominative or accusative. What is the clue that it is an accusative?

52. Expressions of Time

1. Which two cases express time in Latin?
2. What are the three types of time that Latin expresses?
3. Which case goes with each of these three types?
4. Which Latin preposition can sometimes be used to express extent of time?

- The English preposition used to translate the ablative of time when will depend on the specific time word being used and the English preposition that goes with that time word:

  <u>On</u> Friday
  <u>At</u> two o'clock
  <u>In</u> the summertime

Expressions of Time Text

Martial 2.5.1-2. Martial enjoys spending time with Decianus, but Decianus lives far away and is often busy or unavailable. Martial resents having to go all the way there and to return without seeing him. Martial doesn't mind the distance to Decianus' house, but he does mind the distance there and back if he can't see him. In this excerpt, Martial admits how fond he is of Decianus.

Nē valeam, sī nōn tōtīs, Deciāne, <u>diēbus</u>
et tēcum tōtīs <u>noctibus</u> esse velim.

---

1. The underlined words are time words: *diēbus* = "day" and *noctibus* = "night." What adjective modifies them (*diēbus*, a fifth declension noun, is an ablative plural)?
2. Translate the two noun - adjective pairs.

Expressions of Time Text

Pliny, *Epistulae* **9.36.1.** Pliny describes his summer vacation, which he will spend *in Tuscīs*, or at his Tuscan villa.

Quaeris, quemadmodum in Tuscīs diem aestāte dispōnam.

---

1. What are the two time nouns in the above excerpt?
2. What case are each of them in?

3. Complete the following translation by translating the time nouns in brackets.

> You ask how I will spend _____ [*diem* = day] in my Tuscan villa _____ [*aestāte; aestās, -ātis* = summer]

4. Does the ablative noun express time when, time within which, or length of time? Explain your answer.

4. Is *diem* used in a time expression? Explain your answer.

Expressions of Time Text

Pliny, *Epistulae* **2.17.3.** Pliny in this letter describes the pleasant features of his seaside villa in the town of Larentum near Rome's port town of Ostia. In this excerpt, he describes the animals that live nearby.

Multī gregēs ovium, multa ibi equōrum boum armenta, quae montibus hieme dēpulsa herbīs et tepōre vernō nitēscunt.

1. There are four ablative nouns in the above excerpt. What are they? (The form *vernō* is an ablative adjective, and so should not be included in the four.)

2. Which of the four is an ablative of time when? Explain your answer.

3. What kind of ablative could the other three be? Explain your answer.

Expressions of Time Texts

Martial 5.29. Martial here recalls a superstition that says that eating a hare will make the eater beautiful for a week or more. He then quips that if the superstition is indeed true, then Gellia, the addressee of the poem, has evidently never eaten a hare.

Sī quandō leporem mittis mihi, Gellia, dīcis:
     "Formonsus septem, Marce, diēbus eris."
Sī non dērīdēs, sī vērum, lux mea, narrās,
     edistī numquam, Gellia, tū leporem.

Ovid, *Metamorphoses* **10.72-74.** Ovid's poetic hero Orpheus has just turned back to look at his wife Eurydice, whom he was allowed to lead from the underworld back to life, provided that he did not look until they were out. Immediately, she was taken from him back to the world of the dead. The excerpt below describes his tragic reaction.

Orantem frūstrāque iterum trānsīre volentem
portitor arcuerat. Septem tamen ille diēbus
squālidus in rīpā Cereris sine mūnere sēdit;

---

1. What is the time expression in line 2 of Martial and line 73 of Ovid?

2. What is the case of *septem* in both? What does it modify? Explain your answer.

3. If *formonsus* means "handsome" and *diēbus* is "days," translate line 2 of Martial.

4. Complete the following translation of Ovid by translating the time expression in brackets.

   The gatekeeper [of the underworld] had driven him back, begging in vain and wanting to return: Orpheus, then, despondent, sat on the bank of the river without food
   _____ [*septem diēbus*].

5. What does the *septem diēbus* of line 2 of Martial and line 73 of Ovid express? What is unexpected about your answer? How does this time expression seem not to align with the description of the time expressions in the textbook?

CHAPTER 13

The fourth conjugation is the last of the Latin conjugations. It will be formed almost identically to the third -iō verbs that you learned in Chapter 11. Interrogative pronouns and reflexive pronouns each present their own difficulty. Interrogative pronouns in English violate the usual rules of English word order. Reflexive pronouns require an understanding of context for their translation; their form alone will not indicate how they will be translated. Interrogative adjectives, a variation of interrogative pronouns that was not included in the textbook, are summarized briefly. Possession and the Ablative of Specification (Respect) are also introduced.

> **Terms to Know**
>
> fourth conjugation
> interrogative pronoun
> reflexive pronoun
> possessive adjectives
> ablative of specification
> (respect)

53. Fourth Conjugation

1. With what vowel does the stem of fourth conjugation verbs end?

54. Interrogative Pronouns

1. What two questions does the interrogative pronoun ask?

2. Are the singular or plural forms more common?

- Interrogative pronouns (and relative pronouns, as you will learn later) hold a unique place in English grammar: they are the two forms that reveal their grammatical function through their form, or ending, rather than their word order or placement in their clause.

- Other pronouns change form depending on their grammatical function (e.g. I/me, she/her, they/them), but still for the most part follow standard English word order.

- Interrogative pronouns do not follow standard English word order; whatever their grammatical function, they will always appear at the beginning of their clause.

- Consider the following examples (with the pronouns underlined):

  □ <u>Who</u> went to the movies? <u>He</u> went to the movies.

  Both pronouns are the subjects of their sentences, and both occur at the beginning of the sentence.

▫ <u>Whom</u> did you see?   We saw <u>them</u>.

Both pronouns are the direct objects of their sentences. While the personal pronoun (them) appears in the standard grammatical position for English direct objects (after the verb), the interrogative pronoun remains at the beginning of the sentence; its form ("whom" with its "m" ending) indicates that it is the direct object rather than its position in the word order of the sentence.

• The neuter interrogative pronoun causes even more difficulty because in both English and Latin its nominative and accusative (subjective and objective) forms are identical.

▫ <u>What</u> did that?   <u>It</u> did that.

▫ <u>What</u> did you see?   We saw <u>it</u>.

• This violation of word order violates every linguistic instinct of English speakers. Thus, it is imperative to be very careful to identify the case of the interrogative pronoun, and to translate it accordingly. Do not assume that because the interrogative pronoun occurs first in the sentence it will be the subject; it will always be first in the sentence, whatever its grammatical function.

• A good rule of thumb is the following:

▫ A nominative Latin interrogative pronoun will be followed in the English version by the main verb (not just a helping verb).

Who <u>saw</u> it?   What <u>did</u> it?

▫ An accusative (or non-nominative) Latin interrogative pronoun will be followed in the English version by a helping verb (not a main verb), then the subject of the sentence, then the main verb.

Whom did you see?
What did you see?
[did = helping verb; you = subject; see = main verb]

• Dative and ablative interrogative pronouns work similarly to accusative interrogative pronouns in that they come first in the sentence (in both Latin and English) and will be followed in English by a helping verb, the subject, and then the main verb.

Cui cōpiam dedistī?   *To whom did you give the resources?*

Quō cōpiās impedivistī?   *With what did you hinder the troops?*

Quōcum cōpiās impedivistī?   *With whom did you hinder the troops?*

[did = helping verb; you = subject; give/hinder = main verb]

Note the difference in the second and third examples between the ablative of means and the ablative of accompaniment: while both are translated with the English "with," only the Latin ablative of accompaniment is used with the preposition *cum*.

- The genitive interrogative pronoun is translated in two ways: "whose," which is the equivalent of the apostrophe "s" form or the possessive adjective, i.e. whose book = her book = the woman's book; or "of whom" / "of which"= the book of the woman.

- The formula for translating the genitive interrogative pronoun differs slightly from the accusative and the dative/ablative.

- In English, "whose" will be followed directly by whatever noun it is modifying. That noun can be in any case, which then will follow the above formulae.

Cuius cōpiae dormiunt?	*Whose troops are sleeping?*
Cuius iter impedīvistī?	*Whose journey did you hinder?*

Interrogative Adjectives

- Compare the following questions:

  Who went to the store?
  Which person went to the store?

  The first sentence begins with the interrogative pronoun; in Latin, it would be *quis*.

  The second sentence, however, illustrates the interrogative adjective. As its name implies, the interrogative adjective is a word that introduces a question by agreeing with a noun: "who" operates by itself and asks a general question; "which" agrees with "person" and asks a more specific question.

- The interrogative adjective has forms similar to the interrogative pronoun. Their plurals are identical; their singular varies in only a few places. The forms unique to the interrogative adjective are bolded in the paradigm below.

quī	**quae**	**quod**
cuius	cuius	cuius
cui	cui	cui
quem	**quam**	**quod**
quō	**quā**	quō
quī	quae	quae
quōrum	quārum	quōrum
quibus	quibus	quibus
quōs	quās	quae
quibus	quibus	quibus

- The interrogative adjective, unlike the interrogative pronoun, has separate singular forms for all three genders; most of the differences between their forms stem from this difference.

- The interrogative adjective in English will be translated by "which" ("what" is a less formal substitute for "which"). The noun that it modifies will determine case and how that case is translated.

Quī senex dormit?	*Which old man sleeps?* (nominative)
Cuius senis gens intelligit?	*The family of which old man understands?* (genitive)
Cui senī gens cōpiam dedit?	*To which old man did the family give their wealth?* (dative)
Quem senem gens impedit?	*Which old man does the family hinder?* (accusative)
Quōcum sene gens discēdit?	*With which old man does the family leave?* (ablative)

Interrogative Pronoun Text

Catullus 1.1-5. The excerpt below is the opening five lines of the opening poem of the Roman poet Catullus' *carmina*. In them, and throughout the rest of the poem, Catullus unmistakably signals the type of poetry that he will be writing. Words like *lepidum, libellum,* and *expolitum* in lines 1-2 recall the poetry of the Greek poet Callimachus and the poetic approach that he advocated, that eschewed the ponderousness of epic for a more light-hearted and poetically compressed approach. The word *nugas*, "trifles," in line 4 likewise recalls Callimachus: while others might consider this poetry trifling (such as Cicero, who criticized Catullus and his literary coterie), Catullus saw the trifling nature of such poetry as the very quality that made it great.

Cuī dōnō lepidum novum libellum
āridā modō pūmice expolītum?
Cornēlī, tibi: namque tū solēbas
meās esse aliquid putāre nūgās
iam tum,…

Vocabulary

dōnō, -āre. to dedicate   **libellus, -ī.** little book
lepidus, -a, -um. charming   **Cornēlius, -ī.** [*name*]

1. What is the interrogative pronoun in the above passage? What case is it in?
2. Translate line 1, and then translate the answer to the question in the first half of line 3.
3. What case is *Cornēlī* in line 3?

Interrogative Pronouns and Adjectives Text

Catullus 8.15-18. Catullus 8 is perhaps his most despondent and resentful poem toward Lesbia. He steels himself (though we are given the impression that he will be unsuccessful) against a life without Lesbia. Here in this excerpt he imagines for Lesbia, perhaps optimistically, what her life will be without him.

Scelesta, vae tē, <u>quae</u> tibi manet <u>vīta</u>?
<u>Quis</u> nunc tē adībit? <u>Cui</u> vidēberis bella?
<u>Quem</u> nunc amābis? <u>Cuius</u> esse dīcēris?
<u>Quem</u> bāsiābis? <u>Cui</u> labella mordēbis?

Vocabulary

scelesta = "wicked one"
vae tē = "go to hell"
adībit = *future tense of* **adeō, -īre:** to approach, to court
vidēberis = *future tense of* **videor, -ērī:** to seem

bellus, -a, -um. beautiful, pretty
cuius esse dīcēris = "____ [*cuius*] will you be said to be"
bāsiō, -āre. to kiss
labella, -ae. lip
mordeō, -ēre. to nibble

1. Identify the case of the underlined words. (In line 1 *quae* agrees with *vīta*.)
2. Translate the passage.

Interrogative Pronoun and Adjective Text

Catullus 62.19-30. Catullus 62 is a wedding hymn sung by chorsues of boys and girls. In this song-competition between the two groups, the boys open with the rising of the evening star, Hesperus. The star then becomes the subject of each group's song. This excerpt opens with the refrain of the hymn, which also punctuates the interval between the two choruses. The girls in the first section focus on the violent nature of the star, while the boys in the second focus on the joyful.

[**Refrain.**] Hymēn ō Hymenaee, Hymēn adēs ō Hymenaee!   20
Puellae. Hespere, <u>quis</u> caelō fertur crūdēlior ignis?
Quī nātam possis complexū āvellere mātris,
complexū mātris retinentem āvellere nātam,
et iuvenī ardentī castam dōnāre puellam?
<u>Quid</u> faciunt hostēs captā crūdēlius urbe?   25
[**Refrain.**] Hymēn ō Hymenaee, Hymēn adēs ō Hymenaee!
Puerī. Hespere, quis caelō lūcet iūcundior ignis?
Quī desponsa tuā firmēs cōnūbia flammā,
quae pepigēre virī, pepigērunt ante parentēs,
nec iunxēre prius quam sē tuus extulit ardor.   30
<u>Quid</u> dātur ā Dīvīs fēlīcī optātius hōrā?

---

1. Translate the underlined forms. In lines 20 and 26, *quis* is functioning as an interrogative adjective; sometimes poets will use the pronoun form as an adjective, as Catullus is doing here.
2. With what noun does *quis* in lines 20 and 26 agree?
3. What is the case of each *quid* in lines 24 and 30?
4. What are the clues in lines 24 and 30 that help to determine the case of each *quid*?

(In lines 21 and 27, *quī*, even though it appears to be an interrogative adjective, is a relative pronoun. You will learn later that the relative pronoun uses the same forms as the interrogative adjective.)

Interrogative Adjective Text

Cicero, *In Catilinam.* **1.13.** Through a series of rhetorical questions, Cicero points out that Catiline is disgraced among everyone except those who are part of his conspiracy, and that this loss of reputation is a natural outgrowth of the inherent evil of Catiline's character.

<u>Quae</u> *nota* domesticae turpitūdinis nōn inusta vītae tuae est? <u>Quod</u> prīvātārum rērum *dēdecus* nōn haeret in fāmā? <u>Quae</u> *libīdō* ab oculīs, quod facinus ā manibus umquam tuīs, quod flāgitium ā tōtō corpore āfuit? <u>Cui</u> tū *adulēscentulō*, quem corruptēlārum inlecebrīs inrētīssēs nōn aut ad audāciam ferrum aut ad libīdinem facem praetulistī?

Vocabulary

nota, -ae. mark, signal

dēdecus, dēdecoris (*n.*). disgrace, shame, vice

libīdo, libidinis (*f.*). desire

adulēscentulus, -ī. young man

---

1. Identify all possible cases, numbers, and genders for the underlined interrogative adjectives.
2, Using the italicized nouns and their vocabulary information above, identify the gender, number, and case of each noun-adjective pair.
3. Translate each noun-adjective pair.

Interrogative Adjective Text

Catullus 64.154-157. In the midst of Ariadne's invective against Theseus, for abandoning her on an island after she helped him defeat the Minotaur, she questions what kind of inhuman parentage he must have had to have acted in such a way. The association of the disgraceful behavior of men with some questionable parentage is a common trope among their betrayed or embittered women.

Quaenam tē genuit sōlā sub rūpe leaena,
quod mare conceptum spūmantibus exspuit undīs,   155
quae Syrtis, quae Scylla vorax, quae vasta Charybdis,
tālia quī reddis prō dulcī praemia vītā?

Vocabulary

gignō, gignere, genuī. to give birth to

leaena, -ae. lioness

mare, maris. sea

exspuō, -ere, -uī. to spit out, to expel

Syrtis, -is. [*name*: a sand bank on the northern coast of Africa known for beaching ships]

Scylla, -ae. [*name*: a legendary sea-monster that supposedly lived in the Straits of Messina, where the toe of Italy meets the tip of Sicily]

Charybdis, -is. [*name*: a legendary whirlpool in the Straits of Messina, which, along with Scylla, proved deadly to passing ships]

---

1. Translate the underlined pairs of interrogative adjectives and their corresponding nouns, and their verbs. (*Exspuit* is the verb for all pairs except for the first, and the *tē* of line 154 is the object of all verbs.)
2. Identify their gender and number (they are all nominative).

55. The Reflexive Pronoun

1. For what is the reflexive pronoun used?
2. Which case does the reflexive pronoun not have?
3. Which two reflexive pronouns use the same forms as their personal pronouns?

• The reflexive pronoun forms do not indicate the gender of their translation. That gender must be understood from their antecedent.

Reflexive Pronoun Text

Cicero, *In Catilinam* 1.30. Cicero is delivering a lengthy response to the question of whether Catiline should be put to death or exiled. Cicero feels that he should not be put to death because of the fervor it would instill in his allies, but rather he should be exiled so that he and his co-conspirators can be dealt with as a whole; Cicero is assuming that they will inevitably come together and attack the city. In this excerpt, Cicero outlines his plan using the metaphor of a plant: to kill Catiline would only lop the flower off without pulling out the roots.

Quodsī sē ēiecerit sēcumque suōs ēdūxerit et eōdem cēterōs undique collēctōs naufragōs adgregārit, extinguētur atque dēlēbitur nōn modo haec tam adulta reī pūblicae pestis, vērum etiam stirps ac sēmen malōrum omnium.

---

1. Identify the two reflexive pronouns and the one reflexive possessive adjective.
2. Identify the case and number of each.

Reflexive Pronoun Text

Martial 1.41.14-17. A certain Caecilius thinks himself urbane and cultured; Martial strongly disagrees, and spends the bulk of the poem before this excerpt comparing Caecilius to other buffoons: street performers and cheap salesmen. In this excerpt, Martial advises Caecilius to get real; he will never be like the truly cultured, two of whom (Gabba apparently was a court entertainer of Augustus) Martial mentions by comparison.

Quārē dēsine iam tibi vidērī,
quod sōlī tibi, Caecilī, vidēris,   15
quī Gabbam salibus tuīs et ipsum
posses vincere Tettium Caballum.

---

1. Fill in the blanks in the translation below with the correct form of the pronoun / adjective.
2. Identify whether the pronouns and possessive adjective are reflexive or not. Explain your answer.

   Therefore, stop at this point appearing _____ [*tibi*] to be that which you seem only _____ [*tibi*], Caecilius, i.e. one who can surpass Gabba and Tettius Caballus with _____ [*tuīs*] wit.

Reflexive Pronoun Text

Vergil, *Aeneid* **4.24-29.** Book 3 of the *Aeneid* concludes with Aeneas finishing his lengthy tale of the fall of Troy and his journey from Troy to Carthage (the tale comprising books 2 and 3 of the *Aeneid*). Book 4 opens with Dido struggling with her feelings for Aeneas; apparently, she has fallen in love with him. The problem is, however, that she vowed to remain faithful to her first husband Sychaeus, whom her brother Pygmalion (unrelated to Ovid's mythological sculptor) killed. In this excerpt, the conclusion to Dido's lengthy speech, she reaffirms her commitment to her pledge of fidelity to her dead husband. Her sister Anna, in response, will encourage her to embrace her feelings for Aeneas, which of course Dido will, culminating in his departure and her tragic suicide.

Sed mihi vel tellūs optem prius īma dehīscat,
vel pater omnipotēns adigat mē fulmine ad umbrās,   25
pallentes umbrās Erebi noctemque profundam,
ante, Pudor, quam tē violō aut tua iūra resolvō.
Ille meōs, prīmus quī mē sibi iūnxit, amōrēs
abstulit; ille habeat sēcum servetque sepulcrō.

---

1. Identify the forms of *ego* and *tū* in the first four lines.
2. Identify their cases.
3. Identify whether they are personal or reflexive.

4. Identify the two reflexive forms in the last two lines.

5. Identify their case.

6. Complete the translation below by translating the pronouns in brackets.

   He, who first joined _____ [*mē*] _____ [*sibi*], took away _____ [*meōs*] love; may he have my love _____ [*sēcum*] and may he keep my love in his tomb.

7. Are *meōs* and *mē* in line 28 personal or reflexive? Explain your answer.

Reflexive Pronoun Text

Plautus, *Miles Gloriosus* **496-513.** Palaestrio, the clever slave, and Periplectomenus, the kindly old man, are conspiring against the Miles Gloriosus' slave Sceledrus. Philocomasium, the unwilling girl of the Miles Gloriosus, pretends never to have seen Sceledrus before, which angers him to the point that he forces her back into the house of the Miles. Only she escapes into the house of Periplectomenus, where she maintains she has been staying all along. Sceledrus, on the advice of Palaestrio, goes into the house of the Miles to get a sword; they will remove her from the house of Periplectomenus by force if they have to. Only, when Sceledrus returns, he reports seeing Philocomasium in the house of the Miles (she used a passageway between the two houses known only to Palaestrio and Periplectomenus). Now, Periplectomenus is angrily asking Sceledrus why he assaulted one of his house guests. Sceledrus has no good answer.

Sceledrus. Vīcīne, auscultā quaesō. **Periplectomenus.** Ego auscultem <u>tibi</u>?
Sceledrus. Expurgāre volō <u>mē</u>. **Periplectomenus.** <u>Tūn</u> <u>tē</u> expurgēs,
quī facinus tantum tamque indignum fēceris?
An quia latrōcināminī, arbitrāminī
quidvīs licēre facere <u>vōbīs</u>, verberō?   500
Sceledrus. Licetne? **Periplectomenus.** At ita <u>mē</u> dī deaeque omnēs ament,
nīsī <u>mihi</u> supplicum virgārum dē <u>tē</u> dātur
longum diūtinumque, ā māne ad vesperum,
quod <u>meās</u> confrēgistī imbricīs et tēgulās,
ibi dum condignam <u>tē</u> sectātus sīmiam: 505
quodque inde inspectāvistī <u>meum</u> apud <u>mē</u> hospitem
amplexam amīcam, quom osculābātur, <u>suam</u>:
quod concubīnam erīlem insimulāre ausus es
probrī pudīcam <u>mē</u>que summī flāgitī,

tum quod tractāvistī hospitam ante aedīs <u>meām</u>:   510
nisi <u>mihi</u> supplicium stimuleum dē <u>tē</u> dātur,
dēdecoris plēniōrem erum faciam <u>tuom</u>
quam magnō ventō plēnumst undārum mare.

---

1. Fill in the chart below. Identify the case of each pronoun and, using the included verb form, identify the subject of the verb and whether each pronoun is the reflexive or the personal pronoun.

2. The subject of any verb form with endings you have not learned yet has been included.

3. If a form is a possessive adjective, identify which noun that adjective modifies in the last column.

Line #	Pronoun	Verb	Subject of Verb	Case	Reflexive or Personal	Modifies? (only for adjectives)
496	ego	auscultem				
496	tibi	auscultem				
497	mē	volō				
497	tū	expurgēs				
497	tē	expurgēs				
500	vōbīs	arbitrāminī	*you (pl.)*			
501	mē	ament				
502	mihi	dātur	*it*			
502	tē	dātur	*it*			
504	meās	confrēgistī				
505	tē	sectāris				
506	meum	inspectāvistī				
506	mē	inspectāvistī				
507	suam	amplexum	*he*			
509	mē	ausus es	*you*			
510	meam	tractāvistī				
511	mihi	dātur	*it*			
511	tē	dātur	*it*			
512	tuom = tuum	faciam				

56. Possessive Adjectives and Possession Using *Eius*

1. What is the difference between *suus, -a, -um* and *eius* in terms of both forms and meaning?

- As with the reflexive pronoun, possessive adjectives and *eius* do not take the gender of their translation from the noun that they modify. Rather, that gender must be understood from the word to which the adjective refers.

- Compare the following sentences:

Senex suum iter impedit.	*The old man hinders his (own) journey.*
Māter suum iter impedit.	*The mother hinders her (own) journey.*
Māter eius iter impedit.	*The mother hinders her (someone else's) journey.*
Māter eius iter impedit.	*The mother hinders his (someone else's) journey.*

  □ In the first two sentences, because the adjective is reflexive, the subject determines its gender: because *senex* is masculine, *suum* means "his"; because *māter* is feminine, *suum* means "her."

  □ In both sentences, however, even though the translation changes, the Latin form does not because, independent of its antecedent, it still must agree with the neuter, singular, accusative noun *iter*.

  □ In the last two sentences, even though *eius* is the same form, there is nothing in the sentence itself to say whether it refers to the journey of a man or a woman. Context, and an antecedent from another sentence or clause, will determine the gender of the translation of *eius*.

Possessive Adjectives Text

Syracuse University Motto

Suōs cultōrēs scientia corōnat.

Vocabulary

cultor, -ōris. adherent
scientia, -ae. knowledge

corōnō, -āre. to crown, to encourage

1. Translate the motto.

Possessive Adjectives Text

Tulane University Motto

Nōn sibi sed suīs.

1. Both *sibi* and *suīs* are reflexive. What is the difference between them (they are in the same case)?
2. Translate the motto. (Hint: *suīs* is a substantive form.)

57. Ablative of Specification (= Ablative of Respect)

1. Does the ablative of specification use a preposition? If so, which one?
2. What two adjectives take the ablative case?

- The ablative of specification will often be used with adjectives to specify or focus their meaning.

Vir magnus currit.	*The big man runs.*
Vir pedibus magnus currit.	*The man, big with respect to his feet, runs. / The man with big feet runs.*

Ablative of Specification / Respect Text

Caesar, *De bello Gallico* 1. This short excerpt is from the opening to Caesar's *De bello Gallico*. Considered an important text because of its anthropological content, it opens with a description of the peoples that Caesar will be describing. He describes where they live, who lives around them, and the differences among them (the latter in this excerpt).

Hī omnēs linguā, institūtīs, legibus inter sē differunt.

1. What are the three nouns used as ablatives of specification?
2. Complete the following translation by filling in the blanks with each of the ablatives of specification. (While you might not know the vocabulary for the ablatives, using cognates and context should help you with them.)

    All of these people differ _____, _____, _____.

Ablative of Specification / Respect Text

Anonymous, *Miraculum Sancti Nicholai* **30-34.** The son of Getron and Euphronia has just been kidnapped. In this excerpt, the kidnappers describe him and their intentions for him.

Puer iste, vultū laudābilis,
sensū prudēns, genere nōbilis,
bene dēbet, nostrō iūdiciō,
subiacere vestrō servitiō.

Vocabulary

iste, ista, istum. that
vultus, -ūs. face, appearance
laudābilis, -e. praiseworthy

sensus, -ūs. sense, common sense
genus, -eris. birth, family
nōbilis, -e. noble

1. Translate the first two lines.
2. Identify the three ablatives of specification.

Ablative of Specification / Respect Text

Martial 4.5.1-2. Martial here satirizes city life by advising a certain Fabianus to stay out of the city. Fabianus apparently is too good; he will not flatter, he will not impeach his intregity. Rome is no place for such a man. In the opening couplet to the poem, excerpted here, Martial describes Fabianus' positive qualities.

Vir bonus et pauper linguāque et pectore vērus,
        quid tibi vīs urbem quī, Fabiāne, petis?

Vocabulary

pauper, pauperis. poor
lingua, -ae. speech, language

pectus, pectoris. chest, heart
vērus, -a, -um. true, honest

1. What are the two ablative nouns in line 1 (Hint: one will look more like an ablative than the other)?
2. Translate line 1.
3. If the subject of the verb *vīs* in line 2 is you (sing.), is *tibi* in line 2 a reflexive or personal pronoun? Explain your answer.

Ablative of Specification / Respect Text

Cicero, *In Catilinam* 2.18. Catiline has been forced out of Rome, and Cicero takes solace in his absence, if only temporarily; Cicero still fears, at least rhetorically, retaliation from Catiline and his allies. But here Cicero introduces a new cause of concern: those who remain in Rome who might still be sympathetic to Catiline's cause. He outlines the different types of men from whom Catiline drew his allies. In this excerpt, he describes the first type.

Tū agrīs, tū aedificiīs, tū argentō, tū familiā, tū rēbus omnibus ōrnātus et cōpiōsus sīs, et dubitēs dē possessiōne dētrahere, adquīrere ad fidem? Quid enim expectās? Bellum? Quid ergō?

Vocabulary

aedificium, -ī. building, property

argentum, -ī. silver, money

familia, -ae. family

rēbus = "matters"
 [*a fifth declension abl. pl.*]

ōrnātus, -a, -um. outfitted, equipped

cōpiōsus, -a, -um. plentiful, rich

sīs = "may you be"
 [*with* tū *as its subject*]

1. Translate line 1 (*Tū agrīs…cōpiōsus sīs*).

Ablative of Specification / Respect Text

Cicero, *In Catilinam* 4.18. By Cicero's fourth oration against Catiline, overwhelming evidence of Catiline's conspiracy to take over Rome has come to light. At this point, five men have been convicted; all that is left to debate is their punishment: death or exile. Caesar favors exile, while Cato, another senator, favors death. Cicero, though attempting impartiality, clearly favors death. In response especially to Cato's speech, the death penalty is handed down and the five men (Catiline not one of them) are immediately killed. (Catiline will be killed in battle outside of Rome some weeks later.) In this excerpt, Cicero acknowledges, as he weighs the two punishments against each other, that the state is in agreement that these men must be punished.

Omnēs ōrdinēs ad cōnservandam rem pūblicam mente, voluntāte, studiō, virtūte, vōce cōnsentiunt.

The words *studiō* and *virtūte* are not included in the Oxford Classical Text, but are included in other editions. They are included here because of the extra grammatical reinforcement they provide.

1. Compare the two translations below of the above excerpt.

    a. Identify which translates the underlined ablatives as ablatives of respect and which translates them as ablatives of means.

    b. Determine which is the more viable translation of the ablatives. Explain your answer.

Every class agrees to save the Republic with their mind, with their good will, with their enthusiasm, with their virtue, with the voice.

Every class agrees to save the Republic in mind, in good will, in enthusiasm, in virtue, in voice.

CHAPTER 14

The imperfect and future of the fourth conjugation represent the final tenses to be formed from the present stem. They are formed in a way identical to those of the third *-iō* conjugation. The accusative is used to express extent of space and degree.

Terms to Know

extent of space
(accusative of)
degree (accusative of)

58. Imperfect Active Indicative (Fourth Conjugation)

1. What is the tense sign for the imperfect?
2. What are three ways to translate the imperfect?

59. Future Active Indicative (Fourth Conjugation)

1. What vowel does the future tense of the fourth conjugation use?
2. What is the one person and number where this vowel is not used? Which is used instead?
3. To which conjugation is the future of the fourth conjugation identical?

- Now that you have learned all three present-stem tenses (present, imperfect, and future), you might have noticed that the third *-iō* conjugation and the fourth conjugation are alike in all personal formations, and most other forms.

- They differ in their present infinitives (both active and passive, though you have not yet learned the passive), and any forms that will use the infinitive as a stem (which you will learn later); otherwise, their forms are identical.

Future Active Indicative (Fourth Conjugation) Text

Martial 8.31.5-6. A certain Dento apparently is seeking custody of his three sons from his now-estranged wife. Martial, however, advises Dento to return home to tend to his affairs or he might find one more son when he eventually gets there.

Nam dum tū longē dēsertā uxōre diuque   5
trēs <u>quaeris</u> nātōs, quattuor <u>inveniēs</u>.

1. One of the underlined verbs is present and one is future. Which is which? Explain your answer.

2. One of the underlined verbs is third conjugation and one is fourth. Which is which? Explain your answer.

Future Active Indicative (Fourth Conjugation) Text

Catullus 62.11-18. Catullus 62 is a wedding hymn sung by chorsues of boys and girls. In this song-competition between the two groups, the boys open with the rising of the evening star, Hesperus. The star then becomes the subject of each group's song. In this excerpt, the boys somewhat playfully steel themselves against the girls; it appears as if they have a contest on their hands.

Nōn facilis nōbīs, aequālēs, palma parāta est;
aspicite, innuptae sēcum ut meditāta requīrunt.
Nōn frustrā meditantur: habent memorābile quod sit;
nec mīrum, penitus quae tōtā mente labōrant.
Nōs aliō mentes, aliō dīvīsimus aurēs;
iūre igitur vincēmur: amat victōria cūram.
Quārē nunc animōs saltem convertite vestrōs;
dīcere iam incipiēnt, iam respondēre decēbit.

1. Using your prior knowledge of verb forms of all conjugations, identify the following and answer the accompanying questions:
   a. One fourth conjugation indicative
      What tense is the verb? How do you know?
   b. One first conjugation present indicative
      What identifies it as first conjugation?
   c. One second conjugation future indicative
      What identifies it as a future verb?
   d. One third conjugation indicative
      What identifies it as a third conjugation?
      What would the future tense form of this verb be?
   e. One infinitive
   f. Two imperatives

60. Accusative of Extent and Degree

1. For what other expression of extent (length) does Latin use the accusative?

2. Do any of the extent expressions with the accusative use a preposition in Latin? If so, which ones?

3. With what English words is the accusative of extent and degree often used?

4. Which Latin words are given as examples in the book as uses of the accusative of extent and degree?

CHAPTER 15

The perfect active of the third and fourth conjugations as well as the pluperfect and future perfect of all conjugations completes the indicative forms of the third principal part/perfect stem. These three tenses, plus the tenses of the present stem, represent all six tenses of Latin verbs; the passive voice of these tenses will be introduced in later chapters. The perfect active infinitive of third and fourth conjugation verbs is also introduced.

Terms to Know

perfect active
    indicative
pluperfect active
    indicative
future perfect
    indicative
perfect active infinitive

61. Perfect Active Indicative

1. How is the perfect tense formed?

2. How is the stem of the third principal part found?

3. What are two ways to translate the perfect tense?

- Now that the perfect tense for all four conjugations has been learned, it should be pointed out that the formation of the perfect tense is identical for all verbs, including all four conjugations and irregular verbs. While the formation of present-stem tenses (present, imperfect, and future) varies according to conjugation, the formation of the perfect (all of its tenses, the other two of which will be learned in this chapter) is the same for all conjugations and irregular verbs.

- The irregularity, or difficulty, in the formation of the perfect tense lies not in the formation itself but rather in the stems. Verbs will often change their stems between the second and third principal parts. While some of these changes are regular and predictable (most first conjugation verbs follow the same pattern), many are not. The difficulty then lies in remembering and recognizing a third principal part.

Perfect Active Indicative Text

    Bryn Mawr College (PA) Motto

    Veritātem dīlexī.

1. Translate the motto in three different ways. (*dīligō, -ere, dīlexī* = to cherish)

2. Which of these three translations would best represent the value that the motto captures? Explain your answer.

Perfect Active Indicative Text

Martial 6.88. Martial fails to address a certain Caecilianus, apparently a patron of his, in respectful terms, and is forced to pay a sum of money in reparation. On the other hand, the sum that Martial pays is the standard fee that clients pay to their patron. Martial then is juxtaposing the societal expectations against the financial realities of the patron-client relationship. The latter appears more important than the former.

Māne salūtāvī vērō tē nōmine cāsū
    nec dīxī dominum, Caeciliāne, meum.
Quantī lībertās constet mihi tanta, requīris?
    Centum quadrantes abstuli illa mihi.

1. What are the three perfect tense verbs in the poem? (Hint: Their subject is "I.")

Perfect Active Indicative Text

Vergil, *Aeneid* **2.774.** In Aeneas' rush to move his family out of the burning Troy, and in the tumult around him, his wife Creusa becomes separated from him. He rushes back to find her but is stopped by her ghost who tells him that his fate lies elsewhere and with another. In this excerpt, he reacts to seeing her ghost.

Obstipuī, steteruntque comae, et vōx faucibus haesit.

1. What are the three perfect verbs in the above excerpt?
2. What are their subjects?

Perfect Active Indicative Text

Seneca, *Phaedra* **296-316.** Phaedra has just revealed her feelings for Hippolytus to her nurse, who counsels her to try to ignore them. Phaedra half-heartedly agrees but threatens suicide. The chorus then follows with a description of Cupid's power. In this excerpt, they describe the power of Cupid even over the gods. The following stories are alluded to:

296-298: Alcestis, who agreed to go to the underworld in the place of her husband Admetus, a deal he had acquired from Apollo, who was sentenced to be Admetus' slave for killing the Cyclopes who made Zeus' thunderbolts.

301-302: Leda, whom Jupiter seduced in the form of a swan. She also lay with her husband that night and so bore four children, two immortal and two mortal: Helen and Polydeices the former, and Clytemnestra and Castor the latter.

303-309: Europa, whom Jupiter carried off in the form of a bull. He would ultimately carry her to the island of Crete, where she would establish the house of Minos. Because Crete was thought to be the home of the first Greeks, it is from Europa's name that Europe and European are derived.

310-316: Endymion, whom Diana (or Semele) loved and who was put to deathless sleep to preserve his youth and beauty.

Chorus. Thessalī Phoebus pecoris magister
ēgit armentum positōque plectrō
imparī taurōs calamō <u>vocāvit</u>.
<u>Induit</u> formās quotiens minōrēs
ipse quī caelum nebulāsque <u>fecit</u>:   300
candidās āles modo <u>mōvit</u> ālās,
dulcior vōcem moriente cygnō;
fronte nunc torvā petulans iuvencus
virginum <u>strāvit</u> sua terga lūdō,
perque frāternōs, nova regna, fluctūs   305
ungulā lentōs imitante rēmōs
pectore adversō <u>domuit</u> profundum,
prō suā vector timidus rapīnā.
<u>Arsit</u> obscūrī dea clāra mundī
nocte dēsertā nitidōsque frātrī   310
<u>trādidit</u> currūs aliter regendōs:
ille nocturnās agitāre bīgās
<u>discit</u> et gӯrō breviōre flectī,
nec suum tempus <u>tenuēre</u> noctēs
et diēs tardō <u>remeāvit</u> ortū,   315
dum <u>tremunt</u> axēs graviōre currū.

1. Fill in the chart below with the tense and translation of the verb forms from the passage.

   Pay close attention to the differences in stem between present tense verbs and perfect tense verbs. This is an essential reading skill to develop.

Line #	Verb	Principal Parts & Meaning	Tense	Translation
298	vocāvit			
299	induit	induō, induere, induī, indūtus. *to put on*		
300	dūcit			
301	mōvit			
304	strāvit	sternō, sternere, strāvī, strātus. *to level*		
307	domuit	domō, domāre, domuī, domitus. *to tame*		
309	arsit	ardeō, ardēre, arsī, arsus. *to burn*		
311	trādidit	trādō, trādere, trādidī, trāditus. *to hand over*		
313	discit	discō, discere, didicī, -. *to learn*		
314	tenuēre			
315	remeāvit	remeō, -āre, -āvī, -ātus. *to return*		
316	tremunt	tremō, tremere, tremuī, tremitus. *to tremble*		

Perfect Active Indicative Text

Aulus Gellius, *Noctes Atticae* **18.2.9.** Gellius here is describing how he and friends passed the time at a dinner party. In this excerpt, Gellius quotes one of the philosophical conundra posed to the guests.

"Quod nōn perdidistī, habēs; cornua nōn perdidistī: habēs igitur cornua."

Vocabulary

quod = "that which"
perdō, perdere, perdidī, perditus.
   to lose [*this verb is here being used as an antonym to* habeō]

cornū, cornūs. horn
   [*a fourth declension neuter noun; this is the accusative plural*]
igitur. therefore, and so

1. This brief excerpt illustrates nicely the distinction between the perfect and the present tenses.
2. Translate the above passage.

Perfect Active Indicative Text

Cicero, *In Catilinam.* **1.9.** Cicero has begun detailing his evidence against Catiline, beginning with a meeting of the conspirators at the house of a certain M. Laeca. In this excerpt, Cicero turns and addresses Catiline directly with seven verbs in quick succession.

Fuistī igitur apud Laecam illā nocte, Catilīna, distribuistī partīs Italiae, statuistī, quō quemque proficīscī placēret, dēlēgistī quōs Rōmae relinquerēs, quōs tēcum ēdūcerēs, dīscrīpsistī urbis partēs ad incendia, cōnfirmāstī tē ipsum iam esse exitūrum, dīxistī paulum tibi esse etiam nunc morae, quod ego vīverem.

Vocabulary

fuistī. [*from* sum]
distribuō, -ere, distribuī, distribūtus. to divide
statuō, statuere, statuī, statūtus. to decide
dēlēgō, dēlēgere, dēlēgī, dēlēctus. to choose
dīscrībō, dīscrībere, dīscrīpsī, dīscrīptus. to assign
cōnfirmō, -āre, -āvī, -ātus. to confirm [cōnfirmāsti = cōnfirmāvistī; *a common contraction occurs in Latin whereby the* -vi *of the perfect stem drops out*]

1. Fill in the blanks in the translation below with the correct forms of the bracketed perfect tense verbs. [I have used semi-cola instead of commas to separate clauses for increased clarity.]

    Therefore, Catiline, _____ [*fuistī*] at the house of Laeca that night; _____ [*distribuistī*] parts of Italy; _____ [*statuistī*] how and whom you wanted to depart (Rome); _____ [*dēlēgistī*] whom you wanted to leave behind at Rome and whom you wanted to bring with you; _____ [*dēscrīpsistī*] parts of the city on fire; _____ [*cōnfirmāstī*] that you yourself would now leave; _____ [*dīxistī*] that even now you would hardly delay because I live.

62. Pluperfect Active Indicative

1. What is an alternate name for the pluperfect?
2. What is the tense sign for the pluperfect?
3. What endings are used with this tense sign?

- The term "pluperfect" is a compound of "perfect" and "plus." If you remember, the term "perfect" refers to an action that has been completed. A pluperfect action, then, is one that is more (the Latin *plūs* for "more") completed, i.e. an action that happens farther in the past than a perfect action or an action that happens before another perfect action. A timeline illustrating all of the tenses will be included below with the future perfect, the last Latin tense to be learned, to illustrate the six tenses and their relationship to one another.

- As with the perfect tense, the formation of the pluperfect is regular and predictable, i.e. every verb forms the pluperfect tense in the same way; any irregularities occur because of changes in stem between the second and third principal parts.

Pluperfect Active Indicative Text

Seneca, *Phaedra* **530-539.** Hippolytus is delivering a lengthy speech on the merits of the country life. He extols a simple life lived off of the land without the ostentation and greed that accompanies city life. In this excerpt, he harkens back to the mythic four ages of man, successive mythological periods in which people lived in better states than they live in today, albeit progressively worse until the present state. One conspicuous and relatively consistent feature of this golden age was a lack of ships, which ultimately would put people in contact with one another, thereby creating envy and conflict, and a lack of cities and fortifications because such protection was not yet necessary.

Hippolytus. Nōndum <u>secābant</u> crēdulae pontum ratēs: 530
sua quisque <u>nōrat</u> maria. Nōn vastō aggere
crēbrāque turre <u>cinxerant</u> urbēs latūs;
nōn arma saeva mīles <u>aptābat</u> manū
nec torta clausās <u>frēgerat</u> saxō gravī
ballista portās, iussa nec dominum patī   535
iunctō <u>ferēbat</u> terra servitium bove:
sed arva per sē fēta poscentēs nihil
<u>pavēre</u> gentēs, silva nātīvās opēs
et opāca <u>dederant</u> antra nātīvās domōs.

Vocabulary

secō, -āre. to cut, to cleave, to sail

noscō, noscere, nōvī, nōtus. to know, to be familiar with

cingō, cingere, cinxī, cinctus. to surround

aptō, -āre. to put on, wear

frangō, frangere, frēgī, fractus. to break, to shatter

ferō, ferre, tulī, lātus. to tolerate

pascō, -ere, pāvī, pastum. to feed, to nourish

1. Fill in the blanks in the translation below with the correct translation of the verbs in brackets.

> Trustworthy boats _____ not yet _____ [*secābant*] the sea:
> each _____ [*nōrat = nōverat*] his own sea; cities _____ [*cinxerant*]
> their border with wide trenches and tall towers;
> the soldier _____ [*aptābat*] armor with his savage hand
> and a cocked ballista _____ not _____ [*frēgerat*] closed gates
> with a heavy stone and the furrowed land _____ not _____ [*ferēbat*]
> to endure the servitude of masters with yoked oxen:
> but fields, fruitful of their own volition, _____ [*pāvēre*; not an infinitive]
> families that demanded nothing; forests _____ [*dederant*] natural wealth
> and shady caves _____ [*dederant*] natural homes.

Pluperfect Active Indicative Text

Martial 8.74. Martial creates a pun on a type of gladiatorial combatant (the *oplomachus*, who wielded a small, round shield with a spear and sword) and an eye doctor (*opthalmicus*). The subject of Martial's poem apparently was the latter but is now the former. Martial says, however, that his actions as a gladiator and a doctor bear little distinction from one another.

> Oplomachus nunc es, fuerās opthalmicus ante.
>   Fēcistī medicus quod facis oplomachus.

Vocabulary

oplomachus, -ī. gladiator
opthalmicus, -ī. eye-doctor
ante (*adv.*). before, in the past
medicus = "as a surgeon" [*with the subject of* fecisti]

quod = "that which" [*the object of* fecisti]
oplomachus = "as a gladiator" [*with the subject of* facis]

1. Translate the passage.

2. Identify the four verbs in the passage with the following information:

   a. principal parts

   b. tense

   c. subject

Pluperfect Active Indicative Text

Plautus, *Menaechmi* 716-717. Sosicles returns from town with the gown of Menaechmus' wife. Menaechmus' wife sees him and, thinking that he is Menaechmus, wonders how he can be so brazen about bringing her dress back to her from his mistress. Sosicles, never having seen Menaechmus' wife before, only knows that he's being verbally assaulted by an unknown woman. In this excerpt, he likens her to Hecuba, who apparently was similarly abusive to any random passerby.

Sosicles. Quia idem faciēbat Hecuba, quod tū nunc facis: omnia mala ingerēbat, quemquem aspexerat:

---

1. Fill in the following chart with the required information.

Verb	Principal Parts & Definition	Subject	Tense	Translation
faciēbat				
facis				
ingerēbat	ingerō, -ere, ingessī, ingestus. *to bestow*			
aspexerat	aspiciō, -ere, aspexī, aspectus. *to see*			

Pluperfect Active Indicative Text

Vergil, *Aeneid* 4.6-7. It is the morning after Aeneas has told his lengthy tale of the fall of Troy and his journey from Troy to Carthage. Dido prepares to reveal to her sister Anna her feelings for Aeneas.

Postera Phoebēā lūstrābat lampade terrās
ūmentemque Aurōra polō dīmōverat umbram,

---

1. Identify the tense of *lūstrābat* in line 6 and *dīmōverat* in line 7.

2. Complete the translation below with the correct translation of the verbs in brackets. Make sure to distinguish in your translation the two different tenses of each verb.

Next, Aurora _____ [*lūstrābat; lūstrō, -āre* = to illuminate] the land with the lamp of Phoebus [i.e. the sun] and she _____ [*dīmōverat; dīmōveō, -ēre* = to remove] the dew-causing dark from the sky.

Pluperfect Active Indicative Text

Vergil, *Aeneid* 2.757. Aeneas has just realized that his wife Creusa is no longer with him and his family as they flee Troy. In this excerpt, he has hurried back to the tumult of the burning city to find her.

inruerant Danaī, et tēctum omne tenēbant.

Vocabulary

inruō, -ere. to rush in   **tēctum, -ī.** roof, house
Danaus, -ī. Greek

1. Using the vocabulary above, translate the above line.
2. What does the difference in tense of *inruerant* and *tenēbant* indicate about the chronology of these actions? What is the status of Troy according to these tenses?

63. Future Perfect Active Indicative

1. What is the tense sign for the future perfect active?
2. What endings does the future perfect active use?
3. What is the one person and number where the future perfect endings do not coincide with the future of *sum*?

- The future perfect takes its name from the fact that it refers to an action in the future that occurs before another future action, i.e. it is future because it happens in the future but it is perfect because it happens before another action.

- The future perfect is not very common in Latin or English, though perhaps less common in English: "By tomorrow, I will have read three books."

- More common in English, however, is future perfect action that is expressed by a present tense verb: "If I study for three hours, I will do fine." The "do" of the second clause is both happening in the future and a future tense verb. The "study" of the first clause is a present tense verb, but refers to an action that hasn't happened yet and happens before the "do" of the second clause, i.e. a future perfect action.

- Even though the first verb indicates future perfect action, the English "If I will have studied for three hours, I will do fine," sounds stilted and unnatural.

Latin Tense Summary

- With the future perfect, you have now learned all six tenses of the Latin indicative (other moods will have fewer tenses):

  - present: an action happening now

  - imperfect: a repeated or continuous action happening in the past

  - future: an action happening in the future

  - perfect: a completed or singular action happening in the past

  - pluperfect: a past action before another past action

  - future perfect: a future action before another future action

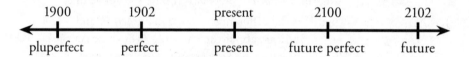

| 1900 | 1902 | present | 2100 | 2102 |
| pluperfect | perfect | present | future perfect | future |

- The above timeline illustrates the relationships among the tenses. The imperfect would fall between the perfect and the present.

64. Perfect Active Infinitive

1. What is the ending for the perfect active infinitive?

_____

- As with all other formations using the third principal part, the formation of the perfect active infinitive is regular and predictable across all conjugations, including irregular verbs. Any irregularities occur because of stem changes between the second and third principal parts.

Perfect Active Infinitive Text

Aulus Gellius, *Noctes Atticae* **17.9.16-17.** Gellius here provides a brief history of encoded writing. In the paragraph prior to this excerpt, he describes how Caesar used a system of transposed letters to encode his writing. In this excerpt, he describes how a

Carthaginian, who may have been Hannibal's brother, hid his writing under the wax of a wax tablet: he would etch his message into the wood of the tablet itself, and then cover the wood with wax. The recipient would then remove the wax and read the message underneath.

Legēbāmus id quoque in vetere historiā rērum Poenicārum, virum indidem quempiam inlūstrem - sīve ille Hasdrubal sīve quis alius est, nōn retineō - epistulam scrīptam super rēbus arcānīs hōc modō abscondisse: pugillāria nova, nōndum etiam cērā inlita, accēpisse, litterās in lignum incīdisse, posteā tabulās, utī solitum est, cērā conlēvisse eāsque tabulās, tamquam nōn scrīptās, cui factūrum id praedīxerat, mīsisse; eum deinde cēram dērāsisse litterāsque incolumēs lignō incīsās lēgisse.

1. Identify the seven perfect active infinitives in the passage above.
2. Is *vetere* in line 1 a present infinitive? Explain your answer.

Perfect Active Infinitive Text

Ovid, *Amores* **1.1.1-4.** Ovid as a young poet, at least according to *Amores* 1.1, wanted to write epic poetry. Cupid, however, intervened and forced him to write love poetry; he stole a metrical foot from the dactylic hexameter of epic poetry, making it a pentameter line of the elegiac couplet.

Arma gravī numerō violentaque bella parābam
    ēdere, māteriā conveniente modīs:
pār erat īnferior versus. Rīsisse Cupīdō
    dīcitur atque ūnum surripuisse pedem.

Vocabulary
rīdeō, -ēre, rīsī, rīsus. to laugh
surripiō, -ere, surripuī, surreptus. to steal away

1. Identify the two perfect active infinitives in the above excerpt.

2. Fill in the blanks in the following translation with the correct
translation of the bracketed perfect infinitives.

I was preparing to write about arms and violent war in a serious meter,

with my material being appropriate for the metrical feet.

The next verse was the same - Cupid is said _____ [*rīsisse; rīdeō, -ēre* = to laugh]

and _____ [*surripuisse; surripiō, -ere* = to steal] one metrical foot.

CHAPTER 16

The fourth and fifth declensions represent the final sets of noun endings to be learned. The nouns of these declensions, with a few exceptions, are relatively uncommon. Nonetheless, both introduce endings that are used in other declensions for different cases; the overlap of endings used for different cases introduces the potential for confusion. The locative case, a relatively rarely used case that expresses place, is also introduced.

Terms to Know

stem
fourth declension
fifth declension
locative
place where

65. Fourth Declension Nouns

1. What is the characteristic vowel of the fourth declension stem?
2. What is the most common gender for fourth declension nouns?
3. What are the two most common fourth declension feminine nouns? neuter nouns?
4. What is unique about *domus, -ūs*?

Fourth Declension Nouns Text

Vergil, *Aeneid* 2.298-303. Aeneas has just received a dream-vision from Hector, the great Trojan warrior, who urges him to flee Troy; he cannot save it. In this excerpt, Aeneas wakes up and connects the sights and sounds around him to what Hector reported to him in his dream.

> Dīversō intereā miscentur moenia lūctū,
> et magis atque magis, quamquam sēcrēta parentis
> Anchīsae domus arboribusque obtēcta recessit,   300
> clārēscunt sonitūs, armōrumque ingruit horror.
> Excutior somnō, et summī fastīgia tēctī
> ascēnsū superō, atque arrēctīs auribus astō;

---

1. Identify the two ablative fourth declension nouns in the above excerpt.
2. Identify the one nominative singular fourth declension noun in the above excerpt.

3. Identify the one nominative plural fourth declension noun in the above excerpt.

4. Explain how you distinguished between 2 and 3 above.

Fourth Declension Nouns Text

Vergil, *Aeneid* 4.333-336. Dido has confronted Aeneas about his leaving Carthage and her. Aeneas here opens his response to her, in which he explains that, while he does indeed love her, his first duty must be to the gods and his destiny to reach Italy.

> ʻEgo tē, quae plūrima fandō
> ēnumerāre valēs, numquam, Rēgīna, negābō
> prōmeritam, nec mē meminisse pigēbit Elissae   335
> dum memor ipse meī, dum spīritus hōs regit artūs.

1. Explain why *dum spīritus hōs regit artūs* in line 336 is confusing because of fourth declension endings.

2. How would you tell which is nominative and which is accusative? Explain your answer.

Fourth Declension Nouns Text

Vergil, *Aeneid* 4.421-423. Dido's sister Anna was instrumental in convincing her to pursue her feelings for Aeneas, despite her pledge of fidelity to her dead husband Sychaeus. At this point in Book 4, Dido knows that Aeneas is leaving, and is distraught. In this excerpt, she asks Anna to try to convince Aeneas to stay.

> Sōlam nam perfidus ille
> tē colere, arcānōs etiam tibi crēdere sēnsūs;
> sōla virī molles aditūs et tempora nōrās.

Mollīs in line 423 is an accusative plural, third declension adjective. Poets will sometimes use a long *-īs* ending in place of the more customary *-ēs* ending of the third declension.

1. *Sēnsūs* in line 422 and *aditūs* in line 423 are accusative plural, fourth declension nouns. Which other word in each clause confirms the case and number of these nouns? Explain your answer.

Fourth Declension Nouns Text

Cicero, *Pro Archia* 17. Cicero has been establishing the importance of poetry and the role it plays in civic virtue. In this excerpt, he alludes to the recent death of Roscius, a friend of his, who, because of his physical abilities, was popular and well liked by all. Cicero connects the popularity and importance of Roscius' physical condition to a similar importance that should be attached to the intellectual and literary abilities of Archias.

Ergō ille corporis mōtū tantum amōrem sibi conciliārat
ā nōbis omnibus; nōs animōrum incrēdibilīs mōtūs
celeritātemque ingeniōrum neglegēmus?

1. There is one fourth declension noun in the above excerpt that is used in two different cases. Identify each form and its case and number.

Fourth Declension Nouns Text

Seneca, *Phaedra* lines 70 and 72. Hippolytus prefaces Seneca's *Phaedra* with an extended speech in which he disavows women and marriage, and pledges fidelity to Diana. In this excerpt from the latter part of the speech, he is finishing his description of Diana's dominance over animals: where they cannot hide and where her bow will always find them.

Hippolytus. ...sīve Hyrcānī cēlant saltūs,
arcūs metuit, Diāna, tuōs.

In the excerpt above, the verb *cēlant* does not have an expressed direct object, and the verb *metuit* does not have an expressed subject.

1. With this in mind, what are the two fourth declension nouns in the above passage?
2. What case are they?
3. What is the clue elsewhere in its line to the case of each noun, beyond its ending?
4. What other cases could each of these fourth declension nouns be, based on their ending?

Fourth Declension Nouns Text

Seneca, *Phaedra* 854-855. Phaedra's husband Theseus has just heard the wailing that signals Phaedra's impending suicide, but does not yet know why she is so distraught. In this excerpt, the Nurse tells Theseus of Phaedra's desire to die. In the dialogue that follows, the Nurse will avoid revealing the reason; Phaedra will soon emerge and eventually reveal to Theseus her illicit passion for his son.

Nutrix. Tenet obstinātum Phaedra consilium necis
flētūsque nostrōs spernit ac mortī imminet.   855

Vocabulary

obstinātus, -a, -um. obstinate, stubborn

Phaedra, -ae. [*name*]

nex, necis (*f*). death

flētus, -ūs. weeping, tears

spernō, -ere, sprevī, sprētus. to reject, to spurn

ac (*conj.*). and

imminō, -ere, imminuī, -. to insist on (+ *dat.*)

1. Using the vocabulary above, translate the excerpt.
2. Identify the fourth declension noun in the excerpt and its case and number.

Fourth Declension Nouns Text

Seneca, *Phaedra* 1050-1056. A messenger has just arrived to tell Theseus of Hippolytus' death. Theseus knows this but wants to know how it happened: a horrid monster in the form of a bull emerged from the sea. Everything ran, animals and people alike, except for Hippolytus. But the horses that pulled his chariot could not remain steadfast and, as the bull charged, they panicked. In the tumult of their panic, Hippolytus was tossed about and eventually died. In this excerpt, the horrified reaction of nature itself to the arrival of the bull from the sea is described.

Tremuēre terrae, fūgit attonitum pecus   1050
passim per agrōs, nec suōs pastor sequī
meminit iuvencōs; omnis ē saltū fera
diffūgit, omnis frigīdō exsanguis metū
vēnātor horret. Sōlus immūnis metū
Hippolytus artis continet frēnīs equōs   1055
pavidōsque nōtae vōcis hortātū ciet.

1. Identify the three fourth declension nouns and their cases in the above passage.

Fourth Declension Nouns Text

Martial 8.65.5-6. Martial here describes monuments to the campaign of the emperor Domitian against the Sarmatians, a people living north and east of the Black Sea. In this excerpt, Martial describes a statue of Rome herself greeting the emperor triumphantly.

hīc laurū redimīta comās et candida cultū   5
   Rōma salūtāvit vōce manūque ducem.

Vocabulary

Rōma, -ae. [*name*]
salūtō, -āre, -āvī, -ātus. to greet

1. Identify the three fourth declension nouns and their cases in the above passage.
2. Translate line 6.

66. Fifth Declension Nouns

1. With what vowel does the stem of fifth declension nouns end?

- The majority of fifth declension nouns are feminine. (*Diēs* is an exception: it is treated by Latin authors as either masculine or feminine.)

- Fifth declension nouns are not very common. The graphic below, now that you have learned all five declensions, illustrates the relative frequency of nouns of the five declensions.

12**3**45

Fifth Declension Nouns Text

Livy, *Ab urbe condita* 1.12.2-3. The Sabines, neighbors of the Romans, had taken the Capitol through the treachery of Tarpeia, a woman who opened the gate to the Sabines in exchange for jewelry; she was killed instead. The Romans, despite their lack of an advantageous position, attempted to retake it. In this excerpt, the bravery of Hostius is described as he temporarily allows the Romans to gain some ground. With his death, however, the Romans lose their momentum and fall back.

Hīc rem Rōmānam inīquō locō ad prīma signa animō atque audāciā sustinēbat. Ut Hostius cecidit, cōnfestim Rōmāna inclīnātur aciēs fūsaque est.

---

1. Identify the two fifth declension nouns in the above excerpt.
2. Identify their cases and numbers.

67. Locative

1. What does the locative express?
2. What are the two categories of places that use the locative instead of the ablative?
3. What are the endings (or rules for endings) for the locative?
4. In what other place expressions do towns and small islands omit Latin prepositions?

- The locative (and the lack of a preposition for place to which and place from which) is used with cities, towns, small islands, and the Latin nouns *domus* and *rus* (*bellum* and *humus* are included in the textbook as examples, but these uses of the locative are less common).

- The term "small islands" might seem arbitrary and imprecise. But there is a grammatical (not necessarily a geographic or demographic) designation for a small island.

  An island is grammatically small if:

  a. it only has one major city or town, and

  b. the name of that city or town is the same as the island

  Off of the coast of Massachusetts' Cape Cod lie two islands: Martha's Vineyard and Nantucket. The former is a grammatically large island; it has four towns and none are named Martha's Vineyard. The latter is a grammatically small island; it has one major town and its name and the island's name are the same. Nantucket would use the locative for place where and no preposition for place to which or from which because it is a grammatically small island. Martha's Vineyard would use the Latin prepositions *in, ad*, and *ab* for place where, to which, and from which because it is a grammatically large island.

- It is important to keep in mind that the rules of the locative apply consistently to common and well-known places: Rome, Athens, etc. The rules of the locative become less consistent the less well known a place is. A common phenomenon occurs in English in the titles for inhabitants of places (English doesn't use a locative, though it does express place to which without a preposition with the word "home": "I'm going home"). I teach near Boston in a town called Wayland. If I live in Boston, I am of course a Bostonian. If I live in Wayland, however, am I a Waylander, a Waylandite, or a Waylandinian? Because there is no concensus (because there doesn't need to be), there is no "rule" per se. Latin will handle the locative of less common places much the same way.

Locative Text

Cicero, *Pro Archia* 4-5. Cicero here describes not only Archias' intellectual training but also the locations that, because of Archias' impressive training and accomplishments, have already granted him citizenship, the very issue for which he's now on trial in Rome.

Nam ut prīmum ex puerīs excessit Archiās, atque ab eīs artibus quibus aetās puerīlis ad hūmānitātem īnfōrmārī solet, sē ad scrībendī studium contulit, prīmum Antiochīae nam ibi nātus est locō nōbilī—celebrī quondam urbe et cōpiōsā atque ērudītissimīs hominibus līberālissimīsque studiīs adfluentī, celeriter antecellere omnibus ingenī glōriā coepit. Post in cēterīs Asiae partibus cūnctaque Graeciae sīc eius adventūs celebrābantur ut fāmam ingenī exspectātiō hominis, exspectatiōnem ipsīus adventus admīrātiōque superāret. Erat Italia tum plēna Graecārum artium ac disciplīnārum, studiaque haec et in Latiō vehementius tum colēbantur quam nunc isdem in oppidīs, et hic Rōmae propter tranquillitātem reī pūblicae nōn neglegēbantur. Itaque hunc et Tarentīnī et Locrensēs et Rēgīnī et Neōpolitānī cīvitāte cēterīsque praemiīs dōnārunt, et omnēs quī aliquid dē ingeniīs poterant iūdicāre cognitiōne atque hospitiō dignum exīstimārunt.

---

1. All of the place words have been underlined in the above excerpt. Identify which of them is locative and which is not, and explain your answer.

Locative Text

Plautus, *Menaechmi* 26-40. This excerpt describes the backstory to the *Menaechmi*, how Menaechmus was kidnapped in Tarentum and how Menaechmus' twin brother Sosicles was renamed Menaechmus in his missing twin's honor.

Inpōnit geminum alterum in nāvem pater,
Tarentum āvexit sēcum ad mercātum simul:
illum relīquit alterum apud mātrem domī.
Tarentī lūdī forte erant, quom illūc venit.
Mortālēs multī, ut ad lūdōs, convēnerant: 30
puer aberrāvit inter hominēs ā patre.
Epidamniensis quīdam ibi mercātor fuit:
is puerum tollit āvehitque Epidamnum eum.
Pater eius autem postquam puerum perdidit,
animum despondit; eāque is aegritūdine   35
paucīs diēbus post Tarentī ēmortuost.
Postquam Syrācūsās dē eā rē rediit nuntius
ad avom puerōrum, puerum surruptum alterum
patremque puerī Tarentī esse ēmortuom,
immūtat nōmen avos huic geminō alterī.   40

---

1. Complete the following translation with the correct place
   constructions of the bracketed Latin towns. (Epidamnium
   was a city on the western coast of Greece; Tarentum on
   the arch of Italy; Syracuse in the southeastern corner of
   Sicily.)

The father placed one twin in the ship, and at the same time,
as he brought him with him _____ [*Tarentum*] to the market,
he left the other twin with his mother _____ [*domī*].
By chance, there was a festival _____ [*Tarentī*] when he came there.
Many people had come together, as if they were at the games:
the boy wandered off from his father among the people.
There was a certain merchant _____ [*Epidamniensis*].
He grabbed the boy and took him _____ [*Epidamnum*].
After his father lost the boy,
he was despondent, and he died after a few days
_____ [*Tarentī*] because of this despondency.
After a messenger returned _____ [*Syrācūsās*] to the boys'
grandfather concerning this matter, that one boy had been taken
and that the father of the boy had died _____ [*Tarentī*],
the grandfather changed the name [of the boy at home] to the name
   of his brother.

CHAPTER 17

While the passive forms are formed essentially the same as the active forms (with a few exceptions), their introduction signals a radical change in the relationship between subject and verb: in an active sentence, the subject does the action while in a passive sentence the subject receives the action. It now becomes imperative to distinguish between active and passive verbs; "The woman sees" vs. "The woman is seen" mean two very different things. The ablative of agent is an ablative construction often used with the passive voice to express the doer of a passive action.

68. Passive Voice

1. What does a verb in the active voice indicate?

2. What does a verb in the passive voice indicate?

3. Write down a translation for the present, imperfect, and future passive in English (use a verb of your choice).

4. What are the six passive personal endings?

5. What is the alternate ending for the second person singular? When is this ending often used?

The Middle Voice

- Ancient Greek had not two but three voices: active and passive, plus what's called the middle voice.

- The subject of an active verb performs the action; the subject of a passive verb receives the action. The middle voice, however, is a reflexive voice, i.e. the subject does the action to him or herself (loosely akin in sense to the reflexive verbs of the modern Romance languages, though the middle voice precludes the use of a reflexive pronoun).

- Latin does not have a middle voice in that it does not have middle endings, as Greek does. But Latin will use its passive forms to sometimes indicate middle action.

Terms to Know

voice
active
passive
personal endings
present passive
   infinitive
intransitive
transitive
linking
factitive
agent (ablative of)
means (ablative of)

- There is nothing about the form of any passive verb that will indicate that it is used in a middle sense. Only context will identify that a verb is being used in a middle sense, and most middle verbs can make sense as a passive or a middle (though the middle sense will often work better).

- Some textual examples of the middle will be included after the texts for the present passive below.

69. Present Passive Indicative

Present Passive Indicative Text

Martial 6.70.7-14. Martial marvels at the youthfulness of the 62 year old Cotta, who apparently has never been ill and scorns doctors. Martial contrasts himself and the addressee of the poem, a certain Marcianus, to Cotta, and concludes that it doesn't matter how long one lives but rather how long one lives in good health. In this excerpt, Martial advocates that years spent sick not be counted as years lived, and he alludes to Priam and Nestor, the former the aged king of Troy, the latter the wizened advisor to the Greek army in the Trojan War.

> At nostrī bene computentur annī
> et quantum tetricae tulēre febrēs
> aut languor gravis aut malī dolōrēs
> a vītā meliōre sēpāretur: 10
> infantēs sumus et senēs vidēmur.
> Aetātem Priamīque Nestorisque
> longam quī putat esse, Marciāne,
> multum dēcipiturque falliturque.

1. Identify the five passive verbs in the above excerpt (*languor* in line 9 is not a passive verb).
2. Identify the three active verbs in the above excerpt.
3. Identify the one infinitive in the above excerpt.

Present Passive Indicative Text

Martial 8.61. Charinus envies Martial the material success that his fame has brought him. Martial quips that he wishes he could punish Charinus for his envy with the same material success. The worry and trouble of his country house and his horses are more trouble than they're worth!

Līvet Charīnus, rumpitur, furit, plōrat
et quaerit altōs, unde pendeat, rāmōs:
nōn iam quod orbe cantor et legor tōtō,
nec umbilīcīs quod decōrus et cedrō
spargor per omnēs Rōma quās tenet gentēs: 5
sed quod sub urbe rūs habēmus aestīvum
vehimurque mūlīs nōn, ut ante, conductīs.
Quid inprecābor, ō Sevēre, līventī?
Hoc optō: mūlās habeat et suburbānum.

---

1. Complete the following table with the requested verb information.

Line #	Verb	Principal Parts	Voice	Subject	Translation
1	līvet	liveō, -ēre = *to blush*			
1	rumpitur	rumpō, -ere = *to break*			
1	furit	furō, -ere = *to madden*			
1	plōrat	plōrō, -āre = *to lament*			
2	quaerit	quaerō, -ere = *to look for*			
2	pendeat	pendeō, -ēre = *to hang*			x
3	cantor	cantō, -ere = *to sing*			
3	legor				
5	spargor	spargō, -ere = *to sprinkle*			
5	tenet				
6	habēmus				
7	vehimur	vehō, -ere = *to convey*			
8	imprecābor	imprecor, -ārī = *to curse*			x
9	optō				
9	habeat				x

Pendeat in line 2 and *habeat* in line 9 are subjunctive verbs whose forms and translation you have not yet learned. *Imprecābor* in line 8 is a type of verb not yet learned that is passive in form but active in meaning; do not translate.

Present Passive Indicative Text

Vergil, *Aeneid* **4.1-2.** Aeneas has just finished his two-book long tale of the fall of Troy and his arrival in Carthage. The fourth book of the *Aeneid* will detail both the inception and the tragic conclusion to the amorous relationship between Dido and Aeneas. These two lines set the tone for the book: upon the conclusion of Aeneas' story, Dido is immediately described as in love with Aeneas.

At rēgīna gravī iamdūdum saucia cūrā
vulnus alit vēnīs et caecō carpitur ignī.

1. Complete the translation below with the correct translation of the verbs in brackets. Pay careful attention to the voice of each verb.

    And so the queen, now preoccupied with a grave concern, _____ [*alit; alō, -ere* = to nourish, to nurse] a wound in her veins and _____ [*carpitur; carpō, -ere* = to seize] by a blind passion.

Present Passive Indicative Text

Pliny, *Epistulae* **9.36.4.** Pliny describes how he spends his time while vacationing at his villa in Tuscany, a region of Italy north of Rome. Reading the rest of the letter reveals how little has changed about vacationing across the millenia!

Iterum ambulō, ungor, exerceor, lavor.

Vocabulary

iterum (*adv.*). again; regularly
ungō, -ere. to clean, to cleanse

exerceō, -ēre. to exercise
lavō, -āre. to wash

1. Identify the voice of each of the four verbs above.
2. Identify the subject of each of the verbs.
3. Translate the line.
4. Is Pliny doing the actions of the verbs above, or receiving them? Explain your answer.
5. Identify the sense of each verb as active, passive, or middle.

The Middle Voice Text

Ovid, *Metamorphoses* **10.250-251.** Ovid's mythic sculptor Pygmalion has just finished his statue of the ultimate woman. In this excerpt, both the skill with which he sculpted her and her beauty are described.

Virginis est vērae faciēs, quam vīvere crēdās   250
et, sī nōn obstet reverentia, velle movērī;

---

1. Choose the better translation of the passive infinitive *movērī* from the two choices below. Explain your choice.

   a. Her face is of a true maiden, which you would believe lives and, if reverence didn't get in the way, you would believe wanted <u>to move</u>.

   b. Her face is of a true maiden, which you would believe lives and, if reverence didn't get in the way, you would believe wanted <u>to be moved</u>.

2. Is *movērī* a true passive or a middle? Explain your answer.

The Middle Voice Text

Ovid, *Metamorphoses* **4.91-92.** Ovid's star-crossed lovers Pyramus and Thisbe have just made their plan to meet outside the city walls. In this excerpt, they are happy with the plan, but the wait until its execution that night seems interminable.

Pacta placent; et lūx, tardē discēdere vīsa,
praecipitātur aquīs, et aquīs nox exit ab īsdem.

---

1. Choose the better translation of the present passive *praecipitātur* from the two choices below. Explain your choice.

   a. The plan is pleasing; and the light, appearing to leave slowly, <u>is sunk</u> into the horizon and the night comes from the same horizon.

   b. The plan is pleasing; and the light, appearing to leave slowly, <u>sinks</u> into the horizon and the night comes from the same horizon.

2. Is *praecipitātur* a true passive or a middle? Explain your answer.

71. Future Passive Indicative

1. What is the difference between the formation of the future of first and second conjugation verbs, and the future of third, third -*iō*, and fourth conjugation verbs?

2. There are three exceptions to the use of the -*bi*- as the tense sign for the future of the first and second conjugations? What are they and what are the alternate forms?

Future Passive Indicative Text

Plautus, *Menaechmi* 72-73. In the preface to the *Menaechmi*, the setting of the play is introduced.

haec urbs Epidamnus est, dum haec agitur fābula:
quandō alia agētur, aliud fiet oppidum.

Vocabulary

Epidamnus, -ī. [*name*; a town located on the coast of southwestern Albania]
dum. while
quandō. when

alius, -a, -ud. another [*here modifying an understood* fābula]
fīō, fierī. to be used (*as the stting*)
oppidum, -ī. town

1. What is the tense of *agitur* in line 72?
2. What is the tense of *agētur* in line 73?
3. Translate the passage.

72. Present Passive Infinitive

1. How is the present passive infinitive formed for the first, second, and fourth conjugations?
2. How is it formed for the third conjugation?
3. How is the present passive infinitive translated?

Present Passive Infinitive Text

Wellesley College (MA) Motto

Nōn ministrārī sed ministrāre.

1. If *ministrō, -āre* means "to minister, to serve," translate the motto.

2. How does the juxtaposition of the passive and active reinforce the message of the motto?

Present Passive Infinitive Text

Martial 4.6. Malisianus tries to appear chaste and seemly, but, at least according to Martial, is not. Martial alludes to Malisianus being as uncouth as one reading the poems of Tibullus in the house of a certain Stella.

Crēdī virgine castior pudīcā
et frontis tenerae cupis vidērī,
cum sīs inprobior, Malisiāne,
quam quī compōsitōs metro Tibullī
in Stellae recitat domō libellōs.   5

1. Identify the two present passive infinitives in the above passage.
2. Identify the conjugation of both.

Present Passive Infinitive Text

Pliny, *Epistulae* 10.96.1, 9-10. Pliny was a governor in Bithynia under the emperor Trajan, to whom this famous letter is directed. Pliny is uncertain about how to handle the Christians under his care and asks Trajan for advice: on the one hand, Christianity is growing and its followers are not hurting anyone, but on the other hand being a Christian violates Roman law, which mandates worship of the state gods as much out of patriotism as faith. Trajan responds definitively that any violation of Roman law must be punished.

Cognitiōnibus dē Christiānīs interfuī numquam: ideō
nesciō quid et quātenus aut <u>pūnīrī</u> soleat aut <u>quaerī</u>.

Neque cīvitātēs tantum sed vīcōs etiam atque agrōs
superstitiōnis istīus contāgiō pervagāta est; quae vidētur
<u>sistī</u> et <u>corrigī</u> posse. Certē satis cōnstat prope iam
dēsōlāta templa coepisse <u>celebrārī</u>, et sacra sollemnia
diū intermissa <u>repetī</u> pastumque vēnīre <carnem>
victimārum, cuius adhūc rārissimus ēmptor inveniēbātur.
Ex quō facile est <u>opīnārī</u>, quae turba hominum <u>ēmendārī</u>
possit, sī sit paenitentiae locus.

The underlined words in the excerpt are present passive infinitives.

1. Write each of the infinitives next to the number of their appropriate conjugation below. Not every conjugation will be represented by the underlined infinitives.

   First _____

   Second _____

   Third _____

   Fourth _____

2. Identify the one present active infinitive in the passage.

3. Identify the one imperfect passive verb in the passage.

Present Passive Infinitive Text

Cicero, *In Catilinam* **4.6.** The case against Catiline has been won; Cicero is now urging the senate to take swift and decisive action against him. In this excerpt, he expresses his surprise at how many unexpected conspirators existed among the Roman citizenry; with this statement, he hopes that the senate will take this opportunity to show such citizens what will happen to them if they, like Catiline, conspire against Rome.

Ego magnum in rē pūblicā <u>versārī</u> furōrem et nova quaedam <u>miscērī</u> et <u>concitārī</u> mala iam prīdem vidēbam, sed hanc tantam, tam exitiōsam <u>habērī</u> coniūrātiōnem ā cīvibus numquam <u>putāvī</u>.

Most but not all of the words underlined above are present passive infinitives.

1. Which are not present passive infinitives? Explain your answer.

Present Passive Infinitive Text

Aulus Gellius, *Noctes Atticae* **4.10.8.** Gellius here relates the story of an ancient filibuster when, to prevent a law from being passed and taking advantage of a provision that allowed a senator to speak on any matter for any length of time prior to addressing the motion on the senate floor, Cato began to speak at length to stall the proceedings. In this excerpt, Caesar, frustrated with Cato, imprisons him but, seeing how the rest of the Senate reacted to his hasty action, relents.

Caesar cōnsul viātōrem vocāvit eumque, cum fīnem
nōn faceret, prēndī loquentem et in carcerem dūcī
iussit. Senātus cōnsurrēxit et prōsequēbātur Catōnem in
carcerem. Hāc," inquit, "invidiā factā Caesar dēstitit et
mittī Catōnem iussit."

---

1. Complete the following translation by translating the
   infinitives in brackets.

   Caesar as consul called a messenger and, since he
   [Cato] didn't finish, ordered him, still speaking, _____
   [*prēndī; prēndō, -ere* = to take away] and _____ [*dūcī*]
   to jail. The Senate dispersed and followed Cato to the
   jail. Caesar stopped because such resentment had been
   created, and ordered Cato _____ [*mittī*; i.e. out of
   jail].

Present Passive Infinitive Text

Seneca, *Phaedra* 370-372. This excerpt comes from the opening
of Act 2 of Seneca's tragedy. The Chorus has just inquired of
the Nurse how Phaedra is doing, and the Nurse replies with a
description of the physical and emotional toll her illicit, and as yet
unrevealed, passion is taking on her. In this excerpt, the Nurse
describes how fickle Phaedra can be about her appearance.

> **Nutrix.** Attollī iubet   370
> iterumque pōnī corpus et solvī comās
>   rursusque fingī;

---

1. Fill in the blanks below with the correct translation of the
   bracketed infinitive.

   She orders her body _____ [*attollī; attollō, -ere* = to
   lift, to raise] and, likewise, _____ [*pōnī*; here used
   as the action opposite to *attollī*] and her hair _____
   [*solvī; solvō, -ere* = to loosen, to undo] and again _____
   [*fingī; fingō, -ere* = to arrange].

Present Passive Infinitive Text

Ovid, *Metamorphoses* 10.56-59. The hero-poet Orpheus
successfully journeyed to the Underworld to recover his
prematurely deceased wife. He swayed Hades and Persephone, the

king and queen of the underworld, with his stirring music. They released his wife Eurydice to him with one condition: that he not turn to see her until he emerges from the underworld. Here, Ovid describes the moment that Orpheus gives in to the temptation to turn and immediately sees his wife taken from him forever.

hīc, nē dēficeret metuēns, avidusque videndī,
flexit amāns oculōs; et prōtinus illa relāpsa est,
bracchiaque intendēns prēndīque et prēndere certāns
nīl nisi cēdentēs īnfēlīx adripit aurās.

Vocabulary

flectō, -ere, flexī, flectus.
  to bend, to turn
amāns, amāntis. lover
prōtinus. immediately

relāpsa est = "she slipped back"
prēndō, -ere. to grab, to hold
adripiō, -ere, adripuī,
  adreptus. to grab at, to
  snatch

1. Translate the second line of the passage.
2. Complete the blanks in the translation of the third and fourth lines of the passage with the correct form of the verb.

   … and streching his arms out and trying _____ [*prēndī*] by her and _____ [*prēndere*] her, he _____ [*adripit*] nothing but empty air.

Present Passive Infinitive Text

Cato, *De agri cultura* 2. Cato here describes the role of the estate's owner. He describes how the owner should assess the status of his estate when he arrives, noting what work has been done and what needs to be done. He should discuss with the manager of the estate these issues, as well as why certain work was not done. If work cannot be done outside because of rain, there is plenty of work to be done inside. Finally, in one of Cato's more controversial statements, he describes how, if slaves become ill, they can be underfed; they can resume their normal diet when they are again healthy.

Pāter familiās, ubi ad villam venit, ubi larem familiārem
salūtāvit, fundum eōdem diē, sī potest, circumeat;
sī nōn eō diē, at postrīdiē. Ubi cognōvit quō modō
fundus cultus siet, opera quaeque facta infectaque sient,
postrīdiē eius diēī vīlicum vocet, roget quid operis siet

factum, quid restet, satisne temperī opera sient confecta, possitne quae reliqua sient <u>conficere</u>, et quid factum vīnī, frūmentī aliārumque rērum omnium. Ubi ea cognōvit, ratiōnem <u>inīre</u> oportet operārum diērum. Sī eī opus nōn appāret, dīcit vīlicus sēdulō sē <u>fēcisse</u>, servōs nōn <u>valuisse</u>, tempestātēs malās <u>fuisse</u>, servōs <u>aufūgisse</u>, opus pūblicum <u>effēcisse</u>. Ubi eās aliāsque causās multās dīxit, ad ratiōnem operum operārumque revocā. Cum tempestātēs pluviae fuerint, quae opera per imbrem fierī potuerint: dōlia <u>lavārī</u>, <u>picārī</u>, villam <u>purgārī</u>, frūmentum <u>transferrī</u>, stercus forās <u>efferrī</u>, stercilīnum <u>fierī</u>, sēmen <u>purgārī</u>, fūnēs <u>sarcīrī</u>, nōvōs <u>fierī</u>, centōnēs, cucūliōnēs familiam <u>oportuisse</u> sibi <u>sarcīre</u>; per fēriās <u>potuisse</u> fossās veterēs <u>tergērī</u>, viam pūblicam <u>munīrī</u>, veprēs <u>recidī</u>, hortum <u>fodīrī</u>, prātum <u>purgārī</u>, virgās <u>vincīrī</u>, spīnās <u>runcārī</u>, expinsī far, munditiās <u>fierī</u>; cum servī aegrōtārint, cibāria tanta dārī nōn <u>oportuisse</u>. Ubi cognīta aequō animō sient quae reliqua opera sient, <u>cūrārī</u> uti perficiantur.

1. Fill in the table below with the requested information.

Verb Form	Conjugation	Tense	Voice
conficere			
inīre			
fēcisse			
valuisse			
fuisse			
aufūgisse			
effēcisse			
lavārī			
picārī			
purgārī			
transferrī			
efferrī			
fierī			
purgārī			
sarcīrī			
fierī			
oportuisse			
sarcīre			

Verb Form	Conjugation	Tense	Voice
potuisse			
tergērī			
munīrī			
recidī			
fodīrī			
purgārī			
vincīrī			
runcārī			
fierī			
oportuisse			
curārī			

2. Translate any verbs whose meaning you know.

73. Sentence Pattern: Passive

1. What are the five sentence patterns that you have learned so far?

2. What are the two elements of the passive sentence pattern?

3. What element of the transitive sentence pattern becomes the subject in the passive sentence pattern?

4. What happens to the doer of the action of a passive sentence, i.e. the subject in a non-passive sentence pattern?

74. Ablative of Agent

1. What does the ablative of agent express?

2. Which preposition does the ablative of agent use?

3. Which ablative construction is used if the action is performed by a thing rather than a person?

  - The ablative of agent requires three criteria:

    □ a passive verb

    □ the preposition *ā/ab*

    □ an animate object as the object of *ā/ab*

  - As is pointed out on page 132 of your textbook, the preposition *ā/ab* can be used with a passive verb without being an ablative of agent. Which of the above three criteria, however, does the example from the textbook, repeated below, not meet?

    Fēminae **ab agrīs** mittuntur.

Ablative of Agent Text

Cicero, *Pro Archia* **6.** Cicero establishes, despite his foreign status, the high esteem in which Archias was held by prominent Romans.

…audiēbātur ā M. Aemiliō, vīvēbat cum Q. Catulō et patre et filiō, ā L. Crassō colēbātur…

1. Which of the above ablatives are ablatives of agent? Explain your answer.
2. What kind of ablative is the non-ablative of agent? Explain your answer.

Latin first names, called the *praenōmen*, are rarely spelled out in texts. Rather, they are expressed by their first initial, each of which was recognizable as standing for the larger name. In the above excerpt, "M" = "Marcus," "Q" = "Quintus," "L" = "Lucius." The case of the abbreviated name, however, is the same as the *nōmen*.

3. Write out each of the abbreviated *praenōmina* above with their appropriate ending.

CHAPTER 18

While a simple sentence consists of a subject and a verb with no other clauses, a complex sentence includes both an independent clause, with a main subject and verb, and at least one dependent clause or subordinate clause. These dependent clauses express different categories of information: place, cause, time, condition, but will always be introduced by a subordinate conjunction. The use of the dative with adjectives is also introduced.

75. Dependent Clauses

1. What is a dependent (= subordinate) clause?

2. What constitutes a complex sentence?

3. What is the function of a dependent clause in a complex sentence?

4. What kind of words are the dependent clauses in this chapter used like?

5. What questions do the dependent clauses in this chapter answer?

6. What are coordinating conjunctions?

7. What do subordinating conjunctions do?

8. What does the textbook call subordinating conjunctions? Why?

9. What is the difference between the placement of Latin subordinating conjunctions and English subordinating conjunctions?

10. Complete the following table, based on the list of subordinating conjunctions on page 138 of the textbook.

Adverbial Clause Marker	English Meaning	Category
		place
		cause
		cause
		time
		time
		time
		time
		condition

11. Why is *cum* a confusing word? What two very different functions can it serve and meanings does it have?

12. How should verbs used with *dum* be translated in English?

Dependent Clauses Text (Conditional)

Martial 1.68.1-4. The above poem introduces Rufus and Naevia. Apparently, "Whatever Rufus does, it is nothing if he doesn't have Naevia." (line 1).

> Quidquid agit Rūfus, nihil est nisī Naevia Rūfō.
>   Sī gaudet, sī flet, sī tacet, hanc loquitur.
> Cēnat, propīnat, poscit, nēgat, innuit: ūna est
>   Naevia; sī nōn sit Naevia, mūtus erit.

Vocabulary

gaudeō, -ēre. to rejoice
fleō, -ēre. to weep
loquor, loquī. to speak [*a special kind of verb that will be learned later, passive in form but active in meaning;* loqu<u>itur</u> *then will be translated actively, despite the passive ending*]

1. Translate line 2; Naevia is the subject of the first three verbs.

The *sī* clause in line 4 introduces the subjunctive mood, which you will learn later. The subjunctive introduces to a conditional the concept that the condition might not be true:

> sī nōn sit Naevia, mūtus erit = *if it is not Naevia (but it is), he will be quiet*
>
> sī nōn est Naevia, mūtus erit = *if it is not Naevia (and indeed it is not), he will be quiet*

Dependent Clauses Text (Conditional)

Martial 2.53. Maximus wants to be free (what exactly Martial means by free is not clear) but is not willing to do what he must to achieve it. Martial advises him to live humbly, not to live ostentatiously, and to not set his social aspirations too high. Through this humility, Maximus might become free in the way that he wants.

> Vīs fierī līber? Mentīris, Maxime, nōn vīs:
>   sed fierī sī vīs, hāc ratiōne potes.

Līber eris, cēnāre forīs sī, Maxime, nolis,
   Vēientana tuam sī domat ūva sitim,
sī rīdēre potes miserī chrȳsendeta Cinnae,   5
   contentus nostrā sī potes esse togā,
sī plēbēia Venus geminō tibi vincitur asse,
   sī tua nōn rectus tecta subīre potes.
Haec tibi sī vīs est, sī mentis tanta potestās,
   līberiōr Parthō vīvere rēge potes.   10

---

1. How many *sī* clauses are in the above passage?
2. Of the *sī* clauses, which is the longest? Which is the shortest? (Answer based on number of words.) Explain how you determined the beginning and end of each clause.

Conditions Text

Cicero, *In Catilinam* **1.12.** Cicero has just declared that Catiline is to be exiled. In this excerpt he introduces why Catiline should not be killed.

Nam sī tē interficī iusserō, residēbit in rē pūblicā reliqua coniūrātōrum manus; sīn tū, quod tē iam dūdum hortor, exieris, exhauriētur ex urbe tuōrum comitum magna et perniciōsa sentīna reī pūblicae.

Vocabulary

interficiō, -ere, -fēcī, -factus. to kill

---

1. Use the chart below to identify the dependent and independent verbs in the above excerpt. Make one column for dependent *sī* clause verbs and one for independent main clause verbs, and list the verbs from the excerpt that correspond to each.
2. Translate the first *sī* clause, from *Nam...iusserō*.
3. What is the tense of *iusserō* in Latin? In what tense will this verb be translated in English?
4. What form is *interficī*? With which other, more commonly used, form of this verb could this form be easily confused? What word serves as the clue that it is not this easily confused form? Explain your answer.

Dependent Clauses Text (Time)

Martial 5.17. Martial criticizes here a certain Gellia for professing lofty social aspirations for her marriage, but ultimately marrying someone well below her supposed station.

Dum proavōs atavōsque refers et nōmina magna,
  dum tibi noster equēs sordida condicio est,
dum tē posse negas nisi lātō, Gellia, clāvō
  nūbere, nupsistī, Gellia, cistiberō.

---

1. Identify the beginning and end words of the three dependent time clauses in the above passage.
2. Identify the beginning and end word of the one independent clause.
3. How many direct objects are in the first dependent time clause? What are they?
4. How many infinitives are in the third dependent time clause? What are they?
5. What case is *Gellia* in lines 3 and 4? How do you know?

Dependent Clauses Text (Time)

Ovid, *Metamorphoses* **4.99-104.** Pyramus and Thisbe arrange to meet in the woods outside Babylon at the tomb of King Ninus, a former King of Babylon. Thisbe arrives first and, as she waits, a lioness, fresh from the kill, arrives to sate her thirst at a nearby fountain. In this excerpt, Thisbe, afraid, flees, and in her flight drops her shawl. The lioness finds the shawl and shreds it with her bloody mouth. This bloodied shawl will begin the series of events that ultimately will lead to the tragic suicides of both Pyramus and Thisbe.

Quam procul ad lūnae radiōs Babylōnia Thisbē
  vīdit et obscūrum timidō pede fūgit in antrum,   100
dumque fugit, tergō vēlāmina lapsa relīquit.
Ut lea saeva sitim multā compēscuit undā,
  dum redit in silvās, inventōs forte sine ipsā
ōre cruentātō tenuēs laniāvit amictūs.

1. Fill in the blanks in the translation below with the correct translation of the dependent time clauses in brackets.

   One of the clause markers (*ut*) is not one that is covered in this chapter (but will be in Chapter 32). See if you can figure out its meaning by context. It also is a clause marker that introduces a dependent time clause.

   > Babylonian Thisbe saw from afar the lioness by the light of the moon and fled on scared feet to a dark cave, and, _____ [*dum fūgit*], she left behind her shawl which had fallen from her back. _____ [*Ut*] the fierce lioness quenched her thirst with a lot of water, _____ [*dum redit in silvās; redeō, -īre* = to return], she tore apart with her bloody mouth the fine shawl found by chance with its owner absent.

Dependent Clauses Text (Time)

Martial 9.1. Martial jokingly catalogs the imperial and divine origins of the names of the months as a satirical commentary on the reach of influence of the emperor.

Dum Iānus hiemēs, Domitiānus autumnōs,
Augustus annīs commodābit aestātēs,
dum grande famulī nōmen adseret Rhēnī
Germānicārum magna lux Kalendārum,
Tarpēia summī saxa dum pātris stābunt,   5
dum voce supplex dumque tūre placābit
matrōna dīvae dulce Iūliae nūmen:
manēbit altum Flāviae decus gentis
cum sōle et astrīs cumque lūce Romānā.
Invicta quidquid condidit manus, caelī est.   10

1. Identify the four verbs used with the subordinating conjunction *dum* in the above poem.
2. Identify the tense of each of these verbs.

   Three of the four should be easily identifiable without vocabulary information; explain how you determined the tense of the fourth without vocabulary information.

3. Identify the two verbs not used in a subordinating clause.

Dependent Clauses Text (Time)

Ovid, *Metamorphoses* 10.8-10. Orpheus and Eurydice have just married. In this excerpt, she, with some friends, is bounding about the fields when suddenly she is killed by a snake hiding in the grass. It is her sudden death that will spur Orpheus to the underworld to attempt, and ultimately fail, to get her back.

nam nūpta per herbās
dum nova Nāiadum turbā comitāta vagātur,
occidit, in tālum serpentis dente receptō.   10

Vocabulary

nam. for
nupta, -ae. bride, wife
herba, -ae. grass, field
Nāiad, Nāiadis (*f.*). Naiad, river nymph
comitō, -āre, -āvī, -ātus. to accompany
vagātur = "…wanders…" [*this is a type of verb, not yet learned, that looks passive but is translated active*]

occidō, -ere. to die
tālum, -ī. ankle
serpens, serpentis (*m./f.*). snake, serpent
dente receptō = "after/because the tooth [*serpentis*] was received [*in tālum*]"

1. Translate the excerpt.

Dependent Clauses Text (Time)

Cicero, *In Catilinam* 1.21. Catiline is trying to avoid his exile, and has asked that a vote on it be put to the Senate. Cicero refuses, on principle he says, but in this excerpt also points out that their silence, their not siding with Catiline on the need for a vote, signals their opinion as much as any vote could.

Dē tē autem, Catilīna, cum quiēscunt, probant, cum patiuntur, dēcernunt, cum tacent, clāmant, neque hī sōlum quōrum tibi auctōritās est vidēlicet cāra, vīta vīlissima, sed etiam illī equitēs Rōmānī, honestissimī atque optimī virī, cēterīque fortissimī cīvēs, quī circumstant senātum, quōrum tū et frequentiam vidēre et studia perspicere et vōcēs paulō ante exaudīre potuistī.

1. Identify the six verbs used in a *cum* clause.

76. Dative with Adjectives

1. What are the nine categories of adjectives that often take the dative case?

Dative with Adjectives Text

Cicero, *Pro Archia* 5-6. Cicero has been establishing the fame and talent of Archias, both to aggrandize Archias before the court and to transition into the tangible benefits of such fame and talent that Archias has already realized, most notably citizenship from other cities. In this excerpt, Cicero focuses on the social benefits of that fame and talent: not only those reputable Romans who patronized him but also his relationship with the Luculli, in whose house he stayed when he was young and in whose house he still stays now that he is old.

Dedit etiam hoc nōn sōlum lumen <u>ingenī</u> ac <u>litterārum</u>, vērum etiam <u>nātūrae</u> atque <u>virtūtis</u> ut domus, quae huius <u>adulēscentiae</u> prīma fāvit, eadem esset familiārissima <u>senectūtī</u>. Erat <u>temporibus</u> illīs iūcundus Q. <u>Metellō</u> illī Numidicō et eius <u>Piō</u> <u>filiō</u>…

The underlined words are nouns that are neither nominative nor accusative.

1. Determine which four nouns are datives with adjectives.
   a. There are two adjectives on which the four nouns are dependent.
   b. The first adjective governs only one dative.
   c. The second adjective governs three datives, but one is an appositive to another.
2. Identify on which adjectives each dative is dependent.

CHAPTER 19

That Chapter 19 is entirely devoted to relative pronouns should indicate their importance. Like interrogative pronouns, relative pronouns in English are somewhat unique in that, no matter their case or use, they occur at the beginning of their clause; this causes some difficulty when dealing with the non-nominative uses of the relative pronoun.

Terms to Know

relative pronoun
interrogative pronoun
adjectival use (of
   relative pronoun)
dependent clause
noun use (of
   relative pronoun)

77. Relative Pronoun

1. What are the five English relative pronouns?

2. What is the objective (accusative) relative pronoun in English?

3. What is the possessive (genitive) relative pronoun in English?

4. How does the preposition *cum* work with the ablatives of the relative pronoun?

The Relative Pronoun and Word Order

- The relative pronoun (and the interrogative pronoun from Chapter 13) are unique in English because they are the only instances in English when form rather than word order indicates meaning.

- The relative pronoun uses form to indicate meaning because it must occur at the beginning of its clause, whatever its grammatical function.

- This phenomenon proves difficult because it violates every instinct of the English speaker (even in English; 'whom' is rarely used in all but the most formal English).

- Consider the following examples (with the pronouns underlined):

    The boy loves Latin. <u>He</u> studies hard.

    The boy, <u>who</u> loves Latin, studies hard.

    The girl loves Latin. Her teacher admires <u>her</u>.

    The girl, <u>whom</u> her teacher admires, loves Latin.

    The boy loves Latin. His friends study with <u>him</u>.

    The boy, with <u>whom</u> his friends study, loves Latin.

The girl loves Latin. <u>Her</u> friends study hard.

The girl, <u>whose</u> friends study hard, loves Latin.

- It is imperative, when dealing with the Latin relative pronoun, to identify the case of the Latin pronoun and translate that case accordingly.

- Although "whom" is a rarely used form in English, it is a helpful form to use when translating. Consider the following Latin sentence.

> Puer, <u>quem</u> puella videt, currit = *The boy, whom the girl sees, runs.*

Although such a sentence will often become in English "The boy, who the girl sees, runs," the use of "who" as a (grammatically incorrect) translation for the accusative is a dangerous translation. When you begin a relative clause with "who," your English brain will want to put the verb next; often that sentence then will (incorrectly) become "The boy, who sees the girl, runs." The use of "whom" then becomes a trigger for your English brain to not automatically translate the relative pronoun as a subject. Just as you would never say "Him goes to the store" you would likewise never say "whom sees the girl" (not to mention, of course, that *puella* is not accusative).

- A good approach is this: when faced with a nominative relative pronoun, translate the pronoun first with the verb immediately following; when faced with an objective relative pronoun (dative, accusative, ablative), translate the relative pronoun with the subject immediately following, i.e. an objective relative pronoun when translated into English will be followed by another noun.

78. Relative Clause - Adjectival Use

1. In English, where does the relative pronoun occur in relation to what it modifies?

2. What is the term for the word that the pronoun modifies?

3. In what two categories will a pronoun agree with the word that it modifies?

The Relative Pronoun and Gender

- Compare the following fragments:

    i. Caesar, quī…   iv. Memoria, quae…

    ii. Clāmor, quī…   v. Auxilium, quod…

    iii. Soror, quae…

- Of *quī*, *quae*, and *quod* in the above examples, which are translated "which?"

- It might be tempting to think that only the last is translated as "which" because of the gender of the Latin relative pronoun, and of course the gender of its antecedent (*auxilium*, a neuter noun). But when the relative pronoun is translated into English, because of Latin's use of grammatical gender and English's lack of use of grammatical gender, it is the gender of the English noun that determines the translation of the relative pronoun.

- In the odd numbered examples above, the gender of the Latin noun matches the gender of the English noun: *quī* = masculine = "who"; *quae* = feminine = "who"; *quod* = neuter = "which."

- In the even numbered examples above, the gender of the Latin noun does not match the gender of the English noun, i.e. *clāmor* is masculine in Latin but neuter in English: *quī* = "which"; *memoria* is feminine in Latin but neuter in English: *quae* = "which."

Relative Clause - Adjectival Use Text

Horace, *Carmina* 3.30.1-5. Known as a *sphragis* poem because it seals the collection of poetry shut (*sphragis* is the Greek word for a seal), the final poem of Horace's third book of odes in fact did not "seal" his collection. He decided he wanted to write more than his originally planned three books and circulated a fourth book of poetry. Nonetheless, in these first five lines of the poem, Horace illustrates a primary theme of the *sphragis* poem: the ability of the poet's poetry to survive well beyond the lifetime of the poet himself.

Exegī monumentum aere perennius
rēgālīque sitū pȳramidum altius,
quod nōn imber edax, nōn Aquilō impotens
possit dīruere aut innumerābilis
annōrum seriēs et fuga temporum.   5

1. Identify the relative pronoun in the above excerpt.
2. Identify its gender.
3. Identify the two nouns in lines 1-2 that it could have as its antecedent.

4. Choose from among the translations below which best translates the following Latin (paraphrased from above):

Exēgī monumentum, quod nōn imber edax, [quod] nōn Aquilō impotens possit dīruere aut [quod] innumerābilis annōrum seriēs et [quod] fuga temporum [possit dīruere].

   a. I have built a monument which is able to withstand the driving rain and the powerless west wind and an innumerable series of years and the flight of time.

   b. I have built a monument which the driving rain can't destroy, which the powerless west wind can't destroy, or which the innumerable series of years and the flight of time can't destroy.

   c. I have built a monument which drives the rain, is not able to rush into the powerless west wind or can't count the years or flee time.

5. What case is *quod*? Explain your answer.

Relative Clause - Adjectival Use Text

Catullus 2.1-4. Catullus opens his collection of poems with a dedicatory poem to a certain Cornelius Nepos. The second poem of his collection introduces Lesbia and their relationship. But Catullus approaches the Lesbia subject-matter obliquely; the poem opens here with her pet sparrow. Via the sparrow, Catullus introduces many of the themes that will characterize his poetic relationship with Lesbia: jealousy, affection, flirtation, isolation. And the potential symbolism of the sparrow, playfully pecking in Lesbia's lap, cannot be ignored: when is a sparrow no longer a sparrow?

Passer, dēliciae meae puellae,
quīcum lūdere, quem in sinū tenēre,   [quīcum = quōcum]
cui prīmum digitum dare adpetentī
et ācris solet incitare morsūs, ...

1. Identify the three relative pronouns in the above passage, as well as their case.

2. If the antecedent for all of the pronouns is in line 1, what noun does it have to be (even if you don't know the vocabulary information for that noun)? Explain your answer.

3. Complete the following translation by filling in the blanks
   with the correct translation of the bracketed relative
   pronoun. Note that all of the blanks will be filled in with
   and English relative pronoun form that refers to the *passer*
   or the sparrow.

   Sparrow, delight of my girl,

   _____ [*quīcum = quōcum*] she commonly plays,

   _____ [*quem*] she commonly holds in her lap,

   _____ [*cui*], as it pecks, she commonly gives the tip
     of her finger

   and who commonly incites sharp pecks.

Relative Clause - Adjectival Use Text

Seneca, *Phaedra* 54-59. Seneca opens his *Phaedra*, as does
Euripides, with an extended speech by Hippolytus in which he
professes his devotion to the huntress goddess Diana. In this
excerpt, Hippolytus declares the omnipotence of Diana over the
earth.

Ades ēn comitī, dīva virāgō,
cuius regnō pars terrārum   55
sēcrēta vacat, cuius certīs
petitur tēlīs fera quae gelidum
pōtat Arāxēn et quae stantī
lūdit in Histrō.

1. Identify all possible cases, numbers, and genders of the
   relative pronouns in the above excerpt.
2. If *fera* in line 58 is the plural, second declension antecedent
   of *quae*, in lines 58 and 59, what is the gender of *quae*?
   Explain your answer.

Relative Clause - Adjectival Use Text

Martial 1.1. This is the opening poem to Martial's collection of fourteen books of epigrams. In it, he announces that his readers are getting what they hoped for: Martial and his poetry. He also looks to the future of this poetry: he has received not unexpected fame for it already, but that sort of fame is rare for poets after they have died.

Hic est quem legis ille, quem requiris,
tōtō nōtus in orbe Martiālis
argūtīs epigrammaton libellīs:
cui, lector studiōse, quod dedistī
vīventī decus atque sentientī,   5
rārī post cinerēs habent poētae.

---

1. Choose the correct translation of line 1. Explain your answer.
   a. Here is that man who reads, who seeks.
   b. Here is that man whom you read, whom you seek.
   c. Here is that man who chooses you, who seeks you.
2. What are the two relative pronouns in line 4? What case are they?
3. How do you know whether the second relative pronoun in line 4 is nominative or accusative?
4. The form *epigrammaton* in line 3 is a Greek accusative, the *-on* ending akin to the Latin *-um* ending. Often Greek words or names will be used with transliterated forms of their Greek endings, especially in the nominative and accusative.

Relative Clause - Adjectival Use Text

Martial 3.63. Martial agrees that a certain Cotilus is an "attractive man" (*bellus homō*), but then questions both the definition of what a *bellus homō* is and, given that definition, whether it is something to which Cotilus, or anyone, should aspire.

Cotile, bellus homō es: dīcunt hoc, Cotile, multī.
   Audiō: sed quid sit, dīc mihi, bellus homō?
"Bellus homō est, flexos quī dīgerit ordine crīnēs,
   balsama quī semper, cinnama semper olet;

cantica quī Nīlī, quī Gādītāna susurrat,   5
  quī movet in variōs bracchia volsa modōs;
inter fēmineās tōtā quī luce cathedrās
  dēsidet atque aliqua semper in aure sonat,
quī legit hinc illinc missās scrībitque tabellās;
  pallia vīcīnī quī refugit cubitī;   10
quī scit quam quis amet, quī per convīvia currit,
  Hirpīnī veterēs quī bene nōvit avōs."
Quid narrās? Hoc est, hoc est homō, Cotile, bellus?
  Rēs pertrīcōsa est, Cotile, bellus homō.

---

1. How many different adjectival relative clauses describe
   bellus homō in line 3?

2. The first and last couplets of the poem are translated here:

   > Cotilus, you are an attractive man: many people say
   > this, Cotilus.
   > I understand: but tell me what an attractive man is.
   > What are you saying? This, this is an attractive man,
   > Cotilus?
   > An attractive man is an odd thing, Cotilus.

   The rest of the poem between the opening and closing
   couplets translated above is an extended quote that begins
   with *Bellus homō est quī....* The quote is comprised of
   a number of successive statements that begin likewise.
   Translate those four words.

Relative Clause - Adjectival Use Text

Cicero, *In Catilinam* **1.30.** Cicero here defends the decision not to
kill Catiline but rather to exile him. In this excerpt, he points out
that there are some in the senate who, by not condemning Catiline
outright, give him hope that he may yet emerge unscathed, and
encourage him and his co-conspirators to continue in their scheming.

Quamquam nōn nūllī sunt in hōc ōrdine <u>quī</u> aut
ea <u>quae</u> imminent nōn videant aut ea <u>quae</u> vident
dissimulent; <u>quī</u> spem Catilīnae mollibus sententiīs
aluērunt coniūrātiōnemque nāscentem nōn crēdendō
conrōborāvērunt; <u>quōrum</u> auctōritāte multī nōn
sōlum improbī vērum etiam inperītī, sī in hunc

animadvertissem, crūdēliter et rēgiē factum esse dīcerent.
Nunc intellegō, sī iste, <u>quō</u> intendit, in Mānliāna castra
pervēnerit, nēminem tam stultum fore, <u>quī</u> nōn videat
coniūrātiōnem esse factam, nēminem tam improbum <u>quī</u>
nōn fateātur.

1. Identify all possible cases, numbers, and genders for the
   underlined relative pronouns.
2. Is *quī* in the first line singular or plural? Explain your
   answer.
3. Is *quae* in the first line feminine or neuter? Explain your
   answer.

Relative Clause - Adjectival Use Text

Martial 5.37.1-17. Martial here mourns the death of a young slave
woman, whom he aggrandizes throughout the first two-thirds of
the poem. His friend Paetus forbids him from mourning a slave,
and uses himself as a parallel: Paetus has lost his wife and, though
sad, continues to live his life. Martial quips at the end how difficult
it must be for Paetus, surrounded, as he is, by so much money.

Puella senibus dulcior mihi cygnīs,
agna Galaesī mollior Phalantīnī,
concha Lucrīnī delicātior stagnī,
cui nec lapillōs praeferās Erythraeōs
nec modō polītum pecudis Indicae dentem   5
nivēsque prīmās līliumque nōn tactum;
quae crīne vīcit Baeticī gregis vellus
Rhēnīque nōdōs aureamque nītellam;
frāgrāvit ōre, quod rosārium Paestī,
quod Atticārum prīma mella cērārum,   10
quod sūcinōrum rapta dē manū glēba;
cui conparātus indecens erat pāvō,
inamābilis sciūrus et frequens phoenix,
adhūc recentī tepet Erōtion bustō,
quam pessimōrum lex amāra fātōrum   15
sextā perēgit hieme, nec tamen tōtā,
nostrōs amōrēs gaudiumque lūsūsque.

1. Identify the seven relative pronouns in the poem above, and complete the following chart.

Line #	Relative Pronoun	All Possible Cases, Genders, and Numbers

79. Relative Clause - Noun Use

1. What is not expressed in this use of a relative clause?

2. What is this use of the relative clause often called?

3. What must you supply in English when you translate these clauses?

Relative Clause - Noun Use Text

Ovid, *Amores* 1.3.21-24. Ovid, in the third poem of his *Amores*, promises poetic and eternal fame to his would-be girlfriend. To convince her of the success of his plan, he alludes to three famous mythological woman, all consorts of the god Jupiter. The passage, however, is laden with a characteristically Ovidian irony: while indeed Ovid is correct that these women have achieved lasting fame through poetry, they are also all women who were forced into an adulterous affair with Jupiter. What does it say then about Ovid's intentions with his would-be girlfriend to allude to perhaps the ultimate adulterer in Jupiter? Such a question is one that Ovid enjoys asking and enjoys even more not answering.

Carmine nōmen habent exterrita cornibus Īō
    et quam flūmineā lūsit adulter ave
quaeque super pontum simulātō vecta iuvencō
    virgineā tenuit cornua vāra manū.

Ovid introduces three women: one in the first line, one in the second line, and one in the third and fourth lines. Only one of the women is named: Io, in the first line. The other two are alluded to only via an indefinite relative clause.

1. Identify the relative pronouns in the second and third lines, as well as their gender and case.
2. Translate both relative pronouns; make certain to include with them an English antecedent and make sure to translate their Latin case into the appropriate English case.

Relative Clause - Noun Use Text

Martial 3.9. Martial scoffs at Cinna's literary assault on him. How bad an assault can it be when Cinna writes that which no one reads?

Versiculōs in mē narrātur scrībere Cinna.
   Nōn scrībit, cuius carmina nēmō legit.

Vocabulary

versiculus, -ī. little verse, epigram   **narrātur** = "is said"
in = "against"   **Cinna, -ae.** [*name*]

Martial generalizes in line 2 about the type of writer that Cinna is (or is not, in this case) by using an indefinite relative clause.

1. Translate the epigram.

CHAPTER 20

The perfect passive system represents a radical change in how Latin verbs are formed. Up to this point, all of your verb forms have consisted of a stem, a characteristic vowel, perhaps a tense sign, and a personal ending. The perfect passive will use none of these but, somewhat akin to English, will use a participle plus a form of *sum* as a helping verb. The perfect passive infinitive will be similarly formed. The forms of the irregular noun *vīs, vis* are also introduced.

80. Perfect Passive Indicative

1. What is the basic formation for the perfect passive?

2. Which form of a verb is the fourth principal part?

3. With what does the fourth principal part agree when used as a perfect passive main verb?

4. Which tense of *sum* is used in the perfect passive?

5. What are two translations for the perfect passive?

Perfect Passive Indicative Text

> **Martial 6.7.1-2.** The *Iūlia lex* (or *lex Iūlia* as it is more commonly known) refers to legislation enacted in 18-17 BCE by Augustus that sought to elevate the social and moral standing of marriage by severely penalizing adultery (either by death or at least exile, to the latter of which Augustus sentenced his own granddaughter for her apparently pervasive indiscretions) and rewarding the bearing of children, especially male children. In this poem, Martial describes a certain Telesilla (not mentioned in this excerpt), who is apparently marrying her tenth husband. Martial quips that he prefers his prostitutes more upfront about their chosen vocation. In this excerpt, Martial introduces to his addressee, a certain Faustinus, the *lex Iūlia* and its purpose to establish the context within which he will discuss Telesilla.

> Iūlia lex populīs ex quō, Faustīne, renāta est
> atque intrāre domōs iussa Pudīcitia est....

1. What are the two perfect passive verbs in the above excerpt?

2. What is the gender of their subject? How do you know?

3. What is the participle that goes with *est* in line 2?

4. Identify the noun that is the subject of both. Explain your answer.

81. Pluperfect Passive Indicative

1. What tense of *sum* is used in the pluperfect passive?

Perfect and Pluperfect Passive Indicative Text

Ovid, *Metamorphoses* **4.65-77.** The forbidden lovers Pyramus and Thisbe lived next door to each other in houses that shared a common wall. In that wall a crack had formed and it is through this crack that they furtively communicated. This excerpt not only describes that communication but also sees Pyramus and Thisbe address the wall directly: they both thank it for allowing them to communicate and wish that it were not there so that they could be together.

Fissus erat tenuī rīmā, quam dūxerat ōlim	65
cum *fieret*, pariēs domuī commūnis utrīque.	
Id vitium nūllī per saecula longa notātum—	
quid nōn sentit amor?—prīmī vīdistis amantēs	
et vōcis fēcistis iter, tūtaeque per illud	
murmure blanditiae minimō *trānsīre* solēbant.	70
Saepe, ubi cōnstiterant, hinc Thisbē, Pȳramus illinc,	
inque vicēs fuerat captātus anhēlitus ōris,	
"Invide" dīcēbant "pariēs, quid amantibus obstās?	
Quantum erat, ut *sinerēs* tōtō nōs corpore *iungī*	
aut, hoc sī nimium est, vel ad ōscula danda *patērēs*!	75
Nec sumus ingrātī; tibi nōs *dēbēre* fatēmur	
quod datus est verbīs ad amīcās trānsitus aurēs."	

1. Fill in the following chart with the requested information about each verb form underlined above. The italicized forms are also verbs, but either non-personal verbs (infinitives) or forms that you have not yet learned (subjunctives).

Line #	Verb Form	Tense	Voice	Subject	Translation
65	fissus erat				
65	dūxerat				
68	sentit				
68	vīdistis				
69	fēcistis				
70	solēbant				
71	cōnstiterant				
72	fuerat				
73	dīcēbant				
73	obstās				
74	erat				
76	sumus				
76	fatēmur				*we confess*
77	datus est				

Fuerat captātus in line 72 is translated as a pluperfect passive: "the breath of their mouth had been captured," but does not follow the convention for forming a pluperfect passive, i.e. according to the rules of grammar its pluperfect passive should read *captātus erat*. In this particular instance, the metrical demands of Ovid's poem perhaps precluded his use of *erat*, or it could be an idiosyncracy. (Compare how English speakers alternately pronounce "neither" with an "ee" sound or an "ay" sound.) Whatever the reason, it is essential to use the rules of Latin grammar judiciously so that they will only help your understanding of the Latin rather then inhibiting it, i.e. even though this verb form does not follow the rules, its meaning still makes sense.

Sumus ingrātī in line 76 looks like a perfect passive but is not. Now that forms of *sum* are used to form perfect passives, it is important to be able to recognize words that are the perfect participle (and so with *sum* will form the perfect passive), and to recognize words, like *ingrātī*, that are not perfect passive participles but might look like them.

82. Future Perfect Passive Indicative

1. What tense of *sum* is used in the future perfect passive?
2. What is the one person and number in which the future perfect passive differs from the future perfect active?

83. Perfect Passive Infinitive

1. What form of *sum* is used in the perfect passive infinitive?

- There are five traditional infinitive forms (a sixth exists, but is rare): the present active and passive; the perfect active and passive; and the future active (the future passive is the very rare sixth).

- The present active and passive infinitives, and the perfect active infinitive are commonly used as objective or subjective infinitives, i.e. they are used in Latin in ways that will be translated into English as infinitives.

Perfect Passive Infinitive Text

Plautus, *Menaechmi* **1126-1136.** Sosicles and Menaechmus are quizzing each other about their pasts to ascertain whether in fact they are long-lost twin brothers. Sosicles has just declared himself Menaechmus' twin, but, in this excerpt, Menaechmus remains confused about how then Sosicles is called Menaechmus.

Menaechmus. Quōmodo igitur post Menaechmō nōmen est factum tibi?
Sosicles. Postquam ad nōs renuntiātum est tē <dēerrasse> et patrem esse
    mortuom,
avos noster mūtāvit: quod tibi nōmen est, fēcit mihi.
Menaechmus. Crēdō ita esse factum ut dīcis. Sed mī hoc respondē.
    Sosicles. Rogā.
Menaechmus. Quid erat nōmen nostrae mātrī? **Sosicles.** Teuximarchae.   1130
Menaechmus. Convenit.
Ō salvē inspērāte annīs multīs post quem conspicor.
Sosicles. Frāter, et tū, quem ego multīs miseriīs labōribus
usque adhūc quaesīvī quemque ego esse inventum gaudeō.
Menaechmus. Hoc erat, quod haec tē meretrix huius vocābat nōmine: 1135
hunc censēbat tē esse, crēdō, quom vocat tē ad prandium.

1. There are perfect passive infinitives in lines 1127, 1129, and 1134. What are they?
2. What is the gender of their subjects?

The Perfect Passive Summary

- The Perfect System of tenses (perfect, pluperfect, and future perfect) utilizes a different approach to formation from the Present System of tenses (present, imperfect, and future).

- In the Present System, the same basic formation is used (stem, characteristic vowel, tense sign if necessary, ending) for both active and passive forms; only the endings change.

- In the Perfect System of tenses, two different formations are used for the active and passive.

- The active perfect tenses are formed from the third principal part; there are no passive forms formed from the third principal part.

- The passive perfect tenses are formed from the fourth principal part. The basic formula remains the same for all three tenses: the perfect participle plus a form of the verb sum.

- The four principal parts, then, can be divided in half. The first two are used for the Present System of tenses; the second two are used for the Perfect System of Tenses.

The Perfect Passive "Formula"

- Understanding the "formula" of how the perfect passive tenses are formed will help you learn not only the perfect passive indicative forms more easily, but also forms yet to be learned that use a similar formula.

- Every perfect passive form uses the perfect participle and a form of *sum*.

    conditus est

- Consider the function of each of the two parts. The participle indicates primarily the meaning of the form, or the verb from which the form is taken; it also indicates the number of the subject and the gender of the subject, although neither of these is essential information (the number is also indicated by the form of *sum*; the gender is helpful for identifying the subject, but not necessary). The form of *sum* indicates the mood and the tense of the verb.

conditus est	conditus esse	[conditus sit]
conditus erat		[conditus esset]
conditus erit		

- In the above grid, each column is a different mood: the left is the indicative, the middle infinitive, and the right subjunctive (bracketed because they have not yet been learned).

- The rows are different tenses: the first is perfect, the second pluperfect, the third future perfect.

1. Based on the "formula," what tense of the subjunctive is *sit*? *esset*? Explain your answer.

2. Based on the "formula," then, what tense is the subjunctive form *conditus sit*? *conditus esset*? Explain your answer. (Remember that there is a difference between the tense of *sum* by itself, asked above, and the tense of the compound verb formed with the perfect passive participle and a form of *sum*, as asked here.)

- Understanding the role of *sum* and its present, imperfect, and future tenses will reduce the amount of memorization required to learn the Perfect System of tenses.

84. Paradigm of *vīs, vis, f.*

1. With what other noun is *vīs, vis* easily confused?

Paradigm of *vīs, vis, f.* Text

Seneca, *Phaedra* 882-893. Theseus is trying to ascertain why Phaedra is so crazed; the nurse will not tell him, and Phaedra keeps trying but ultimately cannot bring herself to do it. In this excerpt, Theseus tells Phaedra that he will bind and beat the nurse until she speaks, but Phaedra stops him, promising herself to tell him of her illicit passion.

Theseus. Silēre pergit. Verbere ac vinclīs anus
altrixque prōdet quidquid haec fārī abnuit.
Vincite ferrō. Verberum vīs extrahat
sēcrēta mentis. **Phaedra.** Ipsa iam fābor, manē.   885
Theseus. Quidnam ōra maesta āvertis et lacrimās genīs
subitō coortās veste praetentā optegis?
Phaedra. Tē tē, creātor caelitum, testem invocō,
et tē, coruscum lūcis aetheriae iubar,
ex cuius ortū nostra dēpendet domus: 890
temptāta precibus restitī; ferrō ac minīs
nōn cessit animus: vim tamen corpus tulit.
Labem hanc pudōris ēluet noster cruor.

1. Identify the two forms of *vīs* in the passage, as well as their case and number.

2. What word, in the first sentence with *vīs*, modifies the form of *vīs*?

CHAPTER 21

The irregular verb *volo*, "to want" or "to wish," as well as its two compounds, *nolo* and *malo*, "to not want" and "to prefer" are introduced. Because of their meanings they will often function with an objective infinitive, which is also introduced. These verbs are consistently irregular only in the present tense.

> **Terms to Know**
>
> objective infinitive
> subject of the infinitive

85. Irregular Verbs: *volō, nōlō, mālō*

1. In what tense do these three verbs have irregular forms?
2. What forms do these verbs not have?

- Each of these verbs will often, though not always, take infinitives following them. When you see these verbs in Latin, prepare for an infinitive to go with it.

- Both *nōlō* and *mālō* are compound forms of *volō*. *Nōlō* is a compound of *nōn* and *volō*, while *mālō* is a comound of *magis* (more) and *volō*. If you say these words quickly (*nōn volō* is an easier example), you can see how the forms contract to make *nōlō* or *mālō*.

Irregular Verbs Text

Martial 1.8. Martial here advises a certain Decianus that thoughtless bloodlust should not and does not bear fame; rather, it is the man who can fight well and return home after the battle that is a hero in Martial's book.

> Quod magnī Thraseae consummātīque Catōnis
>   dogmata sīc sequēris, salvōs ut esse velīs,
> pectore nec nūdō strictōs incurris in ensīs,
>   quod fēcisse velim tē, Deciāne, facis.
> Nōlō virum facilī redimit quī sanguine fāmam,   5
>   hunc volō, laudārī quī sine morte potest.

1. What are the two irregular verbs that appear in the above passage?
2. What is their tense and their subject?
3. There are two other forms of *volō* in the above passage, but they are subjunctive forms (which you haven't learned yet). Try to identify which two verbs are the present subjunctive of *volō*.

Irregular Verbs Text

Martial 1.75. Martial advises not to give a certain Linus half, because that half will be lost. He does seem to imply, however, that giving Linus all is a safer bet. Whether Linus is completely untrustworthy (with half or all) or whether Martial is commenting on Linus' penchant for punishing those who don't trust him completely is unclear.

Dīmidium dōnāre Linō quam crēdere tōtum
qui māvolt, māvolt perdere dīmidium.

1. Identify the two forms of *mālō* in the above poem, as well as their tense and subject.
2. Identify the three infinitives in the passage that depend on these forms of *mālō*.

Irregular Verbs Text

Martial 7.77. Martial does not want to give Tucca his books because of what Tucca will do with them.

Exigis ut nostrōs dōnem tibi, Tucca, libellōs.
Nōn faciam: nam vīs vendere, nōn legere.

Vocabulary

exigō, -ere. to ask, to request [*with "me" as an understood object in English*]
dōnem = "to give"

Tucca, -ae. [*name*]
libellus, -ī. book, little book
vendō, -ere. to sell

1. Identify the form of *volō* in the above poem, as well as its subject and tense.
2. Translate the above epigram.

Irregular Verbs Text

Martial 9.10. There is some debate about whether Priscus wants to marry Paula.

Nūbere vīs Priscō: nōn mīror, Paula: sapistī.
    dūcere tē nōn vult Priscus: et ille sapit.

Vocabulary

nubō, -ere. to marry (+ *dat.*)   **dūcō, dūcere.** to marry
Priscus, -ī. [*name*]   [*used with an understood*
nōn mīrōr = "I'm not surprised"   in matrimonium]
sapiō, -īre. to know, to understand

   1. Translate the above epigram.

86. Negative Commands with *Nōlō*

   1. What form of *nōlō* is used in a negative command?
   2. What other verb form is used with this form of *nōlō* in a negative command?

Negative Commands with *Nōlō* Text

Catullus 23.24-27. This is the close to Catullus' sarcastic poem lauding the life of Furius. Catullus has praised Furius' life in all regards: he is financially secure and he is healthy. The latter, however, brings out Catullus' acerbic wit: Furius is apparently so healthy and pure that he rarely defecates, and when he does, it is so clean that it is as if he hadn't. This excerpt delivers Catullus' final, biting message to Furius: you have plenty, so stop begging money from the rest of us.

Haec tū commoda tam beāta, Furī,
nōlī spernere nec putāre parvī:
et sestertia, quae solēs, precārī
centum dēsine; nam sat es beātus.

   1. Identify the three infinitives in the above excerpt.
   2. Identify the infinitives that go with the *nōlī* in line 25.

87. Noun Clause: Objective Infinitive

1. With what types of verbs do objective infinitives often appear?
2. What is the distinction between an objective and a complementary infinitive?
3. What are the three uses of the infinitive that you have learned so far?

Noun Clause: Objective Infinitive Text

Vergil, *Aeneid* **2.146-147.** Aeneas begins his tale of the fall of Troy with the story of Sinon, a Greek purposely left behind with the Trojan Horse to convince the Trojans that the horse was a gift to the gods and not a ruse of any kind. In this excerpt, Priam has just heard Sinon's (fabricated) sad story of betrayal and abuse by the Greeks and now orders his shackles to be removed.

Ipse virō prīmus manicās atque arta levārī
vincla iubet Priamus, dictīsque ita fātur amīcīs:

1. What is the verb that introduces the objective infinitive?
2. What is the objective infinitive?

CHAPTER 22

Indirect Statement is perhaps the most important use of the Latin infinitive to understand; it is both commonly used by Latin authors and does not translate into English as an infinitive. It is imperative, then, that you know the Latin infinitive forms. The final infinitive to be learned, the future active infinitive, is introduced.

88. Infinitive Forms

1. Fill in the table below with correct formations of the infinitives.

Infinitive	Stem	Ending	Translation
present active			
present passive			
perfect active			
perfect passive			
future active			

Infinitive Forms Text

Ovid, *Metamorphoses* **10.25.** In this excerpt, as the hero-poet Orpheus recounts his wife's sudden death, he admits that he tried to move on with his life, that he tried to live without her. Of course, he could not, and so made his heroic journey to the underworld to get her back.

Posse patī voluī, nec mē temptāsse negābō:

---

1. What are the three infinitives in the above line?
2. What are their tenses and voices?

Infinitive Forms Text

Vergil, *Aeneid* **2.185-188.** In this excerpt, the Greek Sinon, left behind by the Greeks to convince the Trojans that the Trojan Horse is a gift to the gods and not a ruse, is describing the construction of the Trojan Horse. The Greek priest Calchas, overseeing the construction because it supposedly is serving as an expiation to the goddess Athena for the defilement of her image, orders the horse to be built so large that it could not be brought into Troy. Sinon goes on to describe how, if the horse were brought into the walls of Troy, it would serve to protect the Trojans.

Hanc tamen immēnsam Calchās attollere mōlem   185
rōboribus textīs caelōque ēdūcere iussit,
nē recipī portīs, aut dūcī in moenia posset,
neu populum antīquā sub rēligiōne tuērī.

1. Identify the two present active infinitives in the above excerpt.
2. Identify the three present passive infinitives in the above excerpt.

Infinitive Forms Text

Livy, *Ab urbe condita* **1.5.** King Aemulius, who had forcibly removed his older brother Numitor from the throne, exposed Romulus and Remus, the twin sons of his niece, to die; they, however, were found by the shepherd Faustulus and raised as his own. As the twins grew, they began to steal from the brigands who lived around Rome. Eventually these thieves attacked Romulus and Remus; only Remus was caught, and was turned over to King Aemulius. The thieves fabricated a charge of raiding Numitor's land against him, and so he was turned over to Numitor. Recognizing in him something that belied his low social standing, and recognizing that he was about the same age as his exposed grandsons, Numitor was about to acknowledge Remus as his grandson. At this point, however, Faustulus had told Romulus the whole story, and Romulus led an attack himself against Aemulius, eventually overthrowing him and becoming the first king of Rome. This excerpt covers the incidents from the successful defense of Romulus against the thieves and the capture of Remus to the realization of Numitor that the captured boy was his grandson.

Huic dēditīs lūdicrō cum sollemne nōtum <u>esset</u> insidiātōs ob īram praedae āmissae latrōnēs, cum Rōmulus vī sē <u>defendisset</u>, Remum cēpisse, captum rēgī Amūliō trādidisse, ultrō accūsantēs. Crīminī maxime dabant in Numitōris agrōs ab iīs impetum fierī; inde eōs collecta iuvenum manū hostīlem in modum praedās agere. Sīc ad supplicium Numitōrī Remus dēditur. Iam inde ab initiō Faustulō spēs fuerat, rēgiam stirpem apud sē ēdūcārī; nam et expositōs iussū rēgis infantēs sciēbat et tempus, quō ipse eōs <u>sustulisset</u> ad id ipsum congruere: sed rem immātūram nisi aut per occāsiōnem aut per necessitātem aperīrī nōluerat. Necessitās prior venit: ita metū subactus Rōmulō rem aperit. Forte et Numitōrī cum in custōdia Remum <u>habēret</u> <u>audisset</u>que geminōs esse frātrēs, comparandō et aetātem eōrum et ipsam minimē servīlem indolem, tetigerat animum memoria nepōtum; sciscitandōque eōdem pervenit ut haud procul <u>esset</u> quin Remum <u>agnosceret</u>.

1. Fill in the chart below with an infinitive from the above excerpt. Not every infinitive in the chart appears in the passage.

	Active	Passive
present		
perfect		
future		

2. The underlined forms are not infinitives, though they may look like infinitives. Explain how you know that they are not infinitives. (They are a verb form that you will learn later.)

Infinitive Forms Text

Cicero, *Pro Archia* 8. Cicero has concluded his defense of Archias' citizenship and here wraps it up with a masterful summary of the facts. In the excerpt below, he begins by saying that if the only topic to discuss were citizenship, then he would be finished. He then continues by reiterating the evidence presented that Archias had already been enrolled as a citizen at Hereclaea.

Sī nihil aliud nisi dē cīvitāte ac lēge dīcimus, nihil dīcō
amplius; causa dicta est. Quid enim hōrum īnfirmārī,
Grattī, potest? Hēraclēaene esse tum ascrīptum negābis?
Adest vir summā auctōritāte et religiōne et fidē, M.
Lūcullus, quī sē nōn opīnārī sed scīre nōn audisse   5
sed vīdisse, nōn interfuisse sed ēgisse dīcit. Adsunt
Hēracliēnsēs lēgātī, nōbilissimī hominēs, huius iūdicī
causā cum mandātīs et cum pūblicō testimōniō vēnerunt;
quī hunc ascrīptum Heracliae esse dīcunt. Hīc tū tabulās
dēsīderās Hēracliēnsium pūblicās, quās Italicō bellō   10
incēnsō tabulāriō interīsse scīmus omnīs? Est rīdiculum
ad ea quae habēmus nihil dīcere, quaerere quae habēre
nōn possumus, et dē hominum memoriā tacēre, litterārum
memoriam flāgitāre et, cum habeās amplissimī virī
religiōnem, integerrimī mūnicipī iūs iūrandum fidemque,   15
ea quae dēprāvārī nūllō modō possunt repudiāre, tabulās
quās īdem dīcis solēre corrumpī dēsīderāre.

1. There are twenty infinitives in the above passage. Write
   them and their line numbers in the chart below, and identify
   their tense and voice.

line #	infinitive	tense	voice

89. Noun Clause: Indirect Statement

1. After what kinds of verbs can an indirect statement be expected?

2. What are two other names for indirect statement?

3. What kind of English verb will translate the Latin infinitive used in indirect statement?

4. What English clause marker is used, where Latin uses none, in indirect statement?

- Indirect statement is reported speech. Rather than directly quoting something, indirect statement reports it secondhand.

  I love Latin. *vs.* He says that he loves Latin

- It is important to understand the differences between how Latin and English express indirect statement.

- In reality, the Latin indirect statement is simply an objective infinitive. The distinction between an objective infinitive and indirect statement exists more because English treats this particular type of objective infinitive so differently.

- The overlap between indirect statement and the objective infinitive can be seen in a verb like *iubeo, -ere*, "to order": "The general orders him to go" [objective] vs. "The general orders that he go" [indirect statement]. Latin would express both of these with an infinitive, whether considered objective or in indirect statement, while English can translate that infinitive in two very different ways.

	Latin	English
main verb of sentence	head verb	head verb
clause marker	none	"that"
mood of verb of indirect statement	infinitive	indicative
case of subject of indirect statement	accusative	nominative

90. Tenses of the Infinitive in Indirect Statement

- The indicative mood utilizes **absolute tense**, i.e. a present verb reflects present tense action; a future verb reflects future tense action; a perfect verb reflects perfect tense action; etc.

- The infinitive in indirect statement, however, introduces the concept of **relative tense**.

- **Relative tense** indicates tense by how it is related to the tense of another verb.

- In indirect statement, the tense of the infinitive will be relative to the tense of the main verb.

- Each of the three infinitive tenses then indicates not an absolute tense but rather a time relationship.

- The three time relationships are same time, before, and after.
  - The present infinitive indicates same time, the perfect before, and the future after.
  - You might also think of each infinitive in mathematical terms: the present is the = infinitive, the perfect is the -1 infinitive, and the future the +1 infinitive.
- The table below illustrates the most common main verb-infinitive tense combinations and the tense of the translation of the infinitive for each.

Tense of Main Verb	Tense of Infinitive Translation		
	present / same time	perfect / before	future / after
present	present	perfect	future
perfect	perfect	pluperfect	"would"

- The future tense as the main verb of an indirect statement is rare; thus it is left out of the above chart. When the future infinitive is used with a perfect main verb, it does not correspond to a standard tense of the indicative; rather, it is translated as "would": "She <u>said</u> that she <u>would</u> be home soon."
- You can also envision these relationships on a timeline.

     pluperfect   perfect   present   future

- Locate the tense of the main verb on the timeline (imperfect would equal perfect in this model). If the infinitive is present, it is translated with whatever tense the main verb is. If the infinitive is perfect, it is translated with the tense one step to the left on the timeline. If the infinitive is future, it is translated with the tense one step to the right on the timeline (with a perfect main verb, however, the future will be translated "would").

Indirect Statement Text

Martial 6.14. Martial encourages Laberius, perhaps mockingly, to do more than just talk about writing poetry; he should actually do it.

Versūs scrībere posse tē disertōs
adfirmās, Laberī: quid ergō nōn vīs?
Versūs scrībere quī potest disertōs,
conscrībat, Laberī: virum putābo.

Vocabulary

versus, -ūs. verse (of poetry)
disertus, -a, -um. eloquent, well-spoken
adfirmō, -āre. to confirm

Laberius, -ī. [*name*]
quid = "why"
ergō. therefore

1. Translate the first two lines of the above poem.

2. What is the infinitive in line 3? What tense and voice is it?

3. What is the tense of *putābo* in line 4?

Indirect Statement Text

Catullus 76.1-6. Catullus' poems 70, 72, 73, and 76 form a series in which Catullus is at a desperate point in his relationship with Lesbia: he feels betrayed and is trying to avoid the reality that, whatever Lesbia might say, they will never truly be together; her actions only reinforce this. In this excerpt, the opening to poem 76, Catullus is reflecting on his relationship with Lesbia: he wants to find something positive, but can only recall betrayal and duplicity.

Sī qua recordantī bene facta priōra voluptās
    est hominī, cum sē cōgitat esse pium,
nec sanctam violasse fidem, nec foedere in ullō
    divum ad fallendōs nūmine abūsum [esse] hominēs,
multa parāta manent in longā aetāte, Catulle,   5
    ex hōc ingrātō gaudia amōre tibi.

1. The *violasse* in line 3 is a contracted form of *violāvisse*. The bracketed *esse* in line 4 is not included in Catullus' original. (Often, forms of *sum* will be omitted, especially in poetry.)

2. Identify the tenses and voices of the three infinitives in lines 2-4.

3. What is the clue that *foedere* in line 3 is likely not an infinitive, despite its ending?

4. Complete the translation of lines 2-4 below by choosing the correct translation of the infinitive in brackets; explain your choice.

> …when he thinks that he _____ [*esse*: is/has been/ had been] faithful, and that he _____ [*violasse*: does not violate/has not violated/had not violated] sacred trust, and that he _____ [*abūsum (esse)*: does not abuse/has not abused/had not abused] the power of the gods to deceive men in any pact…

5. Explain the meaning of *sē* in line 2.

Indirect Statement Text

Catullus 4. Catullus' fourth poem is a lengthy tribute to the *phasēlus*, or little boat, that conveyed him on a long journey. Throughout the poem, the *phasēlus* is personified as the *phasēlus* itself narrates its own story.

Phasēlus ille, quem vidētis, hospitēs,
āit <u>fuisse</u> nāvium celerrimus,
neque ullīus natantis impetum trabis
<u>nequisse</u> praeterīre, sīve palmulīs
ōpus foret volāre sīve linteō.   5
Et hoc *negat* minācis Hadriāticī
<u>negāre</u> lītus insulāsve Cycladās
Rhodumque nōbilem horridamque Thrāciam
Propontida trucemve Ponticum sinum,
ubi iste post phasēlus anteā fuit   10
comāta silva; nam Cytōriō in iugō
loquente saepe sībilum ēdidit comā.
Amastrī Pontica et Cytōre buxifer,
tibi haec <u>fuisse</u> et <u>esse</u> cognitissima
āit phasēlus: ultimā ex orīgine   15
tuō <u>stetisse</u> *dīcit* in cacūmine,
tuō <u>imbuisse</u> palmulās in aequore,
et inde tot per impotentia freta
erum <u>tulisse</u>, laeva sīve dextera
vocāret aura, sīve utrumque Iuppiter   20
simul secundus incidisset in pedem;
neque ulla vōta lītorālibus deīs
sibi <u>esse facta</u>, cum venīret ā marī
nōvissimō hunc ad usque limpidum lacum.
Sed haec prius fuēre: nunc recondītā   25
senet quiēte sēque dēdicat tibi,
gemelle Castor et gemelle Castoris.

---

1. There are four head verbs that introduce different indirect statements in the poem above; they are italicized. (There are three different verbs, one of which is repeated.)

2. Complete the following chart by identifying the tense
(absolute) of each infinitive, the time relationship that each
infinitive shows, the head verb that governs each infinitive,
and the tense of the English translation of each infinitive
based on the tense of the head verb.

Verb	Absolute Tense	Time Relationship	Governing Head Verb	English Translation Tense
fuisse (2)				
nequisse (4)				
negāre (7)				
fuisse (14)				
esse (14)				
stetisse (16)				
imbuisse (17)				
tulisse (19)				
facta esse (23)				

Indirect Statement Text

Catullus 67.1-8. Catullus address his poem 67 to a *iānua* (line 3),
a door, with which (or really with whom) he discusses the history
and former occupants of its house. The door, and the boundary it
represents, becomes a common symbol in elegiac poetry for the
inability of the elegiac lover to be with his love, similar to the way
the wall functions in the Pyramus and Thisbe story. In this excerpt,
Catullus introduces the door, and gives a precis of the history of
the house.

Ō dulcī iūcunda virō, iūcunda parentī,
    salvē, tēque bonā Iūpiter auctet ope,
iānua, quam Balbō dīcunt servisse benignē
    ōlim, cum sēdēs ipse senex tenuit,
quamque ferunt rursus gnātō servisse malignē,   5
    postquam es porrectō facta marīta sene:
dīc agedum nōbīs, quārē mūtāta ferāris
    in dominum veterem dēseruisse fidem.

There are three head verbs in the above passage, one of which
you should recognize. The other two are forms of *ferō, ferre:
ferunt* (5) and *ferāris* (7).

1. What are the three infinitives in the passage that are used in an indirect statement?
2. What time relationship do these infinitives indicate?

Indirect Statement Text

Plautus, *Miles Gloriosus* **126-128.** Palestrio, the unwilling slave of the Miles Gloriosus, opens the play with an extended preface that explains the backstory to the play. In this excerpt, he describes how his former master's love told him how much she wanted to return to Athens and get away from the Miles Gloriosus.

Palestrio. Āit sēsē Athēnās fugere cupere ex hāc domū:
sēsē illum amāre, meum erum, Athēnīs quī fuit,
neque peius quemquam ōdisse quam istum mīlitem.

1. Translate the following paraphrase from the above passage: *āit sēsē ex hāc domū fugere cupere.*
2. Explain the usage of the two infinitives *fugere* and *cupere.* (Each will be used in a different way.)
3. What does *sēsē* mean? Explain your answer.

Indirect Statement Text

Plautus, *Menaechmi* **208-212.** Menaechmus has just arrived at his mistress' house bearing his wife's dress to give to her. In this excerpt, Menaechmus asks her, in return for the dress, to prepare lunch for him and his mooch Peniculus.

Menaechmus. Iubē igitur tribus nōbīs apud tē prandium
    accūrārier,
atque aliquid scītāmentōrum dē forō opsōnārier.
glandionidam, suillam, lāridum pernōnidam,   210
aut sincipitāmenta porcīna aut aliquid ad eum modum,
madida quae mī adposita in mensa miluīnam suggerant;

The *-ier* ending in lines 208 and 209 (*accūrārier* and *obsōnārier*) is an archaic ending for the present passive infinitive.

1. Complete the following translation by filling in the blanks
    with the correct translation of the infinitives in brackets.

    Therefore, order that lunch _____ [*accūrārier: accūrō,
    -āre* = to take care of] for the three of us at your
    house, and that some provisions _____ [*obsōnārier:
    obsōnō, -āre* = to buy] from the forum.

Indirect Statement Text

Vergil, *Aeneid* 2.232-233. In this excerpt, the Trojans are admiring
the Trojan Horse and discussing what should be done with it.

Dūcendum [esse] ad sēdēs simulācrum ōrandaque [esse] dīvae
nūmina conclāmant.

----

1. What is the head verb in the above excerpt? (Hint: it is a
    compound of a familiar verb.)

    The form of the future passive infinitive is rare, and even
    the Romans themselves tended to vary in their formation of
    it. In the above excerpt are two examples of a form that can
    function as a future passive infinitive: *dūcendum* [*esse*] and
    ōranda [*esse*] (the infinitive *esse* does not appear in Vergil's
    original text, but is included here for clarity). The use of
    the future passive participle, or gerundive, a form that you
    have not yet learned, produces a slightly different nuance of
    meaning from other infinitives, but these forms nonetheless
    are infinitives, are future, and are passive, and should be
    translated below as such.

2. Fill in the blanks in the translation below with a correct
    translation of the infinitives in brackets.

    They clamored that the idol _____ [*dūcendum esse*]
    to its appropriate location and that the blessing of the
    goddess _____ [*ōranda esse*].

Indirect Statement Text

Pliny, *Epistulae* **10.96.5.** Pliny was a governor in Bithynia under the emperor Trajan, to whom this famous letter is addressed. Pliny is uncertain about how to handle the Christians under his care and asks Trajan for advice: on the one hand, Christianity is growing and its followers are not hurting anyone, but on the other hand being a Christian violates Roman law, which mandates worship of the state gods as much out of loyalty as faith. Trajan responds definitively that any violation of Roman law must be punished. In this excerpt, Pliny describes the different ways that Christians react to being identified as Christians.

Quī negābant esse sē Chrīstiānōs aut fuisse, cum praeeunte mē deōs appellārent et imāginī tuae, quam propter hoc iusseram cum simulācrīs nūminum adferrī, tūre ac vīnō supplicārent, praetereā male dīcerent Chrīstō, quōrum nihil cōgī posse dīcuntur quī sunt rē vērā Chrīstiānī, dīmittendōs putāvī.

1. Complete the translation below by translating the infinitives in parentheses; they are underlined in the text for reference. Make sure to distinguish in your translation between the tenses of *esse* and *fuisse*.

   Those who continually denied that _____ [*sē*] _____ [*esse*] Christians or _____ [*sē*] _____ [*fuisse*] Christians…

2. Explain the difference in meaning between *esse* and *fuisse*.

3. Identify the other three infinitives in the passage.

CHAPTER 23

The intensives intensify or emphasize the nouns that they modify; they follow a pattern of endings similar to that of *hic* and *ille*. Deponent verbs are those that are passive in form but active in meaning; they appear passive but are translated actively. And a small number of deponent verbs take their objects in the ablative.

> **Terms to Know**
>
> intensive pronouns
> demonstrative
>   (pronouns)
> deponent verb
> semi-deponent verb

91. Intensive Pronoun: *ipse, īdem, quīdam*

1. To what form that you have already learned does *quīdam, quaedam, quoddam* add a *-dam* in its declension?

2. To what form that you have already learned does *īdem, eadem, idem* add a *-dem* in its declension?

3. What is the letter combination that changes in these compound forms?

4. What will determine how the gender of *ipse, ipsa, ipsum* is translated?

The two "selfs": The Intensive (*ipse, ipsa, ipsum*) vs. the Reflexive (-, *suī, sibi, sē, sē*)

- English uses the "-self" form (himself, herself, itself, themselves) in two very different ways: in an intensive use (the Latin *ipse, ipsa, ipsum*) and a reflexive use (-, *suī, sibi, sē, sē*).

- The overlap of the English "-self" forms often makes it difficult to distinguish in translation between the Latin intensive and reflexive. Students will tend to conflate these forms based on assumptions about what the Latin says rather than a careful distinction between the two separate Latin forms.

- You have to be very careful to identify which Latin "-self" form is being used (intensive or reflexive) and then translate it accordingly.

Intensive vs. Reflexive Exercise

Identify the "-self" forms in the following sentences as reflexive or intensive. Not every sentence will contain one, and some will contain both.

1. The president herself will be delivering the speech!
2. One convoy follows the decoy, and the other follows the movie star himself.
3. He turned and was astounded to see himself in the unexpected mirror.
4. Are you going in your car to the wedding, or with your sister herself?
5. I myself found myself doing the work instead of the rest of the group.
6. He saw me standing by the door.
7. He ran to catch her before she left him.
8. She was shocked to turn the corner and see herself so unmistakably in the face of another.
9. Pick yourself up!
10. I swear! It was her! She herself and not an impersonator!

Now, translate each "-self" form into Latin. You may use English gender for the noun that it modifies/refers to, and you should be able to determine case by the context of the English sentence. (The forms of the reflexive pronoun can be found in Chapter 13 of your textbook, beginning on page 97.)

Intensive Pronoun, *ipse, ipsa, ipsum* Text

Pliny, *Epistulae* 1.6.1. In this letter, Pliny is mock-bragging to a friend about a successful hunt he went on, perhaps in a tone similar to the way, for example, one who is not good at golf or basketball might brag about a lucky shot.

Rīdēbis, et licet rīdeās. Ego ille quem nōsti, aprōs trēs et quidem pulcherrimōs cēpī. "Ipse?" inquis. Ipse.

1. Complete the following translation with the correct translation of the intensive in parentheses.

    You will laugh, and you're allowed to laugh. I, that guy that you know, hunted down three boars, and they were truly fine specimens. You will say: "You _____ [*ipse*]?". Yes. I _____ [*ipse*].

2. Explain why the translation of *ipse* in each instance differs even though the forms are exactly the same. What determines the translation of *ipse*?

3. What does the use of the intensive convey here? What is being intensified (beyond the word that it modifies)?

Intensive Pronoun, *ipse, ipsa, ipsum* **Text**

Vergil, *Aeneid* 4.356-359. Aeneas, accosted by Dido for leaving her, tries to mollify her. He is explaining to her why, despite his feelings for her and hers for him, he must leave her to continue his journey to Italy. In this excerpt, he explains how he was visited by Jupiter who encouraged him to go.

Nunc etiam interpres dīvom Iove missus ab ipsō—
testor utrumque caput—celeres mandāta per aurās
dētulit. Ipse deum manifestō in lūmine vīdī
intrantem mūrōs, vōcemque hīs auribus hausī.

1. What are the two intensives in the above excerpt?
2. Identify the case and number of each.
3. Which noun does each modify? Explain your answer.
4. Translate each noun-intensive pair.

Intensive Pronoun, *ipse, ipsa, ipsum* **Text**

Catullus 70. This is one of a series of poems (70, 72, 73, 76) in which Catullus reveals himself at his most despondent with regard to Lesbia. In this poem, Catullus realizes that what Lesbia says does not necessarily indicate what she does; he may want to believe her words, but her actions do not reflect them.

Nullī sē dīcit mulier mea nūbere malle,
    quam mihi, nōn sī sē Iuppiter ipse petat.
Dīcit: sed mulier cupīdō quod dīcit amantī,
    in ventō et rapidā scrībere oportet aquā.

Vocabulary

mulier, -eris (*f.*). woman, girlfriend

nūbō, -ēre. to marry (+ *dat.*)

quam = "other than" [continues the comparison introduced by *malle*]

mihi. [parallel to the *nullī* of line 1]

Iuppiter, Iovis (*m.*). [*name*; the king of the gods]

1. What construction will the *dīcit* in line 1 introduce? What kind of verb is it?

2. What does *sē* indicate about the subject of *dīcit* and the subject of *malle*?

3. What case is *nullī* in line 1? (Hint: it is not genitive.)

4. Translate the first two lines of the poem. The second two lines are translated below for context.

> She says this: but that which a woman says to an eager lover is often written on the wind and in swift-flowing water.

5. What does the *ipse* intensify? What is the effect of Catullus' use of the intensive here?

Intensive Pronoun, *ipse, ipsa, ipsum* Text

Ovid, *Metamorphoses* 8.200-202. The Athenian craftsman Daedalus has just constructed the wings that will carry him and his son Icarus away from Crete, where King Minos has imprisoned them. In this excerpt, he puts the wings on and tries them out.

> Postquam manus ultima coeptis   200
> imposita est, geminās opifex lībrāvit in ālās
> ipse suum corpus, mōtāque pependit in aurā.

---

1. The excerpt above contains both an intensive form and a reflexive form. What are they?

2. Choose the correct translation from the choices below (from *geminās* to *corpus*).

    a.   …the craftsman put his body itself into the wings themselves…

    b.   …the craftsman himself put her body into the wings…

    c.   …the craftsman put his body itself into the wings…

    d.   …the craftsman himself put his own body into the wings…

    e.   …the craftsman put his body itself into his own wings…

3. Explain your answer.

Intensive Pronoun, *quīdam, quaedam, quoddam* Text

Anonymous, *Carmina Burana* III (196): *In taberna*, 9-16. The various kinds of people *in taberna* (in the tavern) are described.

Quīdam lūdunt, quīdam bibunt,
quīdam indiscrētē vīvunt;
sed in lūdō quī morantur,
ex hīs quīdam dēnūdantur,
quīdam ibi vestiuntur,
quīdam saccīs induuntur.
Ibi nullus timet mortem,
sed prō Bacchō mittunt sortem.

Vocabulary

lūdō, -ere. to play (around)   **indiscrētē** (*adv.*). indiscreetly,
bibō, -ere. to drink   without thought

1. What is the number and gender of the forms of *quīdam* in the above excerpt? What determines whether *quīdam* is singular or plural?
2. Translate the first two lines.

Intensive Pronoun, *quīdam, quaedam, quoddam* Text

Ovid, *Amores* 1.8.1-2. Ovid describes at length the old woman Dipsas, introduced in line 2 of the excerpt below; she is a *lena*, a word difficult to translate, that refers to any woman who effected introductions between men and women, from a nurse (think, albeit anachronistically, *Romeo and Juliet*) to a madame overseeing a brothel. Ovid focuses first on the magic that Dipsas apparently possesses: how she knows spells and potions and incantations, and has any number of supernatural phenomena attributed to her. He then reports a conversation he overheard between Dipsas and a young woman in which she advises the young woman on how to deal with her lover. Dipsas' speech then becomes an inadvertent (from Ovid the character's standpoint) lampoon of the elegiac relationship; Dipsas undercuts the social standing of the girl's lover, and introduces her to a number of tricks to be used against the lover to effect what the girl wants. Corinna, Ovid's love, will use some of these same tricks herself against Ovid. In this excerpt, Ovid introduces Dipsas.

Est quaedam—quīcumque volet cognoscere lēnam,
    audiat!—est quaedam nōmine Dipsas anus.

Vocabulary

Dipsas = [*name*]   **anus, -ūs.** old woman

1. What is the case, number and gender of *quaedam* in line 2 of the above excerpt?
2. Translate line 2 from *est...anus*.

92. Deponent Verbs

1. What is the contradictory nature of deponent verbs?
2. Why are they called deponent verbs?
3. How are deponent verbs recognizable in glossary/dictionary entries?
4. How do semi-deponent verbs work?

- Deponent verbs have three active forms that are also translated actively: the present active participle, the future active participle, and the future active infinitive. Participles will be learned in the next chapter; you learned the future active infinitive in the previous chapter.

- The imperative of deponent verbs uses the alternate second person singular passive ending (*-re*), which makes the imperative of a deponent look like a present active infinitive (which of course for a deponent verb, because it is an active form, cannot exist).

arbitror, -ārī	→ arbitrāre	→ Make a decision!
vereor, -ērī	→ verēre	→ Be afraid!
loquor, -quī	→ loquere	→ Speak!
ingredior, -dī	→ ingredere	→ Enter!
potior, -īrī	→ potīre	→ Grab that!

Deponent Verbs Text

Anonymous, *Carmina Burana, The Return of Spring* 21-30. The joys of spring are celebrated, especially in the context of the love that so often blossoms then.

Glōriantur
et laetantur
in melle dulcēdinis
quī cōnantur
ut ūtantur   25
praemiō Cupīdinis;
Simus iussū Cypridis
Glōriantēs

et laetantēs
parēs esse Paridis.   30

Vocabulary

glōrior, -ārī. to rejoice   **mel, mellis.** honey
laetor, -ārī. to be happy   **dulcēdō, -inis** (*f.*). sweetness

1. Translate the first three lines.
2. Why is *praemiō* in line 26 in the ablative? (If you haven't already, review §93 on Special Intransitive Verbs at the end of this chapter.)
3. The forms *glōriantēs* and *laetantēs* in lines 28-29 are present active participles. Although you have not yet learned these participles for non-deponent verbs, it is instructive to see an example of one of the three active forms that deponents will use.

Deponent Verbs Text

Martial 5.83. Martial here describes a dysfunctional relationship in which he only wants Dindymus when Dindymus flees from him, and Martial never wants Dindymus when Dindymus pursues Martial.

Insequēris, fugiō; fugis, insequor; haec mihi mens est:
velle tuum nōlō, Dindyme, nolle volō.

1. Identify the two deponents in the above poem, as well as their tense. (Hint: both forms are from a compound of a verb from the Chapter 23 Vocabulary List.)
2. Translate the passage. (*Tuum* in line 2 = *tē*; Dindyme is the name Dindymus.)

Deponent Verbs Text

Plautus, *Menaechmi* 976-980. Menaechmus has just finished speculating on the strange day he's had; his father-in-law and doctor have just accused him of things that he did not do. Messenio, the slave of Sosicles, hears Menaechmus' soliloquy and responds with his own about the duty of a slave to his master. In this excerpt, Messenio describes how fear of physical punishment keeps him obedient to his master.

Messenio. Id ego male malum metuō.

Proptereā bonum esse certumst potius quam malum.

Nam magis multō patior facilius verba, verbera ego ōdī

nimiōque edō lubentius molitum quam molitum praehibeō.

Proptereā erī imperium exsequor, bene et sēdātē servō id;   980

---

1. Identify the two deponents in the above excerpt (both of which are from your vocabulary list; one is a compound form).

2. Also identify their tense and subject.

3. As deponent verbs, these passive-in-form verbs can take direct objects. What is the direct object for each deponent?

4. The form *certumst* in line 977 is a contraction of two words: *certum* and *est*. They are so contracted because of the metrical demands of Plautus' verse comedy, somewhat similar to the way the English "ever" can be written in poetry as "e'er" if the meter so demands.

Deponent Verbs Text

Seneca, *Phaedra* **110-111.** Seneca opens the play proper (i.e. after the prefatory speech by Hippolytus) with a long speech by Phaedra in which she describes the extent to which her life has been disrupted by her illicit passion for Hippolytus. In this excerpt, she describes how, having lost interest in her domestic duties, she now is interested in nature and the hunt.

iuvat excitātās consequī cursū ferās   110

et rigida mollī gaesa iaculārī manū.

---

1. Translate the two deponent infinitives in the above passage along with *iuvat*, the verb that governs them.

   a. It is pleasing _____ (*consequī*) excited wild beasts in their course.

   b. It is pleasing _____ (*iaculārī* = throw) rigid nets with a soft hand.

2. What conjugation are each of the infinitives? Explain your answer.

Deponent Verbs Text

Cicero, *In Catilinam* 1.10. Cicero has been pushing his sentence of exile for Catiline, which the Senate cannot decree (only the consul can). But Cicero points out that their silence, their choice not to oppose Catiline's exile, is itself an endorsement of it.

Quae cum ita sint, Catilīna perge, quō coepistī: ēgredere aliquandō ex urbe; patent portae; proficīscere.

1. Identify the two deponent imperatives in the above passage.
2. Translate the one from the Chapter 23 Vocabulary List.

Deponent Verbs Text

Cicero, *In Catilinam* 1.20. Cicero turns to Catiline and orders him to leave the city to free the republic from fear.

Ēgredere ex urbe, Catilīna, līberā rem pūblicam metū, in exilium, sī hanc vōcem exspectās, proficīscere.

Vocabulary

ēgredior, -dī. to leave	**Catilīna, -ae.** [*name*]
līberō, -āre. to free	**exilium, -ī.** exile
exspectō, -āre. to wait for	

1. Identify the three imperatives in the above excerpt; the imperatives are not all deponent imperatives.
2. Translate the above excerpt.

Deponent Verbs Text

Vergil, *Aeneid* 4.361 & 381. Aeneas in line 361 concludes his explanation to Dido of why he has to leave her and continue to Italy; line 381 is from her response.

Ītaliam nōn sponte sequor.   361

Ī, sequere Ītaliam ventīs, pete rēgna per undās.   381

Vocabulary

sponte = "of my own volition", "because I want to" [often used with a form of the reflexive possessive adjective: in this case *meā,* but because the expression occurs more often in the third person, *suā* is more commonly used.]

---

1. Translate line 361.
2. Is there an infinitive in line 381? Explain your answer.

The Latin word *Ī* in line 381 is an irregular imperative of a verb that you will learn in Chapter 25.

93. Special Intransitive: Verbs used with an Ablative Object

1. What are the five deponent verbs that take their objects in the ablative?

• These verbs are sometimes referred to as VPUFF verbs or PUFFV verbs, after their first letters: V(*escor*), P(*otior*), Ū(*tor*), F(*ungor*), F(*ruor*).

Special Intransitive: Verbs used with an Ablative Object Text

Martial 3.89. Martial here prescribes to Phoebus a home remedy for constipation.

Ūtere lactūcīs et mollibus ūtere maluīs:
    nam faciem dūrum, Phoebe, cacantis habes.

---

1. Identify the special intransitive deponent verb form (repeated twice) in the above passage.
2. Identify its objects.

CHAPTER 24

Participles are an essential form for understanding Latin. They are commonly used by Latin authors and, perhaps more important, are used more frequently and in more complex constructions in Latin than they are in English. English will often prefer a relative clause or an adverbial subordinate clause, where Latin will use a participle; this is why Latin participles have so many potential translations into English.

> **Terms to Know**
>
> participle
> relative time/time
>   relative to the verb
> ablative absolute

94. Participles

1. What is a participle?
2. What are the nominative and singular forms for the present active participle?
3. On what stem is the present active participle formed?
4. What declension endings are used for the present active participle?
5. On what stem is the perfect passive participle formed?
6. What endings does the perfect passive participle use?
7. On what stem is the future active participle formed?
8. What endings does the future active participle use?
9. What is the tense sign for the future active participle?
10. What are the two tense-voice combinations that don't exist for participles?
11. What is the other name for the future passive participle?
12. What is the only participial form of *sum*?
13. What is the difference between the ablative singular ending *-ī* and *-e* in the present active participle?

Participles Text

> **Catullus 64.86-99.** This excerpt is part of the backstory to Catullus' lament of Ariadne, i.e. how she came to find herself abandoned on an island by the Athenian hero Theseus. In this excerpt, Catullus describes how Ariadne came to fall in love with Theseus.

Hunc simul ac cupīdō conspexit lūmine virgō
rēgia, quam suāvis <u>exspīrans</u> castus odōrēs
lectulus in mollī complexū mātris alēbat,
quālēs Eurōtae progignunt flūmina myrtus
aurave distinctōs ēdūcit verna colōrēs,   90
nōn prius ex illō <u>flāgrantia</u> dēclīnāvit
lūmina, quam cunctō concēpit corpore flammam
funditus atque īmīs exarsit tōta medullīs.
Heu miserē <u>exagitans</u> inmītī corde furōrēs
sancte puer, cūrīs hominum quī gaudia miscēs,   95
quaeque regis Golgōs quaeque Īdalium frondōsum,
quālibus incensam iactastis mente puellam
fluctibus, in flāvō saepe hospite <u>suspīrantem</u>!
Quantōs illa tulit <u>languentī</u> corde timōrēs!

---

1. There are five examples of the present active participle underlined in the above text. Identify the case and number of each.

2. Identify which nouns each participle modifies. (It might be difficult to do this without vocabulary information for the nouns; if you're uncertain about which noun each participle modifies, identify all nouns that could agree with each participle.)

3. The *exagitans* in line 94 looks nominative but is not. What case is it? (Hint: it modifies *puer* in line 95, which is also modified by *sancte*.)

Participles Text

Vergil, *Aeneid* 2.45-49. Perhaps the most famous single quote (albeit in translation) from the *Aeneid* closes the excerpt below. The Trojan priest Laocoön condemns the Trojan horse and strongly advises the Trojans against accepting it. He eventually is killed, along with his two sons, by huge snakes that come from the sea, which the Trojans interpreted as a divine sign to accept the horse against Laocoön's advice. In this excerpt, he correctly surmises the purpose of the horse and expresses his distrust of Greeks in general.

Aut hōc inclūsī lignō occultantur Achīvī,   45
aut haec in nostrōs fabricāta est māchina mūrōs
īnspectūra domōs ventūraque dēsuper urbī,

aut aliquis latet error: equō nē crēdite, Teucrī.
quidquid id est, timeō Danaōs et dōna ferentīs.

1. Identify the two future active participles.
2. Identify a perfect passive participle.
3. Identify a present active participle.

The form *ferentīs* in line 49 is a form largely restricted
to poetry: the nominative and accusative *-ēs* ending will
sometimes be written as *-īs*. The "i" in this ending will scan
long, while the "i" in the genitive singular *-is* ending scans
short.

Participles Text

Ovid, *Amores* 1.5.1-12. *Amores* 1.5 presents a sultry seduction: it
is a hot day, in a dimly lit room, with Ovid sprawled on a bed. In
walks his love, Corinna, who is named here for the first time in
the *Amores*. In this first half of the poem, Ovid sets the scene (and
the tone) and introduces Corinna. In the second half of the poem,
not included here, he will describe in detail her physical perfection,
having removed her already unbelted tunic, and then quip how he
wishes all of his afternoons were as satisfying.

Aestus erat, mediamque diēs exēgerat hōram.
    Adposuī mediō membra lēvanda torō.
pars adaperta fuit, pars altera clausa fenestrae,
    quāle ferē silvae lūmen habēre solent,
quālia sublucent fugiente crepuscula Phoebō   5
    aut ubi nox abiit, nec tamen orta diēs.
Illa verēcundīs lux est praebenda puellīs,
    quā timidus latebrās spēret habēre pudōr.
Ecce Corinna venit, tunicā vēlāta recinctā,
    candida dīviduā colla tegente comā,   10
quāliter in thalamōs fāmōsa Semīramis isse
    dīcitur et multīs Lāis amāta virīs.

1. There are nine participles in the above excerpt. Fill in the
following table with the participial forms from the above
excerpt. Not every participle is necessarily included above.
Fill in each box with as many participles as you can.

	Active	Passive
present		
perfect		
future		

Participles Text

Martial 3.44.10-18. Martial here addresses why everyone flees a certain Ligurinus (not mentioned by name in the excerpt): he is too much the poet. In this excerpt, Martial relates his own experiences of Ligurinus' excessive poetizing: wherever Martial goes, he cannot escape Ligurinus' incessant recitations.

Et stantī legis et legis sēdentī,	10
currentī legis et legis cacantī.	
In thermās fugiō: sonās ad aurem.	
Piscīnam petō: nōn licet natāre.	
Ad cēnam properō: tenēs euntem.	
Ad cēnam veniō: fugās sēdentem.	15
Lassus dormiō: suscitās iacentem.	
Vīs, quantum faciās malī, vidēre?	
Vir iustus, probus, innocens timēris.	

1. The poem above contains participles used as nouns.
2. Identify the case of each participle.
3. Fill in the blanks of the translation below with the correct translation of the participles in parentheses. Don't forget to consider the case of each participle, and remember that Martial himself is speaking about himself; supply the appropriate pronoun for each participle to modify.

> You read _____ [*stantī*] and you read _____ [*sēdentī*],
> you read _____ [*currentī*] and you read _____ [*cacantī; cacō, -āre = to defecate*].
> I flee into the baths: you shout in my ear.
> I head for the pool: I'm not allowed to swim.
> I hurry to dinner: you keep _____ [*euntem; eō, īre = to go*].
> I come to dinner: you refuse _____ [*sēdentem*].
> I sleep worn out: you bother _____ [*iacentem*].
> You want to see how much evil you do?
> You are feared as a just man, a forthright man, a blameless man.

Participles Text

Seneca, *Phaedra* 736-757. Phaedra has revealed to Hippolytus her illicit passion for him. He was horrified, and threatened to kill Phaedra, but ultimately relented. The Nurse, however, protective of her queen, saw the drawn sword of Hippolytus and the disheveled hair of Phaedra as a means of escape for her. The Nurse has just yelled for help: Hippolytus, according to her, has just tried to rape the queen. In this excerpt, the Chorus immortalizes the youth and beauty of Hippolytus, for they know that, with the rape charge, he will never lead the innocent life that he once led.

Chorus. Fūgit insānae similis procellae,
ōcior nūbēs glomerante Cōrō,
ōcior cursum rapiente flammā,
stella cum ventīs agitāta longōs
     porrigit ignēs.   740
   Conferat tēcum decus omne priscum
fāma mīrātrix seniōris aevī:
pulchrior tantō tua forma lūcet,
clārior quantō micat orbe plēnō
cum suōs ignēs coeunte cornū   745
iunxit et currū properante pernox
exerit vultūs rubicunda Phoebē
nec tenent stellae faciem minōrēs.
Tālis est, prīmās referens tenebrās,
nuntius noctis, modo lōtus undīs   750
Hesperus, pulsīs iterum tenebrīs
     Lūcifer īdem.
   Et tū, thyrsigerā Līber ab Indiā,
intōnsā iuvenis perpetuum comā,
tigrēs pampineā cuspide territans   755
ac mitrā cohibens cornigerum caput,
nōn vincēs rigidās Hippolytī comās.

---

1. The underlined words in the reading are participles. Fill in the following table with the requested information.

2. *rubicunda* in line 747 is the future passive participle/ gerundive that will be learned in Chapter 31 and is not included in the table below.

3. Why might *intōnsā* in line 754 be confused with a present active participle (even though it is not)?

4. Even though you don't have vocabulary information for each verb, you should still be able to ascertain the tense and voice of each participle just by its stem.

5. What each participle modifies will be harder to determine without vocabulary information, but do your best. If you can't determine for certain which noun a participle modifies, identify all nouns with which it can agree.

Participle	Tense	Voice	Case	Modifies?
glomerante				
rapiente				
agitāta				
coeunte				
properante				
referens				
intōnsā				
territans				
cohibens				

Participles Text

Seneca, *Phaedra* 1226-1237. Phaedra has just killed herself, Hippolytus is already dead, and Theseus here delivers an extended speech about his fate and, more specifically, his desire to die. He imagines himself descending to the underworld again (he journeyed there before with his friend Pirithoös, who had the not-so-bright idea to carry off the queen of the underworld, Persephone; they were stuck there until Hercules freed them, although in some accounts he only freed Theseus) both to be with his son and to hasten the death which he now so desires. In this excerpt, Theseus catalogs the underworld's most famous inhabitants and their punishments. Theseus, in his grief, offers to assume their punishments to gain admission to the underworld.

1229-1231: Sisyphus. Disclosed to the river god Asopus where Zeus had taken his daughter, and was sentenced to push a rock up a hill and then have it roll back down for him to do it again. Became the symbol of futility for the 20th century philosopher Albert Camus.

1232: Tantalus. Fed Pelops to the gods, and was sentenced to eternity in a pool of water beneath a fruit tree; every time he reached for the fruit, it would blow out of reach, and every time he bent to drink, the water would shrink away from him. The English word "tantalizing" is an eponym from Tantalus.

1233-1234: Tityos. Tried to rape Leto, the mother of Artemis and Apollo, and was sentenced to have his innards repeatedly eaten by a vulture.

1235-1237: Ixion. Tried to rape Hera, and was sentenced to be tied to a rotating wheel for eternity.

Graviōra vīdī, quae patī <u>clausōs</u> iubet
Phlegethon <u>nocentēs</u> igneō cingens vadō.
Quae poena mēmet maneat et sēdēs, sciō:
Umbrae <u>nocentēs</u>, cēdite et cervīcibus
hīs, hīs <u>repositum</u> dēgravet fessās manūs   1230
saxum, senī perennis Aeoliō labor;
mē lūdat amnis ōra vīcīna <u>alluens</u>;
vultur <u>relictō</u> transvolet Tityō ferus
meumque poenae semper accrescat iecur;
et tū meī requiesce Pīrithoī pater: 1235
haec incitātīs membra turbinibus ferat
nusquam <u>resistens</u> orbe <u>revolūtō</u> rota.

---

1. The underlined words above are participles. Fill in the table below with the requested information.

Participle	Tense	Voice	Case	Modifies?
clausōs				
nocentēs				
repositum				
alluens				
relictō				
resistens				
revolūtō				

Even though you don't have vocabulary information about each verb, you should still be able to ascertain the tense and voice of each participle just by its stem.

What each participle modifies will be harder to determine without vocabulary information, but do your best.

95. Tenses of the Participle

1. What kind of time do participles show?
2. What time relationship does the present participle show? the perfect participle?

96. Participle Uses

1. Which three uses of the participle have you already seen?
2. Why is a participle often best translated as a dependent clause in English?

97. Ablative Absolute

1. Why is the ablative absolute called "absolute?"
2. What three aspects of an action does the ablative absolute usually explain?
3. What will an ablative absolute with a linking pattern consist of? Why?

Ablative Absolute Text

Ovid, *Metamorphoses* 10.64-71. Eurydice, the wife of Ovid's hero-poet Orpheus, has just returned to the underworld forever. Ovid describes Orpheus' numbness with two esoteric comparisons: Orpheus' emotional state is compared first to someone who has just viewed Cerberus and has been turned to stone by his gaze (this power is customarily reserved for Medusa, and this appears to be a unique attribution to Cerberus by Ovid), and second to an otherwise unknown story of Olenos and Lethaea, the latter of whom was apparently turned to stone for insulting the gods, and the former of whom wished to share in her fate.

Nōn aliter stupuit geminā nece coniugis Orpheus
quam tria quī timidus, mediō portante catēnās,   65
colla canis vīdit; quem nōn pavor ante relīquit;
quam nātūra prior, saxō per corpus obortō;
quique in sē crīmen trāxit voluitque vidērī
Olenos esse nocēns, tūque, o cōnfīsa figūrae,
īnfēlīx Lēthaea, tuae, iūnctissima quondam   70
pectora, nunc lapidēs, quōs ūmida sustinet Īdē.

1. Identify the ablative absolute in line 65.
2. Identify the ablative absolute in line 67.
3. Identify the tense and voice of each participle in each ablative absolute.

Ablative Absolute Text

Cicero, *In Catilinam* 4.12. Cicero in this excerpt speculates what would happen if Catiline and his co-conspirators were left unchecked.

Etenim quaerō, sī quis pater familiās, līberīs suīs ā servō
<u>interfectīs</u>, uxōre <u>occīsā</u>, <u>incēnsā</u> domō, supplicium
dē servīs nōn quam acerbissumum sūmpserit, utrum
is clēmēns ac misericors an inhūmānissimus et
crūdēlissimus esse videātur?

1. Each of the underlined words above is a participle in an ablative absolute. Identify which noun each participle modifies.
2. Continue the sentence below with a correct translation of each of the ablatives absolute; each blank represents an entire ablative absolute expression.

   For I seek, if any head of the household, _____, _____, _____,

3. How is it made clear that *ā servō* is translated with *interfectīs*?

Ablative Absolute Text

Vergil, *Eclogues* 4.11-14. Vergil's fourth Eclogue is his most famous because of its messianic nature. In this excerpt, Vergil predicts the coming of a boy to bring the world out of its state of moral decay and degeneracy. He identifies the new reformed age as beginning in the consulship of Pollio. Later Christian readers used this Eclogue to confer upon Vergil a near-prophetic status. It is because of this poem (among other reasons of course) that Vergil became Dante's guide for much of his *Commedia*, and it is because of this poem and its prophecy that Vergil enjoyed more sympathetic treatment from Christian readers otherwise hostile toward pagan literature.

Tū modō nascentī puerō, quō ferrea prīmum
dēsinet ac tōtō surget gens aurea mundō,
casta favē Lūcīna: tuus iam regnat Apollō.   10
Tēque adeō decus hoc aevī, tē consule, inībit,
Polliō, et incipient magnī prōcēdere mensēs;
tē duce, sī qua manent sceleris vestīgia nostrī,
inrita perpetua solvent formīdine terrās.

---

1. In the above excerpt, there are two ablatives absolute that
   follow the linking pattern. Identify both of them, and
   translate them.

Ablative Absolute Text

Martial 5.48. Martial centers a collection of allusions around a
bet lost by Eumolpus, who promised to cut his hair and give it
to Phoebus if Phoebus earned his military promotion. Martial
introduces the promise in the first couplet, and the second opens
with Phoebus' grudging acceptance of the hair. The middle two
couplets catalog different instances of the power of long hair, and
symbolically the power of youth: Phaethon boldly asking his father
the sun god if he could drive his chariot; Hylas, an attractive youth
abducted by nymphs; and Achilles, whose mother Thetis dressed
him as a woman to prevent him from fighting in the Trojan War.
Martial closes the poem by encouraging the reader to not yet
consider Eumolpus a man, despite his trimmed hair.

Quid nōn cōgit amōr? Secuit nōlente capillōs
    Encolpōs dominō, nōn prohibente tamen.
Permīsit flēvitque Pudens: sīc cessit habēnīs
    audācī questūs dē Phaethonte pater:
tālis raptus Hylās, tālis deprensus Achillēs   5
    dēposuit gaudens, mātre dolente, comās.
Sed tū nē properā—brevibus nē crēde capillīs—
    tardaque prō tantō mūnere, barba, venī.

---

1. Identify the two ablatives absolute in the first couplet.
2. What ablative noun does *prohibente* in line 2 modify?

3. Finish the translation of the first couplet below with a correct translation of the ablatives absolute (each blank represents one ablative absolute).

What does love not force! Encolpos has cut his hair, _____, _____.

4. Identify the six ablative nouns in the rest of the poem, from line 3 to the end. (The following words are ablative adjectives: *audācī* (4), *dolente* (6), *brevibus* (7), *tardā* (8), *tantō* (8); *tālis* in line 5 is not ablative.)

5. Identify the one ablative absolute in lines 3-8.

Ablative Absolute Text

Plautus, *Menaechmi* 469-470. Sosicles has just happily accepted the dress of Menaechmus' wife from Menaechmus' mistress, ostensibly to get it tailored. In this excerpt, Peniculus, Menaechmus' mooch, who because of the confusion of the twins thinks he was cheated out of his lunch, sees Sosicles, who he thinks is Menaechmus, leaving Menaechmus' mistress' house.

Pallam ad phrygiōnem fert confectō prandiō
vīnōque expōtō, parasītō exclūsō forās.   470

Vocabulary

palla, -ae. shawl, cloak
phrygiō, -ōnis (*m.*). an embroiderer, tailor
fert = "He carries"
prandium, -ī. lunch
vīnum, -ī. wine

expōtō, -āre, -āvī, -us. to drink
parasītus, -ī. parasite, mooch
exclūdō, -ere, -sī, -sus. to shut out, exclude
forās = "outside"

There are three ablatives absolute in the above excerpt.

1. Identify them.

2. Translate the entire excerpt.

Ablative Absolute Text

Livy, *Ab urbe condita* 1.13.1-2. Rome had been supposedly founded by brigands and outlaws; its earliest incarnation was a place of asylum for those whom no one else wanted. These brigands and outlaws, however, were all men, and they could not propagate, of course, without women. They approached the neighboring tribes about marrying their daughters, but were promptly rejected. Instead, they invited the Sabines, a neighboring tribe, to a religious festival. At a signal given by Romulus, the Romans carried off the Sabine women to make them their wives. The Sabine men of course went to war against the Romans to take back their wives, but finally the Sabine women intervened and called for peace.

Tum Sabīnae mulierēs, quārum ex iniūria bellum ortum erat, <u>crīnibus</u> <u>passīs</u> <u>scissā</u>que <u>veste</u>, <u>victō</u> malīs muliebrī <u>pavōre</u>, ausae sē inter tēla volantia inferre, ex transversō impetū factō dirimere infestās aciēs, dirimere irās, hinc patrēs, hinc virōs ōrantēs, nē sanguine sē nefandō socerī generīque respergerent, nē parricīdiō maculārent partūs suōs, nepōtum illī, hī līberum prōgeniem.

Vocabulary

crīnis, -is. hair
pandō, -ere, pandī, passus. to tear, to rend
scindō, -ere, scisī, scissus. to tear

vestis, -is. clothing, clothes
malum, -ī. evil
muliebris, -e. womanly
pavor, -ōris. fear

1. Finish the translation of the first clause below with correct translations of the three ablatives absolute that are underlined in the above excerpt.

   Then the Sabine women, from whose attack the war had begun, dared to put themselves in the middle of the flying arrows, _____, _____, _____...

CHAPTER 25

You have already learned the common irregular verbs *sum*, and its compound *possum*, and *volō*, and its compounds *nōlō* and *mālō*. Chapter 25 introduces two more irregular verbs: *eō*, "to go," and *ferō*, "to bring" or "to carry."

98. *eō, īre, iī (ivī), itūrus* (to go)

1. In what tense is *eō* irregular?

Eō, īre Text

Plautus, *Menaechmi* 1031-1034. Messenio, the slave of Sosicles, has saved Menaechmus from the henchmen of Menaechmus' father, thinking that he was saving his master. Menaechmus, of course, thinks that a complete stranger saved him, and is thankful to him. Messenio, thinking that he saved his master's life, has just asked Menaechmus, who he thinks is Sosicles, for his freedom. Menaechmus, after some confusion, agrees. In this excerpt, Messenio congratulates himself on his new-found freedom, still a bit confused by the exchange with Menaechmus.

Messenio. Salvē, mī patrōne. Cum tū līber es, Messēniō,
gaudeō—crēdō hercle vōbīs—Sed, patrōne, tē obsecrō,
nē minus imperēs mihi quam cum tuos servos fuī.
Apud tēd habitābō et quandō ībis, ūnā tēcum ībō domum.

Vocabulary

apud (*prep.* + *acc.*). at the house of	**habitō, -āre.** to live
tēd = **tē**	**quandō.** when
	ūnā. together

---

1. What is the tense of the two forms of *eō, īre* in the above excerpt? Translate each form.
2. Translate the last line of the excerpt.

99. *ferō, ferre, tulī, lātus* (to carry, bear)

1. In what tense is *ferō* irregular?

Irregular Verbs Text

Martial 4.10. Martial sends an advance copy of his book to a certain Faustinus, who will appreciate it. But Martial also includes a sponge (an ancient eraser) so that any of his jokes that might be offensive to Faustinus might easily be erased. The poem owes much of its language to Catullus' first poem (see Chapter 13 p. 132 in this workbook): *libellus* and *nūgās* figure prominently in Catullus' poem and the idea of still polishing the book, though described with different words, also appears in Catullus 1.

Dum novus est nec adhūc rāsā mihi fronte libellus,
  pāgina dum tangī nōn bene sicca timet,
ī, puer, et cārō perfer leve mūnus amīcō
  quī meruit nūgās prīmus habēre meās.
Curre, sed instructus: comitētur Pūnica lībrum   5
  spongea: mūneribus convenit illa meīs.
Non possunt nostrōs multae, Faustīne, litūrae
  emendāre iocōs: ūna litūra potest.

There are two forms of the irregular verbs in the above poem.

1. What are they?
2. What forms are they?

CHAPTER 26

Adjectives and adverbs exist in three degrees: the positive, the comparative, and the superlative. The Latin forms for the comparative and superlative of all Latin adjectives and adverbs are introduced in this chapter. In both Latin and English, some adjectives do not follow the regular pattern for forming the comparative and the superlative (e.g. "good" and *bonus, -a, -um*); these irregular Latin forms are also introduced. Finally, the two grammatical constructions that Latin uses to make comparisons, i.e. the two ways Latin expresses the English "than," are introduced.

> **Terms to Know**
>
> degree
> positive
> comparative
> superlative
> comparison with *quam*
> ablative of comparison

100. Comparison of Adjectives

1. What are the three degrees of adjectives?
2. What are the two ways that English forms the comparative?
3. What are the endings for the Latin comparative?
4. What declension endings does the Latin comparative use?
5. What are the two ways that English forms the superlative?
6. What is the ending for the Latin superlative?
7. What Latin adjective is the superlative declined like?
8. What are the two regular exceptions to forming the superlative? What letter does their stem end in? And what ending does each use?

Comparison of Adjectives Text

Motto of Cumberland College (KY).

Vīta abundantior

---

1. Translate the motto. The meaning of *abundantior* should be clear from its English derivative.

Comparison of Adjectives Text

Cicero, *Pro Archia* **16.** Cicero has been making the argument for the importance of literature, especially for the Romans, for whom it was an important feature of civic life. In this excerpt, Cicero lists important Romans who advocated the Hellenism of the late Republic. The figure of Cato is treated with some delicacy because, although perhaps the most famous Roman of the list, and the one who most embodied Republican ideals, he was also the one most vocally against the rise of Hellenism because of its perceived damage to Roman virtue.

Ex hōc esse hunc numerō quem patrēs nostrī vīdērunt, dīvīnum hominem, Āfricānum, ex hōc C. Laelium, L. Fūrium, <u>moderātissimōs</u> hominēs et <u>continentissimōs</u>, ex hōc <u>fortissimum</u> virum et illīs temporibus <u>doctissimum</u>, M. Catōnem illum senem; quī profectō sī nihil ad percipiendam colendamque virtūtem litterīs adiuvārentur, numquam sē ad eārum studium *contulissent*. Quod sī nōn hic tantus frūctus ostenderētur, et sī ex hīs studiīs dēlectātiō sōla peterētur, tamen, ut opīnor, hanc animī *remissiōnem* <u>hūmānissimam</u> ac <u>līberālissimam</u> iūdicārētis.

---

1. Complete the table below with the requested information about the underlined adjectives above. The italicized words are used in questions 2 and 3 below.

    a. In the "comparative" column, form the comparative of the adjective in the same gender, number, and case as the superlative.

	Gender	Case	Number	Modifies?	Comparative
moderātissimōs					
continentissimōs					
fortissimum					
doctissimum					
hūmānissimam					
līberālissimam					

2. Why is *remissiōnem* in line 10 not a comparative form?

3. Why is *contulissent* in line 8 not a superlative form?

101. Declension of Comparatives

1. What is the ablative singular ending for comparatives?

2. How is it different from other third declension adjectives?

3. What are the other differences between the forms of comparatives and the forms of other third declension adjectives?

102. Irregular Comparison

1. Which adjectives in the list on page 207 of your text are irregular in both Latin and English?

Irregular Comparison Text

Martial 7.34.1-5. Martial in this poem criticizes Charinus, a builder working during the reign of the emperor Nero, for his sexual activity. In this excerpt, Martial establishes the parameters for this criticism, and introduces Nero's baths as a reference point: if you thought Nero was bad, take a look at Charinus!

Quō possit fierī modō, Severe,
ut vir pessimus omnium Charīnus
ūnam rem bene fēcerit, requiris?
Dīcam, sed cito. Quid Nerōne pēius?
Quid thermīs melius Nerōniānīs?   5

Vocabulary

cito (*adv.*). quickly
Nerō, Nerōnis. [*name*]
therma, -ae. bath [referring to a large public bath complex]
Nerōniānus, -a, -um. Nero's, of or belonging to Nero

---

1. Identify the three irregular adjectives and/or adverbs.

2. Identify whether each is a comparative or a superlative and an adjective or an adverb.

3. Identify which noun each modifies.

4. Translate the last two lines.

5. What is the tense of *dīcam* in line 4?

Irregular Comparison Text

Martial 2.2. Martial here catalogs the *cognōmina* of men who
received them from successful expeditions in battle. The litany
begins in the third century BCE and continues to Martial's own
time. The poem concludes with Martial lauding the emperor: he
has a *cognōmen* all to himself for his defeat of the Chatti in 84 CE.
(The *cognōmen*, or nickname, was an honorific name bestowed
upon someone, whether for a notable deed or a distinguishing
feature. There is no convention within Roman names for which
of the three names to use to refer to someone: Vergil and Ovid are
known by their *nōmina*, Cicero by his *cognōmen* or, sometimes as a
sign of affection from his admirers, by his *nōmen*. Rarely, though,
is the *praenōmen* used to refer to someone.)

Crēta dedit magnum, maius dedit Āfrica nōmen,
    Scīpiō quod victor quodque Metellus habet;
nōbilius domitō tribuit Germānia Rhēnō,
    et puer hōc dignus nōmine, Caesar, erās.
Frāter Idūmaeōs meruit cum patre triumphōs,   5
    quae datur ex Chattīs laurea, tōta tua est.

---

1. What is the irregular comparative that appears in the first
   couplet?
2. What adjective is it the comparative form of?
3. What is its case, number, and gender?

Irregular Comparison Text

Martial 8.54. Martial lauds Catulla for her beauty, but criticizes
her for her morals. He then wishes that she be not as beauitful or
not as corrupt so he wouldn't be as taken by her. Both the use of
the name Catulla in line 3 and the style of the poem recall the
poetry of Catullus.

Formonsissima quae fuēre vel sunt,
sed vīlissima quae fuēre vel sunt,
ō quam tē fierī, Catulla, vellem
formosam minus aut magis pudīcam!

---

1. Identify the two superlative forms.
2. Identify the two irregular comparatives.
3. Complete the following translation of lines 3-4 by translating the modifiers in brackets.

> O how I want you, Catulla, to become _____ [*minus*] beautiful or _____ [*magis*] chaste.

103. Comparison with *quam* and Ablative of Comparison

1. What are the two ways that Latin can express a comparison?
2. In Latin, what do the two items connected by *quam* share?

Comparison with *quam* and Ablative of Comparison Text

Motto of Appalachian State University (NC).

Esse quam vidērī.

1. Translate the motto.
2. What are the implications for the goal of a university, especially one with its origins as a teacher's college, of *esse* and *vidērī*?

Comparison with *quam* and Ablative of Comparison Text

Horace, *Carmina* 3.30.1-5. Known as a *sphragis* poem because it seals the collection of poetry shut (*sphragis* is the Greek word for a seal), the final poem of Horace's third book of odes in fact did not "seal" his collection. He decided he wanted to write more than his originally planned three books and circulated a fourth book of poetry. Nonetheless, in these first five lines of the poem, Horace illustrates a primary theme of the *sphragis* poem: the ability of the poet's poetry to survive well beyond the lifetime of the poet himself.

Exēgī monumentum aere perennius
rēgālīque sitū pȳramidum altius,
quod nōn imber edax, nōn Aquilō impotens
possit dīruere aut innumerābilis
annōrum seriēs et fuga temporum.   5

1. Identify the two comparatives in the above excerpt.
2. Are they adjectives or adverbs? Explain your answer.
3. What are the two ablatives of comparison?

Comparison with *quam* and Ablative of Comparison Text

Catullus 9.10-11. Catullus' good friend Veranius has been on a long journey and has just returned home. In the excerpt below, Catullus rejoices at his good fortune.

Ō quantum est hominum beātiōrum,
quid mē laetius est beātiusve?

1. Identify the three comparative adjectives in the above excerpt.
2. Identify all possible case, numbers, and genders for each adjective.
3. What is the ablative of comparison in the above excerpt?

Comparison with *quam* and Ablative of Comparison Text

Martial 1.109.1-5. Martial describes in loving terms the pet dog of Publius. In this excerpt, Issa, the dog, is described in the language of the elegiac poets, compared in the first line to the sparrow of Catullus 2.

Issa est passere nēquior Catullī,
Issa est pūrior osculō columbae,
Issa est blandior omnibus puellīs,
Issa est cārior Indicīs lapillīs,
Issa est dēliciae catella Publī.   5

Vocabulary

Issa, -ae. [*name*]
passer, -eris. sparrow
nēquam (*indeclinable adj.*).
    worthless, vile
Catullus, -ī. [*name of famous
    Roman poet*]
pūrus, -a, -um. pure, chaste

osculum, -ī. kiss
columba, -ae. dove
blandus, -a, -um. seductive,
    charming
Indicus, -a, -um. Indian, of
    or belonging to India
lapillus, -ī. stone, gem

1. Translate the above excerpt.

104. Comparison of Adverbs

1. What do comparative adverbs end in?
2. What so superlative adverbs end in?
3. How is *quam* + the superlative translated?

Comparison of Adverbs Text

Motto of the Olympics.

Citius. Altius. Fortius.

---

1. Translate the Olympic Motto.

Comparison of Adverbs Text

Martial 7.20.1. A scathing poem aimed at a certain Santra, who is apparently both gluttonous and cheap. He will worm his way into dinner parties, and then carry off any food and drink that he can. After lugging his spoils to his upstairs apartment (and remember that Roman apartments grew cheaper the higher in a building they were located), he turns around and sells them.

Nihil est miserius neque gulōsius Santrā.

---

1. Identify all possible forms of *miserius* and *gulōsius*.
2. Which of these forms are they in this excerpt? Explain your answer.
3. What do they modify?

Comparison of Adverbs Text

Ovid, *Metamorphoses* **1.510-511.** As Apollo chases the uninterested Daphne through the woods, he expresses his concern for her well-being. His concern, of course, is laden with Ovidian irony because of his unmistakable intentions toward her once he catches her. Nonetheless, Apollo warns Daphne about the brambles and thorns that might scratch her, and offers to adjust the speed of his pursuit of her so that she might adjust the speed of her flight accordingly, all of course for her protection and well-being.

Aspera, quā properās, loca sunt. Moderātius, ōrō,   510
curre, fugamque inhibē. Moderātius īnsequar ipse.

Vocabulary

asper, -era, -erum. rough, thick, harsh
quā = "where"
properō, -āre. to hurry, to hasten
moderātus, -a, -um. slow

ōrō = "please"
fuga, -ae. flight
inhibeō, -ēre. to slow
īnsequor, -ī. to pursue, to follow

1. What is the comparative adverb in the above excerpt?
2. Translate the excerpt.

Comparison of Adverbs Text

Seneca, *Phaedra* **1123-1125.** Theseus has just heard how his son Hippolytus was killed and has lamented his fate. The Chorus responds with a speech about the vagaries of Fortune. In this excerpt, they introduce the capricious nature of Fortune.

Chorus. Quantī cāsūs, humana rotant!
Minor in parvīs Fortūna furit
leviusque ferit leviōra deus;   1125

Vocabulary

furō, -ere. to rave, to rage

feriō, -īre. to strike

1. Translate the last two lines.

CHAPTER 27

The present subjunctive will be formed similarly to the present indicative, but with a different characteristic vowel; the perfect subjunctive will use a stem identical in most forms to the future perfect indicative. The present subjunctive is often used in independent, as opposed to subordinate, uses.

Terms to Know

present subjunctive
perfect active
    subjunctive
indicative vs.
    subjunctive mood
hortatory (subjunctive)
jussive (subjunctive)
optative (subjunctive)

105. Present Active Subjunctive

1. What personal endings does the present subjunctive use?
2. What is the characteristic vowel for the present subjunctive?
3. What conjugation is the one that does not use this vowel?
4. What does it use instead?

- Another way to conceive of the formation of the present subjunctive is as a change of characteristic vowel: each conjugation has its characteristic vowel for the indicative, and a different vowel, or an additional vowel, for the subjunctive.

Present Active Subjunctive Text

Plautus, *Menaechmi* **1100.** Menaechmus and Sosicles have just arrived for the first time in the same place along with Messenio, who has now figured out what must be going on. Menaechmus in this excerpt agrees to be interviewed by Messenio to confirm that he and Sosicles are indeed long-lost twins.

Prōmeruistī ut nē quid ōrēs quod velīs quīn impetrēs. 1100

---

1. There are three present subjunctive verbs in the short excerpt above. One should be recognizable from your vocabulary. What is it? To what conjugation does it belong? Who is its subject?

2. There is one present subjunctive form of the irregular verb *volō, velle.* Can you guess what it is?

255

3. There is one more first conjugation present subjunctive form. Can you guess what it is?

Present Active Subjunctive Text

Martial 9.42. Martial here is apparently campaigning for Stella to be made consul. He comprehensively beseeches Apollo to sway Caesar's mind to Stella, and, at the close of the poem, wonders why Apollo hesitates when the sacrifice Martial has prepared for him is ready to go.

Campīs dīves Apollō sīc Myrīnīs,
sīc semper senibus fruāre cygnīs,
doctae sīc tibi serviant sorōrēs
nec Deiphīs tua mentiātur ullī,
sīc Palātia tē colant amentque: 5
bis sēnōs citō tē rogante fascēs
det Stellae bonus annuatque Caesar.
Fēlix tunc ego dēbitorque vōtī
casūrum tibi rusticās ad ārās
dūcam cornibus aureīs iuvencum.   10
Nāta est hostia, Phoebe; quid morāris?

1. Within lines 5-7, there are two first conjugation present subjunctives. What are they?
2. Within lines 5-7, there are also two third conjugation present subjunctives. What are they?
3. Within lines 3-4, there are two fourth conjugation present subjunctives. What are they?
4. *Fruāre* in line 2 is an alternate form for *fruāris*, a present passive subjunctive. Although the passive forms won't be formally learned until Chapter 29, you should see that the formation is identical to the active, except the use of the passive personal endings instead of the active. What conjugation is *fruāris*? What is its subject?

Present Active Subjunctive Text

Vergil, *Aeneid* 4.288-295. The Trojan hero Aeneas has just received a visit from the messenger god Hermes, who reports to him Jupiter's message: leave Carthage and proceed to Italy. Aeneas in this excerpt readies his men and his ships secretly, so that Dido will not know. Following the excerpt, Dido confronts Aeneas with his deception.

Mnēsthea Sergestumque vocat fortemque Serestum,
classem aptent tacitī sociōsque ad lītora cōgant,
arma parent, et quae rēbus sit causa novandīs   290
dissimulent: sēsē intereā, quandō optima Dīdō
nesciat et tantōs rumpī nōn spēret amōrēs,
temptātūrum aditūs et quae mollissima fandī
tempora, quis rēbus dexter modus. Ōcius omnēs
imperiō laetī pārent et iussa facessunt.   295

---

1. Explain why *facessunt* in line 295 cannot be a present subjunctive.
2. Of the other verbs, how many are first conjugation present subjunctives?
3. How many are third conjugation present subjunctive?
4. What is the only first conjugation indicative verb? Third conjugation indicative verb?

Present Active Subjunctive Text

Plautus, *Menaechmi* **110-124.** Peniculus has just finished the speech that opens the play proper in which he introduces himself and, to a lesser extent, Menaechmus. This excerpt represents Menaechmus' first appearance on stage; he is yelling at his wife about how she nags him too much.

Menaechmus.

Nī mala, nī stulta siēs, nī indomita imposque animī,   110
quod virō esse odiō videās, tūte tibi odiō habeās.
Praeterhāc sī mihi tāle post hunc diem
faxis, faxō forīs vidua vīsās patrem.
Nam quotiens forās īre volō, mē retinēs, revocās, rogitās,
quō ego eam, quam rem agam, quid negōtī geram,   115
quid petam, quid feram, quid forīs ēgerim.
Portitōrem domum dūxī ita omnem mihi
rem necesse ēloquīst, quicquid ēgī atque agō.
Nimium ego tē habuī dēlicātam; nunc adeō, ut factūrus, dīcam.
Quandō ego tibi ancillās, penum,   120
lānam, aurum, vestem, purpuram   120a
bene praebeō nec quicquam egēs,
malō cavēbis, sī sapis: 121a

virum observāre dēsinēs.

Atque adeō, nē mē nēquīquam servēs, ob eam industriam

hodiē dūcam scortum ad cēnam atque aliquō condīcam forās.   124

---

1. Put an "x" in the column for indicative or subjunctive based on the verb forms in the above excerpt.

In line 110, *siēs* is an archaic form of *sis*.

In line 113, *faxis* and *faxō* are archaic forms *faciās* and *faciam*.

Only verbs formed from the present stem (i.e. no perfect tenses) have been included.

2. What is the one perfect active subjunctive form?

Line #	Form	Principal Parts	Indicative	Subjunctive
110	siēs			
111	videās			
111	habeās			
113	faxis			
113	faxō			
114	volō			
114	retinēs	retineō, -ēre		
114	revocās			
114	rogitās	rogitō, -āre		
115	eam			
115	agam			
115	geram			
116	petam			
116	feram			
118	agō			
119	dīcam			
121	praebeō	praebeō, -ēre		
121	egēs	egeō, ēre		
121a	sapis	sapiō, -īre		
122	dēsinēs			
123	servēs			
124	dūcam			
124	condīcam			

Present Active Subjunctive Text

Cicero, *In Catilinam* 1.32. Cicero has just advocated that not only Catiline be exiled but also all of his co-conspirators. In this excerpt, he describes the results of such comprehensive exile.

Quā rē sēcēdant improbī, sēcernant sē ā bonīs, ūnum in locum congregentur, mūrō dēnique, [id] quod saepe iam dīxī, sēcernantur ā nōbīs; dēsinant īnsidiārī domī suae cōnsulī, circumstāre tribūnal praetōris urbānī, obsidēre cum gladiīs cūriam, malleolōs et facēs ad īnflammandam urbem comparāre; sit dēnique īnscrīptum in fronte ūnīus cuiusque quid dē rē pūblicā sentiat. Polliceor hoc vōbīs, patrēs cōnscrīptī, tantam in nōbīs cōnsulibus fore dīligentiam, tantam in vōbīs auctōritātem, tantam in equitibus Rōmānīs virtūtem, tantam in omnibus bonīs cōnsēnsiōnem ut Catilīnae profectiōne omnia patefacta, inlūstrāta, oppressa, vindicāta esse videātis.

1. Fill in the table below with the requested information:

   This is a verb review. It includes a number of present subjunctive forms, but also participles, infinitives, and indicatives. One form, *īnflammandam*, has been done for you. It is a form you have not yet learned.

2. An "x" in the subject column indicates that that particular form does not have a personal ending from which to determine its subject. This should also be a clue at least to which moods it is not.

Form	Principal Parts	Mood	Tense	Voice	Subject
sēcēdant	sēcēdō, -ere				
sēcernant	sēcernō, -ere				
congregentur	congregō, -āre				
dīxī					
sēcernantur	sēcernō, -ere				
dēsinant					
īnsidiārī	īnsidior, -ārī				x
circumstāre					x
obsidēre	obsideō, -ēre				x
īnflammandam	īnflammō, -āre	*participle*	*future*	*passive*	x
comparāre					x

Form	Principal Parts	Mood	Tense	Voice	Subject
īnscrīptum					x
sentiat					
polliceor	polliceor, -ērī				
cōnscrīptī					x
fore (= futūrum esse)					x
patefacta (esse)					x
inlūstrāta (esse)	inlustrō, -āre				x
oppressa (esse)	opprimō, -ere				x
vindicāta esse	vindicō, -āre				x
videātis					

106. Perfect Active Subjunctive

1. What stem does the perfect active subjunctive use?

2. What letters does the perfect subjunctive add to this stem?

3. What other form does the perfect active subjunctive look like?

Perfect Active Subjunctive Text

Horace, *Carmina* **1.9.1-4.** Horace uses the snowy peak of Mt. Soracte, a mountain in central Italy, to exemplify his *carpe diem* ("seize the day") philosophy. In this excerpt, Horace describes Mt. Soracte and the imagery of winter and cold that represents the concern and preoccupation that prevents people from living in the now.

Vidēs ut altā stet nive candidum
Sōracte, nec iam sustineant onus
    silvae labōrantēs, gelūque
    flūmina constiterint acūtō.

---

1. Fill in the table below with the requested information.

Form	Principal Parts	Mood	Tense	Subject
vidēs				
stet				
sustineant	sustineō, -ēre			
constiterint	consistō, -ere, constitī			

Perfect Active Subjunctive Text

> **Cicero, *Pro Archia* 12.** Cicero is responding to the question of why
> Archias is so valued, and reponds that literature provides an escape
> for inquisitive and curious minds. In this excerpt, Cicero describes
> his own love of the escape that literature provides, but is careful
> to point out that he does not become so lost in literature that he
> neglects his civic duties.

> Ego vērō fateor mē hīs studiīs esse dēditum. Cēterōs
> pudeat, sī quī ita sē litterīs abdidērunt ut nihil possint
> ex eīs neque ad commūnem adferre frūctum neque in
> aspectum lūcemque prōferre; mē autem quid pudeat
> quī tot annōs ita vīvō, iūdicēs, ut ā nūllīus umquam mē
> tempore aut commodō aut ōtium meum abstrāxerit aut
> voluptās āvocārit aut dēnique somnus retardārit?

1. Complete the following table with the requested
   information.

Verb	Principal Parts	Mood	Tense	Voice	Subject
fateor	fateor, -ērī				
dēditum esse	dēdō, -ere				x
pudeat	pudeō, -ēre				
abdidērunt	abdidō, -ere				
possint					
adferre					x
prōferre					x
pudeat					
vīvō					
abstrāxerit	abstrahō, -ere				
āvocārit	avocō, -āre				
retardit	retardō, -ere				

2. The forms *āvocārit* and *retardārit* are syncopated or
   contracted forms. What would they be written out
   completely?

Perfect Active Subjunctive Text

Horace, *Carmina* 1.8.1-7. Horace here laments the loss of Sybaris to his love for Lydia; Sybaris no longer participates in war games.

Lȳdia, dīc, per omnīs
hoc deōs vērē, Sybarin cūr properēs amandō
    perdere, cūr aprīcum
ōderit campum, patiens pulveris atque sōlis,
    cūr neque mīlitāris   5
inter aequālis equitet, Gallica nec lupātīs
    temperet ōra frēnīs?

1. The verb *dīc* in line 1 governs the subordinate clauses in the rest of the poem.

2. Identify the tense of each subjunctive verb below, and explain your answer.
    properēs [properō, -āre]
    ōderit [ōdī, odisse]
    equitet [equitō, -āre]
    temperet [temperō, -āre]

3. Explain why *properēs* in line 2, and *temperet* in line 7 are not imperfect subjunctive; your explanation should be based on both vocabulary information and grammatical conventions.

4. How does *atque* in line 4 signal that *pulveris* is not a perfect subjunctive, even if you do not know the vocabulary information for *pulveris*?

107. Subjunctive of *sum*

1. What vowel does the subjunctive of *sum* use?

108. Independent Uses of the Subjunctive

1. For what is the subjunctive mood used?

2. What are the four identified uses of the subjunctive as an independent verb?

Independent Uses of the Subjunctive Text

Catullus 64.143-144. Ariadne, as she laments her abandonment by the Athenian hero Theseus, here generalizes her pain and resentment of Theseus to how all women should (or might) feel about all men.

Nunc iam nulla virō iūrantī fēmina crēdat,
nulla virī spēret sermōnēs esse fidēlēs;

1. Choose the correct translation of the above excerpt from the choices below.
   a. Now, no woman believes a man making promises, no woman hopes that what a man says is trustworthy;
   b. At this point, no woman has believed a man making promises, no woman has hoped that what a man says is trustworthy;
   c. Now, no woman may believe a man making promises, no woman may hope that what a man says is trustworthy;
   d. Now, no woman should believe a man making promises, no woman should hope that what a man says is trustworthy;
2. Explain your answer.

Independent Uses of the Subjunctive, Hortatory Text

Vergil, *Aeneid* **2.353.** As Aeneas recalls the fall of Troy to Dido and her assembled guests, he here describes how he exhorted his men to rush into battle with him to save Troy from the marauding Greeks. Ultimately Aeneas will forsake such folly, save his family, and flee Troy.

Moriāmur et in media arma ruāmus.

Vocabulary

ruō, -ere. to rush (into battle)

1. Translate the excerpt.
2. *Hysteron proteron* is a rhetorical device whereby the natural order of events is reversed; a common example in English is to put one's shoes and socks on, when of course socks go on before shoes. Explain how this excerpt is a *hysteron proteron*.

Independent Uses of the Subjunctive, Jussive Text

Motto of the University of Chicago.

Crescat scientia; vīta excolātur.

Vocabulary

crescō, -ere. to grow

scientia, -ae. knowledge

excolō, -ere. to cultivate, to enhance

---

1. Translate the motto.

Independent Uses of the Subjunctive, Jussive Text

Vergil, *Aeneid* **4.232-237.** Jupiter is concerned that Aeneas is spending too much time dallying in Carthage with Dido, thereby forsaking his destiny to travel to Italy and establish his Trojan lineage as the antecedent for the Romans. In this excerpt, he concludes the speech to Mercury in which he tells Mercury to get Aeneas moving with a final comment on Aeneas and his final instructions for Mercury.

"Sī nūlla accendit tantārum glōria rērum
nec super ipse suā mōlītur laude labōrem,
Ascaniōne pater Rōmānās invidet arcēs?
Quid struit? Aut quā spē inimīcā in gente morātur   235
nec prōlem Ausoniam et Lāvīnia respicit arva?
Nāviget! Haec summa est, hic nostrī nūntius estō."

---

1. Complete the translation below by translating the verb in brackets.

If no glory for such things spurs him on, and if he himself does not pursue any longer his task along with his praise, does he, as father, begrudge Roman citadels to his son Ascanius? What is he thinking? Or because of what desire does he delay in a hostile land and does not consider his Italian offspring and Roman land? _____ [*nāviget*]! This is the goal, may you be my messenger.

The form *estō* in line 237 is called the future imperative, recognizable by its *-stō* ending. It is a rare form, more common in poetry than in prose, that is translated very similarly to the jussive subjunctive; the future imperative is a softened form of the more direct present imperative, loosely akin to the distinction modern languages like Italian make between an informal and a formal imperative form.

Independent Uses of the Subjunctive, Jussive Text

Horace, *Carmina* **1.36.10-16.** In this poem, Horace sends greetings to his friend Numida, who has just returned from fighting in Spain. In this excerpt, Horace describes the various ways in which he wants to celebrate Numida's return.

Cressa nē careat pulchra diēs nōta,   10
 neu promptae modus amphorae,
neu mōrem in Salium sit requiēs pedum,
 neu multī Damalis merī
Bassum Thrēiciā vincat amystide,
 neu dēsint epulīs rōsae   15
neu vīvax apium neu breve līlium.

1. Identify the four present subjunctives in the above excerpt.
2. What does the *nē* in line 10 indicate?

Independent Uses of the Subjunctive, Optative Text

Catullus 64.171-176. In this excerpt from Ariadne's lament, she wishes that Theseus had never come to Crete so that she would never have been abandoned by him.

Iuppiter omnipotens, utinam nē tempore prīmō
Gnōsia Cēcropiae tetigissent lītora puppēs,
indomitō nec dīra ferens stīpendia taurō
perfidus in Crētam religasset nāvita fūnem,
nec malus hic cēlans dulcī crudēlia formā
consilia in nostrīs requiesset sēdibus hospes!

1. What are the three subjunctives used in the optative in the above excerpt?
2. What tense are they?

3. Complete the following translation by translating the
words in brackets. Translate each twice, once using a literal
translation of *utinam*, the other using a more colloquial
translation of *utinam*.

> All-powerful Jupiter, _____ [*utinam*] Athenian ships
> _____ [*nē tetigissent; tangō, -ere* = to touch, to
> reach] the shores of Crete way back when, and _____
> [*utinam*] that faithless sailor, bringing harsh payment
> to the indomitable bull, _____
> [*nec religasset = religāvisset; religō, -āre* = to
> bind, to fasten] his mooring line to Crete, and _____
> [*utinam*] this evil man, hiding cruel plans in a sweet
> exterior, _____ [*nec requiesset; requiescō, -ere* = to
> rest] here in our land as a guest!

Independent Uses of the Subjunctive Text

Alcuin, ***Conflictus veris et hiemis* 42-48.** In this excerpt, spring
hopes that all of the natural indicators of her arrival be allowed to
appear and flourish.

Dēsine plūra, hiems, rērum tū prōdigus, atrox:
et veniat cucūlus, pastōrum dulcis amīcus.
Collibus in nostrīs ērumpant germina laeta,
pascuā sint pecorī, requiēs et dulcis in arvīs,
et viridēs rāmī praestent umbrācula fessīs,
ūberibus plēnīs veniantque ad mulctra capellae,
et volucrēs variā Phoebum sub vōce salūtent.

------

1. Identify the six subjunctive verbs in the above excerpt.
2. What are their tense?
3. Of the three independent uses of the subjunctive on page
   216 of your textbook, which use must these verbs be?
   Explain your answer.

CHAPTER 28

Both the imperfect active and the pluperfect active subjunctives are formed by using infinitives as stems. With these two final tenses of the subjunctive, the subjunctive sequence of tense is also introduced. Similar in theory to the infinitive sequence of tense, the subjunctive sequence of tense is slightly more complicated. More often than not, subjunctive verbs will be used in dependent clauses; the most common of these clauses are introduced.

> **Terms to Know**
>
> sequence of tenses
> primary (tense/
>   sequence)
> secondary (tense/
>   sequence)
> purpose clause
> result clause
> result clause "signpost
>   word"
> *cum* clause of
>   circumstance, cause,
>   concession

109. Imperfect Active Subjunctive

1. What is the stem used for the imperfect active subjunctive?

2. When is the *-e-* that precedes the personal endings short? When is it long?

- It might be tempting to mix up the present active infinitive and forms of the imperfect subjunctive. A very simple rule can minimize confusion: if the form has a personal ending, it must be a subjunctive; if it does not, it must be an infinitive (keeping in mind, of course, that occasionally the *-re* ending can be an alternate ending for the second person singular passive indicative).

Imperfect Active Subjunctive Text

Martial 2.1.1-2. Martial opens his second book of epigrams with a self-deprecating assessment of why shorter books are better. In this excerpt, the opening couplet, he points out that a long book may be portable (to an extent) but cannot be read as it is being transported.

Ter centēna quidem poterās epigrammata ferre,
> sed quis tē ferret perlegeretque, liber?

1. There are four verbs in the above excerpt. What are they (include all verb forms in your answer)?

2. How many are subjunctive? What is it/are they?

3. How many are indicative? What is it/are they?

4. How many are infinitive? What is it/are they?

Imperfect Active Subjunctive Text

Livy, *Ab urbe condita* 1.15.3. As the young Rome expanded, its neighbors worried about its growing military power. The Veientes, one of these neighbors, accordingly sent a raiding party into Roman territory to at least announce their willingness to fight. The Romans responded with invasion. In this excerpt, the response of the Veientes to the Roman invasion is described: rather than wait to be besieged within their city, the Veientes elected to meet the Romans in open battle (and were subsequently routed by the Romans).

Quem postquam castra pōnere et ad urbem accessūrum Vēientēs audīvēre, obviam ēgressī ut potius aciē dēcernerent quam inclūsī dē tectīs moenibusque dīmicārent.

1. List the infinitives in the above excerpt.

2. List the imperfect subjunctives in the above excerpt.

3. One form that looks like an infinitive is not. Which one? Why not? What form is it?

Imperfect Active Subjunctive Text

Cicero, *In Catilinam* 3.4. Catiline has left Rome but not as many of his co-conspirators have left as was expected. In this excerpt, Cicero describes how the presence of these co-conspirators in Rome concerns him, and how he is spending his time watching and investigating them to better make a case against them to the Senate.

Atque ego, ut vīdī, quōs maximō furōre et scelere esse īnflammātōs sciēbam, eōs nōbīscum esse et Rōmae remānsisse, in eō omnīs diēs noctēsque cōnsūmpsī ut, quid agerent, quid mōlīrentur, sentīrem ac vidērem, ut, quoniam auribus vestrīs propter incrēdibilem magnitūdinem sceleris minōrem fidem faceret ōrātiō mea, rem ita comprehenderem ut tum dēmum animīs salūtī vestrae prōvidērētis cum oculīs maleficium ipsum vidērētis.

---

1. Identify each verb as infinitive or subjunctive by placing a check in the appropriate column below, and identify the tense of each form.

Verb	Infinitive?	Subjunctive?	Tense
esse			
remānsisse			
agerent			
mōlīrentur			
sentīrem			
vidērem			
faceret			
comprehenderem			
prōvidērētis			
vidērētis			

2. Identify two contextual clues that signal that *scelere* in line 1 is not an infinitive.

110. Pluperfect Active Subjunctive

1. What is the tense sign of the pluperfect active subjunctive?
2. What other form does this stem look like?
3. What endings does the pluperfect active subjunctive use?
4. When is the *-e-* that precedes the personal endings short? When is it long?

---

*   The same rule that applies to the potential confusion between the imperfect subjunctive and the present infinitive applies to the pluperfect active subjunctive and the perfect active infinitive: if it has a personal ending, it must be the subjunctive; if it does not, it must be the infinitive.

*   The use of the infinitive as the stem for the imperfect and pluperfect subjunctive adheres to the following pattern: the addition of endings to the infinitive shifts the tense of the infinitive one step into the past, i.e. the present infinitive plus endings becomes the imperfect subjunctive and the perfect infinitive plus endings becomes the pluperfect subjunctive.

Pluperfect Active Subjunctive Text

Vergil, *Eclogues* **6.43-51.** *Eclogues* 6 is a catalog of allusions to various mythological stories. The Hylas of lines 43-44 is a youth who sailed with the Argonauts on the Quest for the Golden Fleece and was lost. Hercules and the other Argonauts searched for him, calling his name. The bulk of this excerpt, however, is devoted to Pasiphae, the wife of king Minos of Crete who, because either he or she had offended a god (the details vary according to the source) was made to fall in love with a white bull. Daedalus, the court engineer (of Daedalus and Icarus and the man-made wings fame), effected her coupling with the bull and thus the Minotaur was born.

> Hīs adiungit Hylan nautae quō fonte relictum
> clāmassent, ut lītus, Hylā, Hylā, omne sonāret;
> et fortūnātam, sī numquam armenta fuissent,   45
> Pāsiphaen niveī sōlātur amōre iuvencī.
> Ā, virgō infēlix, quae tē dēmentia cēpit?
> Proetides inplērunt falsīs mūgītibus agrōs:
> at nōn tam turpis pecudum tamen ulla secūta
> concubitus, quamvīs collō timuisset arātrum,   50
> et saepe in lēvī quaesisset cornua fronte.

1. Identify the four pluperfect active subjunctive verbs in the above excerpt.
2. Identify the one imperfect active subjunctive.

Pluperfect Active Subjunctive Text

Martial 9.65. Hercules has long been associated with Rome and her early history. The Roman historian Livy tells the story of how Hercules killed the monster Cacus on the banks of the Tiber where the Forum Boarium, Rome's cattle market, was located. A temple dedicated to Hercules still stands in the location today, and the Arch of the Argentarii, an arch in the Forum Boarium, bears the image of Hercules. In this poem, Martial, addressing Hercules by Alcides, his original name, in line 1, details Hercules' accomplishments as he compliments the emperor at the same time. The emperor had a portrait statue of his face on Hercules' body sculpted (described more fully in 9.64); Martial quips that if Hercules had had the emperor's face when he was alive, he never would have had to complete his labors.

Alcīdē, Latiō nunc agnoscende Tonantī,
    postquam pulchra deī Caesaris ōra geris,
sī tibi tunc istī vultūs habitūsque fuissent,
    cessērunt manibus cum fera monstra tuīs:
Argolicō famulum nōn tē servīre tyrannō   5
    vīdissent gentēs saevaque regna patī,
sed tū iussissēs Eurysthea; nec tibi fallax
    portasset Nessī perfida dōna Lichās,
Oetaeī sine lēge rogī sēcūrus adissēs
    astra patris summī, quae tibi poena dedit;   10
Lȳdia nec dominae traxisses pensa superbae
    nec Styga vīdissēs Tartareumque canem.
Nunc tibi Iūno favet, nunc tē tua dīligit Hēbē;
    nunc tē sī videat Nympha, remittet Hylan.

---

1. Complete the table below with the requested information.

Line #	Verb	Principal Parts	Mood	Tense
2	geris			
3	fuissent			
4	cessērunt			
5	servīre			
6	vīdissent			
6	patī			
7	iussissēs			
8	portāsset			
9	adisses			
10	dedit			
11	traxissēs			
12	vīdissēs			
13	favet	faveō, -ēre		
13	dīligit	dīligō, -ere		
13	videat			
14	remittet			

2. Identify the subject of each of the pluperfect active subjunctives.

3. Identify the one present active infinitive.

4. Identify the one present active subjunctive.

111. Subjunctive of *sum*

- Just as the subjunctive of *sum* is regular in the imperfect and pluperfect subjunctives, so too are the other irregular verbs that you have learned:

    Possum (a compound of *sum* whose subjunctive forms are compounds of the subjunctive of *sum*) is covered in Chapter 30.

    volō, velle, voluī = vellem, *etc.*; voluissem, *etc.*
    nōlō, nolle, nōluī = nollem, *etc.*; nōluissem, *etc.*
    mālō, malle, māluī = mallem, *etc.*; māluissem, *etc.*
    eō, īre, iī, itūrus = īrem, *etc.*; īvissem, *etc.*
    ferō, ferre, tulī, lātus = ferrem, *etc.*; tulissem, *etc.*

- Note that even though the infinitive forms themselves are irregular, their use informing the imperfect subjunctive is not.

112. Tenses in Independent Uses of the Subjunctive

1. Which tense is more common in independent uses of the subjunctive, present or perfect? imperfect or pluperfect?

113. Tenses in Dependent Uses of the Subjunctive: Sequence of Tenses

1. What are the three types of relative action?
2. What are the two categories for a Latin verb?
3. Which three tenses are the **primary** tenses?
4. Which three tenses are the **secondary** tenses?

- The subjunctive sequence of tenses is generally only necessary for Latin composition. Latin subjunctives will for the most part be translated into English in whatever tense they are in Latin, i.e. the present Latin subjunctive will remain a present in English, the perfect Latin a perfect in English, the imperfect Latin an imperfect or perfect in English (but this overlap is common with the indicative as well) and the pluperfect Latin a pluperfect in English.

Tenses in Dependent Uses of the Subjunctive: Sequence of Tenses Text

Cicero, *In Catilinam* 3.13. Cicero here offers to recall to the Senate their decision about Catiline, since it has not yet been formally published.

Et quoniam nōndum est perscrīptum senātūs cōnsultum,
ex memoriā vōbīs, Quirītēs, quid senātus cēnsuerit
expōnam.

---

1. What is the tense of the main verb of the sentence,
   expōnam?
2. What sequence does *expōnam* signal?
3. What is the subjunctive verb that depends on *expōnam*?
4. What is its tense?

Tenses in Dependent Uses of the Subjunctive: Sequence of Tenses Text

Pliny, *Epistulae* 5.19.3. Pliny writes to his friend about how he
treats his servants. In this excerpt, Pliny praises the intellect of
Zosimus, one of his slaves.

Īdem tam commodē ōrātiōnēs et historiās et carmina
legit, ut hoc sōlum didicisse videātur.

The principal parts of *legit* are *legō, legere, lēgī, lectus.* The
present and perfect indicative, then, look similar.

1. Is *legit,* in the lines above, present or perfect indicative?
2. How does *videātur* act as a clue?

Tenses in Dependent Uses of the Subjunctive: Sequence of Tenses Text

Pliny, *Epistulae* 1.13.3. Pliny is writing of a particularly fruitful
April for poets and poetic recitations. In this excerpt, he relates
an anecdote about the emperor Claudius who, upon hearing that
a certain poet was giving a public reading, rushed over to hear it,
much to the surprise of the poet.

At hercule memoriā parentum Claudium Caesarem
ferunt, cum in Palātiō spatiārētur audīssetque clāmōrem,
causam requīsīsse, cumque dictum esset recitāre
Nōniānum, subitum recitantī inopinatumque vēnisse.

1. Identify two subjunctive verbs in the above excerpt (*dictum esset* is a third subjunctive verb; it is the pluperfect passive which you will learn in the next chapter).
2. Identify the tense of each verb.
3. Based on the tenses of the subjunctive verbs, is it more likely that they will be dependent of *ferunt* or on *requīsīsse*? Explain your answer.

Tenses in Dependent Uses of the Subjunctive: Sequence of Tenses Text

Cicero, *In Catilinam* **3.8.** Cicero, with the help of ambassadors of the Allobroges, a tribe in Gaul, whom Catiline had hoped to enlist in his conspiracy, but who instead reported to the Senate what Catiline had attempted, has exposed Catiline's plot with damningly specific evidence. In this excerpt, Cicero describes the unravelling of the plot: how he sent the praetor to a house to collect a weapons cache and how he brought someone in for questioning who detailed the plot.

Atque intereā statim admonitū Allobrogum C. Sulpicium praetōrem, fortem virum, mīsī, quī ex aedibus Cethēgī, sī quid tēlōrum <u>esset</u>, <u>efferret</u>; ex quibus ille maximum sīcārum numerum et gladiōrum extulit. Intrōdūxī Volturcium sine Gallīs; fidem pūblicam iussū senātūs dedī; hortātus sum, ut ea quae <u>scīret</u> sine timōre <u>indicāret</u>. Tum ille dīxit, cum vix sē ex magnō timōre <u>recreāsset</u>, ā P. Lentulō sē habēre ad Catilīnam mandāta et litterās, ut servōrum praesidiō <u>ūterētur</u>, ut ad urbe quam prīmum cum exercitū <u>accēderet</u>; id autem eō cōnsiliō ut, cum urbem ex omnibus partibus, quem ad modum dīscrīptum distribūtumque erat, <u>incendissent</u> caedemque īnfīnītam cīvium <u>fēcissent</u>, praestō <u>esset</u> ille quī et fugientīs <u>exciperet</u> et sē cum hīs urbānīs ducibus <u>coniungeret</u>.

1. The underlined verbs above are subjunctive. Complete the table below with the requested information about them. In the third column, identify the verb on which the subjunctive (or its clause) depends. In the fourth column, identify which sequence of tense is being used, and in

the fifth the time relationship of the main verb and the subjunctive verb.

Verb	Tense	Verb on which it Depends	Sequence	Time Relationship
esset				
efferret				
scīret				
indicāret				
recreāsset				
ūterētur				
accēderet				
incendissent				
fēcissent				
esset				
exciperet				
coniungeret				

2. Why is *praesidiō* in line 9 in the ablative?

114. Dependent Uses of the Subjunctive

1. What are three common dependent uses of the subjunctive?

2. Which word introduces a positive purpose clause? a negative purpose clause?

3. Which verb form does English often use to express purpose?

4. Which questions does a purpose clause answer?

- "Why?" is a common question for a purpose clause to answer, but you should be careful not to answer that question with "because." Although "because" is of course a viable answer to the question "why," it is not a viable translation for a purpose clause. Purpose clauses and causal clauses are different grammatically. Although they both answer the same question, they answer it in different ways, the causal clause looking to the past cause of an action, the purpose clause looking to the future purpose of an action.

---

5. Which word introduces a positive result clause? a negative result clause?

6. What is the most common English meaning for the signpost words?

7. Which questions does a result clause answer?

8. Which word introduces a positive clause of circumstance, cause, or concession? What word is used in the negative?

9. What does the subjunctive with *cum* indicate?

10. Which tenses of the subjunctive are typically used with *cum* circumstantial?

Purpose Clause Text

Brevard College (NC) Motto.

Cognosce ut prōsīs.

Vocabulary

cognoscō, -ere. to know   prōsum, prōdesse. to be useful

1. Translate the motto.

Purpose Clause Text

Niagara University (NY) Motto.

Ut omnēs tē cognoscant.

1. Translate the motto.

Purpose Clause Text

University of Leicester (UK) Motto.

Ut vītam habeant.

1. Translate the motto.

Purpose Clause Text

Plautus, *Menaechmi* 387. Menaechmus' mistress Erotium is discussing with Sosicles the lunch that she and Menaechmus had arranged. Sosicles of course knows nothing of it and says as much, but Erotium thinks that he's being coy. In this excerpt, she encourages him to join her.

Erotium. Eāmus intrō, ut prandeāmus.
Sosicles. Bene vocās: tam gratiast.

Vocabulary

intrō (*adv.*). inside   **prandeō, -ēre.** to eat lunch

1. What is the mood and tense of *eāmus*?
2. Which independent use of the subjunctive does *eāmus* illustrate?
3. Translate the excerpt.
4. What does Erotium suggest they do? Why?

Purpose Clause Text

Seneca, *Phaedra* 463-465. The Nurse delivers a lengthy speech to Hippolytus in which she expresses concern about his disavowal of women. In this excerpt, she focuses on the hardships men are forced to undergo when they could be experiencing pleasure.

Nutrix. Hoc esse mūnus crēdis indictum virīs,
ut dūra tolerent, cursibus domitent equōs
et saeva bella Marte sanguineō gerant?   465

1. Identify the three subjunctive verbs in the above excerpt.
2. Identify the tense of each.
3. What sequence does the verb *crēdis* in line 463 put the sentence in?
4. What are the two contextual clues that *tolerent* in line 464 is not an imperfect subjunctive?

Purpose Clause Text

Catullus 101.1-4. This is the opening to perhaps Catullus's most famous poem, a lament over the death of his brother. Catullus, at least fictionally, has travelled to Bithynia, modern-day northern Turkey, where his brother died, to mourn at his brother's tomb. It is a tragic elegy whose universality still resonates with those grieving the loss of loved ones today.

Multās per gentēs et multa per aequora vectus
  adveniō hās miserās, frāter, ad īnferiās,
ut tē postrēmō dōnārem mūnere mortis
  et mūtam nequīquam alloquerer cinerem.

---

1. Complete the following translation by translating the words in brackets; translate each purpose clause in two different ways.

   Carried through many peoples and through many seas I arrive at this miserable tomb, brother, _____ [*ut dōnārem; dōnō, -āre* = to give] you your last rights and _____ [*ut alloquerer; alloquor, alloquī* = to address, to speak to] your mute ashes uselessly.

Result Clause Text

Scholiast on Juvenal. 6.117 (Breviarium 308.29).

Messālīna tantae libīdinis fuit, ut sē immūtāret habitū et cum ūnā ancillā descenderet dē Palātiō atque pūblicē in Circō prostāret per noctem.

---

1. What is the word in the main clause that signals the possibility of a result clause?
2. What are the three results of the *tanta libīdinis Messālīnae* (answer with the Latin result clauses)?

Result Clause Text

Cicero, *In Catilinam* 1.32. Cicero has just advocated that not only Catiline be exiled but also all of his co-conspirators. In this excerpt, he describes the results of such comprehensive exile.

Polliceor hoc vōbīs, patrēs cōnscrīptī, tantam in
nōbīs cōnsulibus fore dīligentiam, tantam in vōbīs
auctōritātem, tantam in equitibus Rōmānīs virtūtem,
tantam in omnibus bonīs cōnsēnsiōnem ut Catilīnae
profectiōne omnia patefacta, inlūstrāta, oppressa,
vindicāta esse videātis.

1. Complete the following translation by translating the
    words in brackets.

    I promise you this, conscript fathers, that there will be
    in my advice _____ [*tantam dīligentiam*], in you
    _____ [*tantam auctōritātem*], in Roman equites
    _____ [*tantam virtūtem*], in all good men _____
    [*tantam cōnsēnsiōnem*], _____ [*ut videātis*] that
    everything has been made clear, that everything has
    been brought to light, that everything has been put
    down, and that everything has been punished.

2. Explain how the sequence of tense works with *polliceor* and
    videātis.

Result Clause Text

Cicero, *In Catilinam* 1.16. Cicero here changes his tune toward
Catiline, addressing him not out of hate but rather out of pity,
wondering what life will be left for him.

Nunc vērō quae tua est ista vīta? Sīc enim iam tēcum
loquar, nōn ut odiō permōtus esse videar, quō debeō, sed
ut misericordiā, quae tibi nūlla dēbētur.

1. Identify two markers that indicate that the clause
    beginning with *nōn ut* is a result clause, rather than a
    purpose clause.

2. Complete the following translation by translating the
    words in brackets.

    Now indeed what life is left for you? For at this point
    I will speak to you _____ [*sīc*] _____ [*ut*] _____
    [*videar*] to be influenced not by hatred, with which I
    should be influenced, but _____ [*ut*] _____ [*videar*]
    to be influenced by pity, none of which is owed to you.

Clause of Circumstance, Cause, or Concession Text

Cicero, *Pro Archia* **6.** Cicero here details the process by which Archias obtained citizenship from the Heracleans.

Interim satis longō intervāllō, cum esset cum M. Lūcullō in Siciliam profectus et cum ex eā prōvinciā cum eōdem Lūcullō dēcēderet, vēnit Hēraclēam. Quae cum esset cīvitās aequissimō iūre ac foedere, ascrībī sē in eam cīvitātem voluit idque, cum ipse per sē dignus putārētur, tum auctōritāte et grātiā Lūcullī ab Hēracliēnsibus impetrāvit.

1. Of the three appearances of *cum* in the first line, how many are conjunctions and how many are prepositions? Explain your answer.

2. Using brackets on the text itself, mark out each *cum* clause from beginning to end. Underline the subjunctive verb in each.

CHAPTER 29

The subjunctive forms its passives in the same way that the indicative does, i.e. the present and imperfect passive subjunctives use the same stem as the active but with the passive personal endings, while the perfect and the pluperfect use the perfect passive participle with a corresponding form of sum. Other uses of the subjunctive in dependent clauses are also introduced, as well as the forms of the irreglar verb *fīō*.

115. Present and Imperfect Passive Subjunctive

1. What is the difference between the active and the passive present and imperfect subjunctives?

116. Perfect and Pluperfect Passive Subjunctives

1. What is the difference between the perfect and pluperfect indicatives, and the perfect and pluperfect subjunctives?

117. Dependent Uses of the Subjunctive - Noun Clauses

1. What is the key to identifying how each dependent subjunctive noun clause is used?
2. What are the three noun clauses included here?
3. By what kind of word is an indirect question introduced?
4. What kind of verbs often accomapny an indirect question?
5. What is the exception to the subjunctive sequence of tense that indirect question exhibits?
6. By what is the positive indirect command introduced? the negative?

- The verbs that introduce indirect questions are broad and varied. The term "verb of asking" more reflects the role of the verb as the lead-in to an indirect question, rather than its meaning as "ask" or something similar.

- The most important signal of an indirect question is not so much the "verb of asking," though certain verbs will be obvious lead-ins to an indirect question, but rather the interrogative word that begins an indirect question.

- There are also certain instances when the indirect question substitues for a neuter relative clause, i.e. "I see that which I want" [neuter relative clause] vs. "I see what I want" [indirect question]. Latin will use both of these constructions, the former with a relative pronoun (*quod*) plus an indicative verb, the latter with the interrogative pronoun (*quid*) plus a subjunctive verb. Even though the latter construction is in the form of an indirect question (interrogative word + subjunctive verb), it does not necessarily reflect the strict meaning of an indirect question.

- Each indirect question will be comprised of three fundamental elements:

  verb of asking + interrogative word + subjunctive verb

7. What kind of verbs often accompany an indirect command

8. What three verbs are followed by an infinitive rather than by an indirect command?

9. By what is the positive noun result clause introduced? the negative?

10. How does a noun result clause function?

A Summary of the Three Indirect Constructions

- With this chapter, you have now learned all three indirect constructions: indirect statement (discourse), indirect question, and indirect command.

- It is worth summarizing the different characteristics of each. They can prove confusing, because some have overlapping features in English, and some have overlapping features in Latin.

	Introductory Verb Type	Introductory Latin Word	Mood of Verb	Translation
indirect statement/ discourse	head verb/verb of saying or speaking	[none]	infinitive	that…
indirect question	verb of asking	[interrogative word]	subjunctive	[interrogative word]
indirect command	verb of ordering	*ut/ne*	subjunctive	that…/to…

- In Latin, indirect question and indirect command both use the subjunctive.

- In English, indirect statement and indirect command both are translated with "that…" (although indirect command can also be translated using the English infinitive).

Indirect Question Text

Horace, *Odes* **1.9.1-4.** Horace uses the snowy peak of Mt. Soracte, a mountain in central Italy, to exemplify his *carpe diem* ("sieze the day") philosophy. In this excerpt, Horace describes Mt. Soracte and the imagery of winter and cold that represents the concern and preoccupation that prevents people from living in the now.

Vidēs ut altā stet nive candidum
Sōracte, nec iam sustineant onus
    silvae labōrantēs, gelūque
    flūmina constiterint acūtō.

1. What are the three subjunctive verbs in the indirect question in the above excerpt?
2. What is the "verb of asking" that introduces the indirect question?
3. What is the interrogative word that begins the indirect question?

Indirect Question Text

Martial 1.23. Cotta apparently only culls her dinner guests from the baths. Since Martial has not been invited to dinner, he concludes that he must be unattractive naked, i.e. when he is at the baths.

Invītās nullum nisi cum quō, Cotta, lavāris
    et dant convīvam balnea sōla tibi.
Mīrābar quārē numquam mē, Cotta, vocassēs:
    iam sciō, mē nūdum displicuisse tibi.

Vocabulary

quārē. why	**nūdus, -a, -um.** naked, nude
Cotta, -ae. [*name*]	**displiceō, -ēre.** to be
vocassēs = **vocāvissēs**	displeasing

1. The indirect question is underlined above. Translate it.
2. Line 4 also includes one of the three indirect constructions. Which one? Explain your answer.
3. Translate line 4.

Indirect Question Text

Plautus, *Menaechmi* 879-881. Sosicles, accosted by the wife of Menaechmus and her father, who of course think that he is Menaechmus, scares them off by acting as if he is possessed by the god Apollo. In this excerpt, he asks the audience not to tell them where he's gone, should they return.

Sosicles. Vōs omnīs quaesō, sī senex revēnerit,	879-880
nē mē indicētis quā plateā hinc aufūgerim.	881

Vocabulary

indicō, -āre. to indicate, to show, to reveal

plateā, -ae. road, path

aufūgiō, -ere. to flee, to leave

---

1. Complete the following translation by filling in the parts of the indirect question indicated in brackets.

   I ask all of you, if the old man returns, not _____ [*indicētis*] _____ [*quā plateā*] _____ [*aufūgerim*] from here.

2. What are the tenses of *indicētis* and *aufūgerim*?

3. *Revēnerit* by form can be either indicative or subjunctive. Which is it? Explain your answer.

Indirect Question Text

Horace, *Odes* 1.8. Horace here laments the loss of Sybaris to his love for Lydia; Sybaris no longer participates in wargames.

Lȳdia, dīc, per omnīs	
hoc deōs vērē, Sybarin cūr <u>properēs</u> amandō	
perdere, cūr aprīcum	
<u>ōderit</u> campum, patiens pulveris atque sōlis,	
cūr neque mīlitāris	5
inter aequālis <u>equitet</u>, Gallica nec lupātīs	
<u>temperet</u> ōra frēnīs?	
Cūr <u>timet</u> flāvum Tiberim tangere? Cūr olīvum	
sanguine vīperīnō	
cautius <u>vītat</u> neque iam līvida <u>gestat</u> armīs	10
bracchia, saepe <u>discō</u>,	
saepe trans fīnem iaculō nōbilis expedītō?	
Quid <u>latet</u>, ut marīnae	

filium <u>dīcunt</u> Thetidis sub lacrimōsa Troiae
    fūnera, nē virīlis   15
cultus in caedem et Lyciās <u>prōriperet</u> catervās?

1. All of the indicative and subjunctive verbs in the above
poem are underlined. Use the vocabulary information
in the table below to determine whether the verbs are
indicative or subjunctive, and whether they are used in an
indirect or a direct question.

Line	Form	Principal Parts	Indicative?	Subjunctive?	Tense	Indirect Question?	Direct Question?
2	properēs	properō, -āre, -āvī, -ātus					
4	ōderit	ōdī, odisse					
6	equitet	equitō, -āre,-āvī, -ātus					
7	temperet						
8	timet						
10	vītat						
10	gestat	gestō, -āre					
11	discō						
13	latet	lateō, -ēre, latuī					
14	dīcunt						
16	prōriperet	prōripiō, -ere, -uī, -reptus					

2. What form is *dīc* in line 1? What form is *perdere* in line 3?

Indirect Question Text

Vergil, *Eclogues* **6.31-40.** *Eclogues* 6 is a catalog of allusions to
various mythological stories. In this excerpt, Vergil describes the
physical origins of the earth.

Namque canēbat utī magnum per ināne coacta
sēmina terrārumque animaeque marisque <u>fuissent</u>
et liquidī simul ignis; ut hīs ex omnia prīmīs
omnia et ipse tener mundī <u>concrēverit</u> orbis;
tum dūrāre solum et disclūdere Nērea pontō   35
<u>coeperit</u> et rērum paulatim sūmere formās;
iamque novom terrae <u>stupeant</u> lūcescere sōlem,
altius, atque <u>cadant</u> submōtīs nūbibus imbrēs,
<u>incipiant</u> silvae cum prīmum surgere, cumque
rāra per ignārōs <u>errent</u> animālia montis.   40

All of the underlined verbs above are subjunctive verbs used in an indirect question.

1. Identify the tense of each verb.
2. Identify the interrogative word that introduces each indirect question.
3. Identify the verb of asking that governs each indirect question.

Some subjunctive verbs may share interrogative words and verbs of asking.

Indirect Command Text

Martial 1.46. Martial is trying to avoid Hedylus, the subject of the poem, by being wherever he is not.

Cum dīcis "Properō, fac sī facis," Hēdyle, languet
  prōtinus et cessat dēbilitāta Venus.
Expectāre iubē: vēlōcius ībo retentus.
  Hēdyle, sī properās, dīc mihi, nē properem.

---

1. The sentence with the indirect command in the above poem is underlined. Is the indirect command positive or negative?
2. Identify the introductory verb (verb of commanding) and the subjunctive verb.
3. Finish the translation of line 4 below by translating the verbs in brackets.

    Hedylus, if you hurry, _____ [*dīc*] me _____ [*nē properem*].

4. What form is *dīc* in line 4?

Indirect Command Text

Martial 3.86. Martial criticizes an unnamed woman, apparently prudish, for complaining about the appropriateness of his poetry, despite being warned by Martial not to read it, and then enjoying the sexually charged performances of the mimes Panniculus and Latinus.

Nē legerēs partem lascīvī, casta, libellī,
praedīxī et monuī: tū tamen, ecce, legis.
Sed sī Panniculum spectās et, casta, Latīnum—
nōn sunt haec mīmīs inprobiōra—lege.

---

1. Finish the translation below with the correct translation of the parts of the indirect command included in brackets.

   Chaste girl, _____ [*praedīxī; praedīcō, -ere* = to encourage] and _____ [*monuī*] _____ [*nē legerēs*] part of a salacious little book. Look! You, however, still read it.

2. What is the tense of *praedīxī* and *monuī*? *legerēs*?

3. How could the clause in lines 1-2 be translated as a purpose clause? Why, however, would that make less sense with *praedīxī* and *monuī*?

Indirect Command Text

Ovid, *Metamorphoses* 4.83-90. Pyramus and Thisbe have devised a plan to steal out of the city and meet in the woods at the tomb of a former king. The plan, and their discussing of it, is described in the excerpt below.

Tum murmure parvō
multa prius questī statuunt ut nocte silentī
fallere custōdēs foribusque excēdere temptent,   85
cumque domō exierint, urbis quoque tēcta relinquant;
nēve sit errandum lātō spatiantibus arvō,
conveniant ad busta Ninī lateantque sub umbrā
arboris: arbor ibī niveīs ūberrima pōmīs,
ardua mōrus, erat, gelidō contermina fontī.   90

Vocabulary

temptō, -āre. to try
exeō, -īre. to leave, to exit
relinquō, -ere. to leave behind, to abandon

conveniō, -īre. to meet, to come together
lateō, -ēre. to hide, to lie hidden

The single sentence above is of a complex structure. Its main verb is *statuunt* (line 84): "they decided..." There are four verbs in an indirect command dependent on *statuunt*. There are two other subjunctive verbs in subordinate clauses (not indirect commands, lines 86-87), as well as two infinitives in line 85.

1. What are the four subjunctive verbs of the indirect command?

2. Translate each of the four verbs in the indirect command with *statuunt*, i.e. "they decided…," "they decided…," etc.

3. What is the one subjunctive verb in a *cum* clause?

4. What is the one subjunctive verb in a purpose clause?

5. With what verb are the two infinitives in line 85 translated?

Indirect Command Text

Livy, *Ab urbe condita* 1.13.1-2. The earliest residents at Rome were, according to legend, brigands and criminals who arrived at Rome as outlaws. Because they were all men, they needed women with whom to procreate; they went to their neighbors to ask for their daughters' hands, but were promptly rejected. Instead, they hosted a religious festival for the neighboring tribes. At a set signal, each Roman carried off a Sabine woman as his wife. The Sabine men, understandably, attacked Rome to recover their daughters. Ultimately, however, the women themselves, unwilling to watch their fathers and brothers and even their new husbands die, intervened to end the fighting. Their intervention is described in the excerpt below.

Tum Sabīnae mulieres, quārum ex iniūriā bellum ortum erat, crīnibus passīs scissāque veste, victō malīs muliebrī pavōre, ausae sē inter tēla volantia inferre, ex transversō impetū factō dirimere infestās aciēs, dirimere īrās, hinc patrēs, hinc virōs ōrantēs, nē sanguine sē nefandō socerī generīque respergerent, nē parricīdiō maculārent partūs suōs, nepōtum illī, hī līberum prōgeniem.

---

1. The indirect command of the excerpt occurs in line 3. What is the verb of ordering that introduces it? And is it a positive or negative indirect command? Explain your answer.

2. What form is *ōrantēs* in line 3?

3. What are the two subjunctive verbs in the indirect command? What tense are they?

Indirect Command Text

CIL I 1210. Roman epitaphs, of which the next two texts are examples, tended to be formulaic: the tomb was often personified and would often address the passerby, asking him to stop and hear the story of the tomb. On the other hand, the personified tomb, after communicating its story to the passerby, often abruptly ends the "conversation" by telling the passerby that it is finished speaking and that the passerby should continue on his way.

Rogat ut resistas, hospes, tē hic tacitus lapis,
dum ostendit quod mandāvit, quoius umbram tegit.
Pudentis hominis frūgī cum magnā fidē,
praecōnis Olī Granī sunt ossa heic sita.
Tantum est. Hoc voluit nescius nē essēs. Valē.

Vocabulary

resistō, -ere. to stop
hospes, hospitis (*m/f*). guest, passerby

tacitus, -a, -um. quiet, mute
lapis, lapidis (*m.*). stone

1. Translate the first line.
2. Why is the subject not initially apparent? Identify two things that might make it difficult to identify the subject.
3. In lines 2 and 4, colloquial spellings occur. Can you tell which words are spelled irregularly and what they would be in their more conventional spelling?

Indirect Command Text

CIL VIII 9691.

Mī filī, māter rogat, ut mē ad tē recipiās.

Vocabulary

mī = *vocative singular of* **meus, -a, -um**
filī = *vocative singular of* **filius, -ī**
recipiō, -ere. to take away, to remove

1. Translate the epitaph in two different ways.

Noun Clauses Text

Pliny, *Epistulae* **9.23.1.** Pliny in this letter describes how happy he is to learn that his name is being used in the same context of fame as that of the historian Tacitus. In this excerpt, he describes how often he receives praise for his work as a lawyer. He will use this description to contrast against how much more pride he feels at being mentioned alongside Tacitus.

Frequenter agentī mihi ēvēnit, ut centumvirī, cum diū sē intrā iūdicum auctōritātem gravitātemque tenuissent, omnēs repente quasi victī coāctīque cōnsurgerent laudārentque;

1. What is the verb that introduces the noun clause?
2. What are the three subjunctive verbs in the noun clause? What is the tense of each?

Noun Clauses Text

Catullus 109. Catullus in this poem expresses hope, but by implication also doubt, that Lesbia's promises of eternal love and devotion will prove reliable.

Iucundum, mea vīta, mihi prōpōnis amōrem
    hunc nostrum inter nos perpetuumque fore.
Dī magnī, facite ut vērē prōmittere possit,
    atque id sincērē dīcat et ex animō,
ut liceat nōbīs tōtā perdūcere vītā
    aeternum hoc sanctae foedus amīcitiae.

1. What is the verb that introduces the noun clause?
2. What are the three subjunctive verbs in the noun clause? What is the tense of each?
3. Finish the translation below with the correct translation of the Latin words in brackets.

> Great gods, _____ [*facite ut*] she _____ [*possit*] to promise this truly and _____ [*ut*] she _____ [*dīcat*] sincerely and from the heart, and _____ [*ut*] _____ [*licet, licēre, licuit* = "it is permitted"] to us to spend our whole life in this eternal bond of sacred union.

Noun Clauses Text

Ovid, *Metamorphoses* 10.50-52. The poet-hero Orpheus, after his wife Eurydice is abruptly killed soon after they are married, travels to the underworld to recover her. He charms Hades and Persephone with his music and they release Eurydice to him, with one condition. Orpheus's acceptance of Eurydice and this condition are described in the excerpt below.

Hanc simul et lēgem Rhodopēius accipit hērōs,   50
nē flectat retrō sua lūmina, dōnec Avernās
exierit vallēs; aut irrita dōna futūra.

The excerpt above contains a noun clause that is not a noun clause of result as described in the book. Rather, the noun clause here functions as an appositive to a noun, i.e. the noun clause expands upon the meaning of a noun.

1. The first line of the excerpt is the main clause: "The Rhodopeian hero accepted her [Eurydice] at the same time as he accepted a stipulation." What then does the noun clause that begins with *nē* in line 51 explain or expand upon? What information does it provide?

118. Forms of *fīō, fierī, factus*

1. What conjugation does *fīō* in general look like?
2. What are the exceptions to this? What conjugation does it look like in these exceptions?
3. What is it used as? What verb's passive forms is it used as?

The subjunctive forms of *possum* are introduced as are two further dependent uses of the subjunctive: fearing clauses and conditionals.

Terms to Know

clause of fearing
verb of fearing
conditional sentence
simple condition
subjunctive condition
protasis
apodosis

119. Subjunctive of *possum*

1. How is the present subjunctive of *possum* formed?

2. How are the rest of the subjunctive forms of *possum* formed?

Subjunctive of *possum* Exercises

- Identify the mood, tense, and subject of the forms of *possum*.

1.	possit	6.	poterunt
2.	poterat	7.	putuerint
3.	possint	8.	possent
4.	potuissēmus	9.	potuerāmus
5.	potuerim	10.	possem

120. Clauses of Fearing

1. What kind of verbs do fearing clauses follow?

2. With what words are fearing clauses introduced?

3. What is unexpected about how *nē* and *ut* will work with fearing clauses?

4. What sometimes replaces *ut*? Under what condition does this always happen?

Clauses of Fearing Text

Pliny, *Epistulae* 9.23.6. Pliny in this letter describes how happy he is to learn that his name is being used in the same context of fame as that of the historian Tacitus. Pliny has just defended his desire for fame, and in this excerpt, the conclusion to the letter, he defends his bragging about his fame to his recipient, both because it is inherently not wrong and because he knows his recipient will read it in the appropriate spirit.

Neque enim vereor nē iactantior videar, cum dē mē
aliōrum iūdicium nōn meum prōferō, praesertim apud tē
quī nec ullīus invidēs laudibus et favēs nostrīs. Valē.

---

1. Identify the verb of fearing that introduces the fearing
   clause in the above excerpt.
2. Identify the beginning and end of the fearing clause.

Clauses of Fearing Text

Ovid, *Metamorphoses* **10.256-258.** In this excerpt, Ovid describes
how Pygmalion lovingly interacts with his statue of the ultimate
woman; he treats her as if she is exceedingly delicate.

Ōscula dat, reddīque putat. Loquiturque, tenetque
et crēdit tāctīs digitōs īnsīdere membrīs:
et metuit, pressōs veniat nē līvor in artūs.

---

1. Identify the verb of fearing that governs the fearing clause.
2. Identify the subjunctive verb in the fearing clause.
3. Identify the full fearing clause with its first and last words.

Clauses of Fearing Text

Plautus, *Menaechmi* **266-267.** Messenio and Sosicles have just
been arguing about the cost, both physical and financial, of
Sosicles' quest to find his long-lost twin. Sosicles has just asked
Messenio for the money bag, which Messenio had told him was
almost empty. In this excerpt, Messenio wants to know why
Sosicles wants it, and Sosicles responds that he doesn't trust
Messenio to spend the little money they have wisely; he's afraid
that Messenio will squander it on women and drink.

Messenio. Quid eō vīs? **Sosicles.** Iam aps tē metuō dē verbīs tuīs.
Messenio. Quid metuis? **Sosicles.** Nē mihi damnum in Epidamnō duis.

---

1. There are two instances of a verb of fearing in the above
   excerpt. Only one of them is used with a fearing clause.
2. The form *duis* in line 267 is an archaic form of the
   subjunctive of *dō, dare*.

3. What is that verb of fearing?

4. What is the fearing clause?

5. How is the act of fearing expressed in the sentence without a fearing clause?

Clauses of Fearing Text

Plautus, *Menaechmi* **420-421.** Erotium, the mistress of Menaechmus, has just been inviting Sosicles in to the lunch he was promised; she of course thinks that Sosicles is Menaechmus. Sosicles, at first confused, eventually relents, just for the meal. In this excerpt, Sosicles is now explaining to Erotium why he was acting so strangely: so that his slave wouldn't tell his wife where he was or what was going on.

Sosicles. Hunc metuēbam, nē meae   420
uxōrī renuntiāret dē pallā et dē prandiō.

Vocabulary

renuntiō, -āre. to report   **prandium, -ī.** lunch
palla, -ae. cloak, dress

1. Translate the above excerpt.

121. Conditions

1. What are the two components to a conditional?

2. What are the two types of Latin conditionals?

3. How do tenses of the indicative in a simple condition generally work?

4. What are the two things that subjunctive conditions imply about their situation?

5. How do tenses of the subjunctive in a subjunctive condition generally work?

6. What are the four words after which the *ali-* of *aliquis, aliquid* drops away?

Conditions Text

Plautus, *Menaechmi* **238-241.** In the following excerpt, Messenio, the servant of Sosicles, is complaining about how difficult it is to find someone who may not even exist.

Messenio. Sī acum, crēdō, quaererēs,
acum invēnissēs, sī appārēret, iam diū.
Hominem inter vīvōs quaeritāmus mortuom: 240
nam invēnissēmus iam diū, si vīveret.

---

1. List the five subjunctive verbs in the passage.
2. List the one indicative verb in the passage.
3. Complete the following translation by translating the
   words in brackets.

   > I think, _____ [*sī*] _____ [*quaererēs*] a needle,
   > _____ [*invenissēs*] a needle,_____ [*sī*] _____
   > [*appārērent; appareō, -ēre* = to be visible, to be
   > apparent], a long time ago. We keep looking for a dead
   > man among the living; for _____ [*invēnissēmus*] him
   > a long time ago, _____ [*sī*] _____ [*vīveret*].

The final conditional, in line 241, is reversed, with the protasis
following the apodosis instead of the more customary other
way around.

The -*om* ending on *mortuom* in line 240 is an archaic form of
the more common -*um* ending.

Conditions Text

Plautus, *Miles Gloriosus* 718-722. Periplectomenus, the kindly
old man trying to reunite Philocomasium and Pleusicles, has been
discussing with Pleusicles why he never had any children. In this
excerpt, he describes how he would worry about any children he
might have had.

Periplectomenus. Pol sī habuissem, satis cēpissem miseriārum ē līberīs:
continuō excruciārer animī: sī forte eī fuisset febris,   719-720
censerem ēmorī; cecidissetve ēbrius aut dē equō uspiam,   721
metuerem nē ibi diffrēgisset crūra aut cervīcēs sibi.

---

1. Fill in the table with the requested information.
2. Write all personal verb forms in the column at left.

Verb Form	Mood	Tense	Type of Conditional

3. Circle the verbs used in the protasis, and underline the verbs used in the apodasis.

Conditions Text

Cicero, *In Catilinam* 1.17. Cicero is trying to convince Catiline to leave the city. In this excerpt, he posits how, if he were as reviled as Catiline, he would choose to leave quite willingly.

Et sī mē meīs cīvibus iniūriā suspectum tam graviter atque offēnsum <u>vidērem</u>, carēre mē aspectū cīvium quam īnfestīs omnium oculīs cōnspicī <u>māllem</u>; tū, cum cōnscientiā scelerum tuorum <u>agnōscās</u> odium omnium iūstum et iam diū tibi dēbitum, dubitās quōrum mentīs sēnsūsque volnerās, eōrum aspectum praesentiamque vītāre? Sī tē parentēs <u>timērent</u> atque <u>ōdissent</u> tuī neque eōs ratiōne ūllā placāre <u>possēs</u>, ut opīnor, ab eōrum oculīs aliquo <u>concēderēs</u>.

1. Complete the table below with the requested information. All verbs underlined in the excerpt above are subjunctives. In the far right column, place a check if the verb is used in a conditional; leave it blank if the verb is not used in a conditional.

Verb	Tense	Used in Conditional?
vidērem		
māllem		
agnōscās		
timērent		
ōdissent		
possēs		
concēderēs		

Conditions Text

Vergil, *Aeneid* **4.311-313.** Dido accosts Aeneas when she finds out that he is leaving her. In this excerpt, she wonders about her life if Aeneas had never arrived in Carthage.

> Quid? Sī nōn arva aliēna domōsque
> ignōtās peterēs, et Trōia antīqua manēret,
> Trōia per undōsum peterētur classibus aequor?
> Mēne fugis?

Vocabulary

arvum, -ī. field, land
peterēs. [the "you" is Aeneas]
manēret. [*here,* with the sense of "to still exist"]
classis, -is. fleet [of ships; *here,* referring to the Greek fleet that attacked Troy]

The condition begins with an abbreviated apodasis: the *quid* of line 311 means "what would happen…" with the thought finished by the protasis introduced by *sī*.

1. Without translating the passage literally, answer the following question: What are the three hypotheticals that Dido posits (to this end, only key vocabulary, instead of every word, has been provided above)?

Conditions Text

Vergil, *Aeneid* **4.340-344.** The excerpt below is from Aeneas' response to Dido whom he will leave and who will ultimately commit suicide in her grief. Aeneas here is responding to her accusatory speech, trying to placate her by saying that he too wishes he could have stayed in Troy and never arrived in Carthage.

> Mē sī fāta meīs paterentur dūcere vītam   340
> auspiciīs, et sponte meā compōnere cūras,
> urbem Trōiānam prīmum dulcesque meōrum
> rēliquiās colerem, Priamī tēcta alta manērent,
> et recidīva manū posuissem Pergama victīs.

1. There are four subjunctive verbs in the above excerpt; three of them are the same tense. List them and their tenses.

2. Finish the translation below by translating the verbs used in conditionals; note that the last verb is a different tense from the others. Make sure that your translation reflects this difference.

> _____ [*sī*] the Fates _____ [*paterentur; pateō, -ēre* = to allow] me to live my life the way I wanted to, and to handle my situation on my own, I _____ [*colerem*] the Trojan city first and the sweet ashes of my ancestors; the tall roofs of Priam _____ [*manērent*], and with my own hand _____ [*posuissem; pōnō, -ere* = to establish] rebuilt Troy for the conquered Trojans.

Conditions Text

Cicero, *Pro Archia* 1. The excerpt below is the opening to Cicero's *Pro Archia*, which Cicero opens with a tribute, excerpted below, to his own teacher. He humbly attributes any skill he might possess to his training, establishing the parameters within which he will defend the importance of Archias' skills as a poet for Rome.

Sī quid est in mē ingenī, iūdicēs, quod sentiō quam sit exiguum, aut sī qua exercitātiō dīcendī, in quā mē nōn īnfitior mediocriter esse versātum, aut sī huiusce reī ratiō aliqua ab optimārum artium studiīs ac disciplīnā profecta, ā quā ego nūllum cōnfiteor aetātis meae tempus abhorruisse, eārum rērum omnium vel in prīmīs hic A. Licinius frūctum ā mē repetere prope suō iūre dēbet.

5

1. There are four "q-" words in the above passage: *quid* in line 1, *quod* in line 1, *qua* in line 2, *quā* in line 2, and *quā* in line 5. Which of these are shortened forms of *aliquis, aliquid*? Explain your answer.

Conditions Text

Catullus 92. Catullus, as he does elsewhere (e.g. poem 83), reveals the often contradictory nature of his relationship with Lesbia. On the one hand, he says that he needs Lesbia's love to survive. On the other hand, he says that he needs to love Lesbia to survive. Such an emotional quandary in many ways epitomizes the poetic position of the elegiac poet.

Lesbia mī dīcit semper mala, nec tacet unquam
    dē mē: Lesbia mē dispeream nisi amat.
Quō signō? Quia sunt totidem mea: dēprecor illam
    assiduē, vērum dispeream nisi amō.

---

1. There are two conditionals in the above poem. What is the introductory word for both of these conditionals?
2. Choose the best translation for line 2 (*Lesbia…amat*) from the following choices.
   a. Let me die if Lesbia does not love me.
   b. I will die if Lesbia does not love me.
   c. I will die if Lesbia should not love me.
   d. Lesbia loves me if I should not die.
3. Is *dispeream* or *amat* the verb in this conditional? Explain your answer.

Conditions Text

Cicero, *In Catilinam* **1.12.** Cicero is trying to convince Catiline to leave the city. In this excerpt, he posits how Catiline's co-conspirators would react if Catiline were killed.

Nam <u>sī tē interficī iusserō</u>, residēbit in rē pūblicā reliqua coniūrātōrum manus; sīn tū, quod tē iam dūdum hortor, exieris, exhauriētur ex urbe tuōrum comitum magna et perniciōsa sentīna reī pūblicae.

The conditional is underlined above.

1. Is *iusserō* indicative or subjunctive? Explain your answer.
2. In the previous chapter, the verbs that introduced indirect commands were discussed on page 236 of your textbook. Three verbs that do not use indirect commands but rather use the infinitive were mentioned, one of which is used here with an infinitive.

CHAPTER 31

The gerund represents the final commonly used aspect of verbs to be learned. It is a verbal noun that, unlike the infinitive, which is also a verbal noun but an uninflected verbal noun, will use noun endings to change case. The Latin future passive participle, the final form of the participle to be learned, will both look like and be used in ways similar to the gerund.

> **Terms to Know**
>
> gerund
> participle
> gerundive
> passive periphrastic

122. Gerund

1. What is a gerund?
2. What is its gender and number?
3. With what other form in English can the gerund be confused?
4. What are the two letters that signal the gerund?
5. What stem is used to form the gerund?
6. What endings are used for the gerund?
7. What is the gerund never used for?
8. What form is used instead?
9. What case of the gerund is very rare?
10. What are the three uses of the gerund in the genitive case?
11. The one in the dative case?
12. The one in the accusative case?
13. The two in the ablative case?
14. What are the two ways that the gerund can express purpose?

Gerund Text

The State of New Mexico Motto

Crescit eundō.

---

1. Translate the motto. (The subject of *crescit* is indefinite: "one.")

Gerund Text

Ovid, *Metamorphoses* **10.56-59.** Hades and Persephone, the king and queen of the underworld, gave Orpheus one condition for bringing back to earth his recently deceased wife Eurydice: that he not look back at her until they are out of the underworld. This excerpt describes Orpheus' fatal turning around to see Eurydice just before their exit from the underworld, and the immediate consequences of his folly.

hīc nē dēficeret metuēns, avidusque videndī,
flexit amāns oculōs; et prōtinus illa relāpsa est,
bracchiaque intendēns prēndīque et prēndere certāns
nīl nisi cēdentēs īnfēlīx arripit aurās.

1. There are two *-nd-* forms in the above excpert: *videndī* in line 56 and *prēndī* in line 58. One is a gerund and one is not. What form is the non-gerund (it is not a gerundive, which is covered in the next section and which uses the same *-nd-* that the gerund uses with similar endings)? Explain your answer.
2. What case is the gerund in?
3. Of the uses of the gerund listed in your textbook, which is illustrated here?
4. What kind of clause is *nē dēficeret* in line 56? Explain your answer.

Gerund Text

Pliny, *Epistulae* **1.13.1-2.** Pliny is writing of a particularly fruitful April for poets and poetic recitations. In this excerpt, which opens the letter, he describes the pleasant combination of spring and poetry.

Iuvat mē quod vigent studia, prōferunt sē ingenia hominum et ostentant, tametsī ad audiendum pigrē coitur. Plērīque in statiōnibus sedent tempusque audiendī fābulīs conterunt ac subinde sibi nūntiārī iubent, an iam recitātor intrāverit, an dīxerit praefātiōnem, an ex magnā parte ēvoluerit librum:

1. What are the two gerunds in the above passage?
2. What is their case?
3. How is each being used?

Gerund Text

Livy, *Ab urbe condita* 1.15.1. As the young Rome expanded, its neighbors worried about its growing military power. The Veientes, one of these neighbors, accordingly sent a raiding party into Roman territory to at least announce their willingness to fight. In this excerpt, the goal and method of the raiding party are described.

In fīnēs Rōmānōs excucurrerunt populābundī magis quam iustī mōre bellī.

1. Identify the gerund in the above excerpt.
2. Identify its case. Why is it not nominative?

Gerund Exercises

Circle the letter of the correct gerund form.

1. probō, -āre: *dative singular*
   a. probandī   b. probandō   c. probāre   d. probandum

2. probō, -āre: *nominative singular*
   a. probandī   b. probandō   c. probāre   d. probandum

3. probō, -āre: *ablative singular*
   a. probandī   b. probandō   c. probāre   d. probandum

4. committō, -ere: *genitive singular*
   a. committere   b. committendō   c. committere   d. commitendī

5. committō, -ere: *accusative singular*
   a. committere   b. committendō   c. committere   d. commitendī

6. committō, -ere: *ablative singular*
   a. committere   b. committendō   c. committere   d. commitendī

7. conveniō, -īre: *accusative singular*
   a. conveniendī   b. conveniendō   c. convenenīre   d. conveniendum

8. conveniō, -īre: *genitive singular*
   a. conveniendī   b. conveniendō   c. convenenīre   d. conveniendum

9. conveniō, -īre: *nominative singular*
   a. conveniendī   b. conveniendō   c. convenenīre   d. conveniendum

123. Gerundive

1. What is another name for the gerundive?
2. What does the gerundive look like?
3. What is the difference between the gerund and the gerundive?
4. What endings does the gerundive use?
5. What are the two main uses of the gerundive in Latin?
6. When is the gerundive used to replace the gerund?

Gerund and Gerundive Confusion

- The gerund and gerundive are commonly confused, in form, usage, and translation.

- The term "gerundive" itself often proves confusing; students tend to forget that there is a distinction between the two terms, and that they are not synonymous terms, despite their affinity.

- Remember that, although the terms look very similar, they refer to very different grammatical forms.

- The term "gerundive" strictly applies only to the second use listed on page 256 of your textbook: it refers to when the future passive participle is acting like a gerund, i.e. it is a gerund-ive.

- The future passive participle, when used in the passive periphrastic (below) or as a simple participle, is not functioning like a gerund, and so should not necessarily be called the gerundive.

- I recommend avoiding the term "gerundive" because of the (potentially unnecessary) confusion it causes with the gerund, but your instructor will have his/her own preference.

- From a purely grammatical standpoint, the gerundive, because it is a verbal adjective, must agree with a noun, and the gerund, because it is a verbal noun, cannot agree with a noun and will stand alone (I don't know of any instance of the gerund being modified by an adjective).

- There exists further confusion with the gerund and gerundive because of different overlapping forms in Latin and English.

- In Latin, the gerund and the gerundive both use the *-nd-* tense sign. In English, the gerund and the present active participle both use the *-ing* ending.

- The overlap in English of the gerund and present active participle tends to cause more difficulty when translating the present active participle used as a substantive, i.e. when a present active participle is not agreeing with any visible noun.

- Consider the following sentence fragment from Petronius' *Matron of Ephesus* (a story told within his *Satyricon*): *et [cum] gemitum lūgentis audisset.* Choose the correct translation from among the following choices.

  - and when he had heard the groan of mourning
  - and when he had heard the groan of the mourning woman
  - and when he had heard the mourning groan

  Explain your answer.

- Is *lūgentis* a gerund or a present active participle? Explain your answer.

- The table below summarizes the double overlap of the gerund, gerundive, and present active participle.

	Latin	English
Present Active Participle	-ns, -ntis	-ing
Gerund	-nd-	-ing
Gerundive	-nd-	about to be / must be

Gerundive Text

Cicero, *Pro Archia* 1. The excerpt below comes from the opening to Cicero's *Pro Archia*, in which Cicero offers a tribute to his own teacher. In the excerpt below he recalls how pleasant his youth was, spent with his studies.

Nam quoad longissimē potest mēns mea respicere spatium praeteritī temporis et pueritiae memoriam recordārī ultimam, inde usque repetēns hunc videō mihi prīncipem et ad suscipiendam et ad ingrediendam ratiōnem hōrum studiōrum exstitisse.

---

1. What are the two gerundives in the above passage?
2. What is their case, number, and gender? What do they modify?
3. What use of the gerundive is illustrated?

Gerundive Text

Livy, *Ab urbe condita* 1.15.6. As the young Rome expanded, its neighbors worried about its growing military power. The Veientes, one of these neighbors, accordingly sent a raiding party into Roman territory to at least announce their willingness to fight. The Romans responded with invasion, and easily conquered the Veientes. In this excerpt, Livy summarizes the rule of Rome's first king Romulus, focusing on his military achievements and the divinity that attended his reign.

Haec fermē, Rōmulō <u>regnante</u>, domī mīlitiaeque <u>gesta</u>, quōrum nihil absonum fideī dīvīnae orīginis dīvīnitātisque post mortem <u>crēditae</u> fuit, nōn animus in regnō avītō <u>reciperandō</u>, nōn <u>condendae</u> urbis consilium, nōn bellō ac pāce <u>firmandae</u>.

The underlined words in the above excerpt are participles.

1. Fill in the table below with the correct information.

Participle Form	Participle Tense	Participle Voice	Participle Case	Participle Modifies?
regnante				
gesta				
crēditae				
reciperandō				
condendae				
firmandae				

Gerundive Text

Cicero, *Pro Archia* 14. Cicero in this excerpt describes the benefit of his study of literature for his own civic life, how literature taught him not only the importance of honor and virtue but also the necessity of sacrificing oneself to achieve honor and virtue. He concludes by alluding to specific examples of when he risked his own life for the sake of Rome and the Senate.

Nam nisi multōrum praeceptīs multīsque litterīs mihi ab adulēscentiā <u>suāsissem</u> nihil <u>esse</u> in vitā magnō opere <u>expetendum</u> nisi laudem atque honestātem, in eā autem <u>persequendā</u> omnīs <u>cruciātūs</u> corporis, omnia perīcula mortis atque exsilī parvī esse <u>dūcenda</u>, numquam mē prō

salūte vestrā in tot ac tantās dīmicātiōnēs atque in hōs
prōflīgātōrum hominum cotīdiānōs impetūs <u>obiēcissem</u>.

The verb forms in the above excerpt are underlined. They
comprise various moods.

1. Fill in the chart below with the requested information.

Verb Form	Mood	Tense	Voice	Subject *or* Modifies
suāsissem				
esse				
expetendum				
persequendā				
dūcenda				
obiēcissem				

Gerundive Text

Plautus, *Miles Gloriosus* **79-80.** Palaestrio, the former slave of
Pleusicles and now the slave of the Miles Gloriosus, in this excerpt
asks the audience to please listen to the prefatory speech he is about
to give to introduce the play and its backstory.

Palaestrio. Mihi ad ēnarrandum hoc argūmentumst cōmitās,
sī ad auscultandum vostra erit benignitās;   80

Vocabulary

ēnarrō, -āre. to narrate, to speak
auscultō, -āre. to listen, to hear

---

1. What are the two gerundives in the above excerpt?
2. What do they modify?
3. How are they used?
4. Finish the translation below by translating the gerundives
   in parentheses.

   It is a pleasure to me _____ [*ad ēnarrandum*] this
   introduction, if it will be your pleasure _____ [*ad
   auscultandum*].

Gerundive Text

Ovid, *Amores* **1.5.1-2.** In the opening to this poem, Ovid describes a scene with which we are all familiar: a hot summer day resting on his bed. The rest of the poem, however, takes a sultry turn: his love Corinna enters (named in this poem for the first time in the *Amores*) and they spend, shall we say, an enjoyable afternoon together.

Aestus erat, mediamque diēs exēgerat hōram;
    Adposuī mediō membra levanda torō.

Vocabulary

aestus, -ūs. summer
exagō, -ēre, exēgī, exactus. to pass [with *diēs*]
appōnō, -ere. to put on, to place on

membrum, -ī. limb (of the body)
levō, -āre. to lighten, to take a load off
torus, -ī. bed, sofa

1. What is the gerundive in the above excerpt?
2. What does it modify?
3. Translate the excerpt.

Gerundive Text

Ovid, *Amores* **1.9.11-14.** Ovid's *Amores* 1.9 is an extended poetic examination of the similarities between lovers and soldiers. In these two couplets, Ovid describes how both will battle the elements to accomplish their goals.

Ībit in adversōs montēs <u>duplicāta</u>que nimbō
    flūmina, congestās exteret ille nivēs,
nec freta <u>pressūrus</u> tumidōs causābitur Eurōs
    aptaque <u>verrendīs</u> sīdera quaeret aquīs.

1. Identify the tense, voice, and case of the underlined participles.
2. Identify which noun each participle modifies. (Because you do not have vocabulary information, use sentence structure and endings to help.)

Gerundive Text

Pliny, *Epistulae* 7.20.1. Pliny here writes to the historian Tacitus about his histories. Pliny has read them and has noted his changes.

Librum tuum lēgī et, quam dīligentissime potuī, adnotāvī, quae commūtanda, quae eximenda arbitrārer.

Vocabulary

dīligens, -ntis. careful, diligent
adnotō, -āre. to note, to notate

commūtō, -āre. to change
eximō, -ere. to remove, to expunge

1. Translate the excerpt.

Gerundive Text

Pliny, *Epistulae* 10.97. In this letter, the emperor Trajan responds to Pliny's letter to him about how to handle the Christians in his province of Bithynia-Pontus. Trajan here responds that Pliny has acted appropriately, that he should only persecute those Christians that have been brought to his attention and not go hunting for them.

Āctum quem dēbuistī, mī Secunde, in <u>excutiendīs</u> causīs eōrum quī Chrīstiānī ad tē dēlātī fuerant secūtus es. Neque enim in ūniversum aliquid quod quasi certam fōrmam habeat, cōnstituī potest. <u>Conquīrendī</u> nōn sunt; sī dēferantur et arguantur, <u>pūniendī</u> sunt, ita tamen ut quī negāverit sē Chrīstiānum esse idque rē ipsā manifēstum fēcerit, id est <u>supplicandō</u> dīs nostrīs, quamvīs suspectus in praeteritum, veniam ex paenitentiā impetret. Sine auctōre vērō prōpositī libellī <in> nūllō crīmine locum habēre dēbent. Nam et pessimī exemplī nec nostrī saeculī est.

The underlined forms in the excerpt above are either gerunds or gerundives.

1. Identify all possible cases, numbers, and genders based on the endings.

2. Identify which one of the four must be a gerundive. Explain your answer.

3. Identify whether each of the other three is a gerund or a gerundive based on endings and context. Explain your answer.

Gerundive Text

Aulus Gellius, *Noctes Atticae* **14.5.1.** An interesting excerpt for Latin students: it describes a debate that two grammar teachers are having about the correct form of the vocative case of the adjective *ēgregius, -a, -um*.

Dēfessus ego quondam diūtinā commentātiōne laxandī levandīque animī grātiā in Agrippae campō deambulābam. Atque ibi duōs forte grammaticōs cōnspicātus nōn parvī in urbe Rōmā nōminis, certātiōnī eōrum ācerrimae adfuī, cum alter in cāsū vocātīvō "vir ēgregī" dīcendum contenderet, alter "vir ēgregie."

1. Complete the translation below with the correct translation of the gerundive or gerundive phrase in brackets (*dīcō, -ere* below means here "to use" in the sense of "to use when speaking").

    I, tired, was once walking for my daily reflection in the Campus Agrippa _____ [*laxandī levandīque animī grātiā; laxō, -āre* = to relax; *levō, -āre* = to ease]. And I, having spotted by chance two grammar teachers of not a slight reputation in Rome, was present at a very bitter debate they were having, since one contended that "*vir ēgregī*" _____ [*dīcendum*] in the vocative case, and the other that "*vir egregie*" _____ [*dīcendum*] in the vocative case.

2. Why does the form of *ēgregius, -a, -um* prove troublesome when forming its vocative? Can you think of any other Latin nouns or adjectives that would pose a similar problem?

Gerundive Text

Aulus Gellius, *Noctes Atticae* **17.9.3.** Gellius here provides a brief history of encoded writing. In this excerpt, he describes how Caesar used a system of transposed letters to encode his writing. In the paragraph that follows this, he describes how a Carthaginian, who may have been Hannibal's brother, hid his writing under the wax of a wax tablet: he would etch his message into the wood of the tablet itself, and then cover the wood with wax. The recipient would then remove the wax and read the message underneath.

Erat autem conventum inter eōs clandestīnum de commūtandō sitū littērarum, ut in scrīptō quidem alia aliae locum et nōmen tenēret, sed in legendō locus cuique suus et potestās restituerētur;

1. Identify the two gerund/gerundive forms in the above excerpt.
2. Identify whether they are gerunds or gerundives. Explain your answer.

Gerundive Text

Pliny, *Epistulae* **2.17.8.** Pliny here describes a bookshelf and the books that it holds.

Parietī eius in bibliothēcae speciem armārium īnsertum est, quod nōn legendōs librōs, sed lēctitandōs capit.

1. Finish the translation below by translating the gerundives in brackets.

    …the bookshelf which holds books _____ [*nōn legendōs*] but (books) _____ [*lēctitandōs; lēctitō, -āre* = to recite, to read out loud].

Gerund and Gerundive Text

Aulus Gellius, *Noctes Atticae* **4.10.8.** Gellius here relates the story of an ancient filibuster when, to prevent a law from being passed and taking advantage of a provision that allowed a senator to speak on any matter for any length of time prior to addressing the motion on the senate floor, Cato (not mentioned in this excerpt) began to speak at length to stall the proceedings.

Eius reī dūcendae grātiā longā ōrātiōne ūtēbātur eximēbatque dīcendō diem.

1. What is the gerundive in the above excerpt? the gerund?
2. How can you tell the difference between them?
3. What is the case of each?
4. How is the the gerundive being used? the gerund?

Gerund and Gerundive Text

Pliny, *Epistulae* **1.13.5.** Pliny is writing of a particularly fruitful April for poets and poetic recitations. In this excerpt, Pliny writes of encouraging poets to write; the more support they receive, the more they will write and recite, and the more such Aprils will continue to happen.

Sed tantō magis laudandī probandīque sunt, quōs ā scrībendī recitandīque studiō haec audītōrum vel dēsidia vel superbia nōn retardat.

1. Identify the four gerund/gerundive forms in the above excerpt.
2. All of them have the same ending, but two are gerunds and two are gerundives. Which are which? Explain your answer.
3. Translate *laudandī probandīque sunt*. (*probō, -āre* = to commend) What use of the gerund/gerundive is this?
4. Translate *ā scrībendī recitandīque studiō*. (*recitō, -āre* = to recite; *studium, -ī* = enthusiasm) What case are *scrībendī* and *recitandī*? Explain your answer.

124. Passive Periphrastic

1. With what verb is the gerundive used in the passive periphrastic?
2. What does the passive periphrastic express?
3. With what construction is the person who does the action of the passive periphrastic expressed?

Passive Periphrastic Text

Cicero, *In Catilinam* 4.6. In Cicero's extended plea to the senate to decide Catiline's fate, here he summarizes by saying a decision must be made one way or another.

Id opprimī sustentandō aut prōlātandō nūllō pactō potest; quācumque ratiōne placet celeriter vōbīs vindicandum est.

---

1. Identify the passive periphrastic in the above excerpt.

Passive Periphrastic Text

New England College (NH) Motto

Dūra dūranda, alta petenda.

Vocabulary

dūrō, -āre. to endure [the form *dūra* does not come from this verb, but their meanings are related]

---

1. Translate the motto.

Passive Periphrastic Text

Horace, *Carmina* 1.37.1-4. Horace is perhaps best known for his *carpe diem*, from poem 1.11. But the philosophy behind *carpe diem*, that of seizing the day, of taking advantage of opportunities when they present themselves, of enjoying life while you can, permeates much of Horace's collection of odes, and can be seen in the following excerpt.

Nunc est bibendum, nunc pede lïberō
pulsanda tellus, nunc Saliāribus
　　ornāre pulvīnar deōrum
　　tempus erat dapibus, sodālēs.

Vocabulary

bibendum. [Has as its subject an understood *vinum*, "wine."]
pulsō, -āre. to strike, to beat [with *pede lïberō*, refers to dancing]

1. What are the two gerundives used in the passive periphrastic?
2. Translate lines 1-2 (*Nunc…tellus*).
3. How does the use of the passive periphrastic, instead of the simple future indicative, emphasize the philosophy Horace is here espousing?

Passive Periphrastic Text

Pliny, *Epistulae* **10.39.2.** In this letter, Pliny expresses concern about a new theater being built in Nicaea, a city in the northwestern corner of modern-day Turkey. The foundation, he reports, is already cracking, perhaps because too much money was spent on unnecessary extravagances and not enough on its more fundamental aspects. In this excerpt, Pliny suggests possible solutions to the problem.

Dignum est certē dēlīberātiōne, sitne faciendum an sit
relinquendum an etiam dēstruendum.

Vocabulary

relinquō, -ere. [*here*, to leave behind, to abandon]
dēstruō, -ere. to destroy

1. What are the three gerundives used in a passive periphrastic? Finish the translation below by translating the passive periphrastics in parentheses.

   Certainly it is worthy of consideration, whether this _____ [*sit faciendum*] or _____ [*sit reliquendum*] or even _____ [(*sit*) *dēstruendum*].

2. Why is *sit* subjunctive?

Passive Periphrastic Text

Plautus, *Menaechmi* **860-861.** Sosicles has just been accosted by the wife of Menaechmus and her father, who of course think that he is Menaechmus. Sosicles scares them off by acting as if he were possessed by the god Apollo. In this excerpt, the father of Menaechmus' wife expresses concern that the crazed Sosicles might actually carry out his threats.

Senex. Enim vērō illud praecavendumst, atque adcūrandumst mihi.   860
Sānē ego illum metuō, ut minātur, nē quid male faxit mihi.

1. Identify the two passive periphrastics in the above excerpt.
2. Translate the first line.

Gerundives and Passive Periphrastic Exercises

- Form the gerundive to agree with the specified noun.

  1. probō, -āre: amīcitiam
  2. conspiciō, -ere: iūdicēs
  3. appropinquō, -āre: oppidīs
  4. līberō, -āre: canum
  5. requīrō, -ere: victōriae

  6. colō, -ere: amīcitiā
  7. metuō, -ere: imperātōrī
  8. vereor, -ērī: gladiī
  9. quaerō, -ere: pontibus
  10. dō, dare: poenās

- Select the correct form to complete each sentence.

  1. Amīcitia inter imperātōrem senātōrēsque [colendae / colenda /colendī] sunt.
  2. Canis quī in oppidō habitat [līberandus / līberandīs / līberandō] est.
  3. Imperātōr et iūdicēs [metuendae / metuendī / metuendōs] sunt.
  4. Oppida quae contra Rōmam iunguntur convenienda [est / sunt].
  5. Vīnum dīrum [tibi / ā tē / tē] bibendum est.
  6. Oppidum [ab imperātōribus / imperātōribus / imperātōrēs] appropinquandum est.

CHAPTER 32

The final chapter is a clean-up chapter: it introduces a number of disparate constructions to conclude your introduction to Latin grammar. Some are more common than others.

125. Supine

1. What is the supine?
2. What endings does the supine use?
3. What stem does the supine use?
4. What cases is the supine found in?
5. After what kind of verbs is the accusative of the supine used? What does it express?
6. What are the five verbs commonly used in the ablative of the supine?
7. In which ablative does the supine appear?

Supine Texts

Livy, *Ab urbe condita* 1.15.5. As the young Rome expanded, its neighbors worried about its growing military power. The Veientes, one of these neighbors, accordingly sent a raiding party into Roman territory to at least announce their willingness to fight. In this excerpt, the Veientes sue the Romans for peace.

eaque clāde haud minus quam adversā pugnā subactī
Vēientēs pācem petītum ōrātorēs Rōmam mittunt.

Vergil, *Aeneid* 2.785-787. In Aeneas' rush to move his family out of the burning Troy, and in the tumult around him, his wife Creusa becomes separated from him. He rushes back to find her but is stopped by her ghost, who tells him that his fate lies elsewhere and with another. In this excerpt, she comforts him, to whatever extent possible, by saying that because she is dead she will not be enslaved to the Greeks. (Creusa's "comforting" words here recall Hector's fears for his wife Andromache in the *Iliad*.)

Nōn ego Myrmidonum sēdēs Dolopumve superbās   785
aspiciam aut Grāīs servitum mātribus ībō,
Dardanis et dīvae Veneris nurus;

Vergil, *Aeneid* **4.117-118.** Juno has plotted the relationship of
Aeneas and Dido, with Venus' "blessing"; Venus agrees, knowing
full well what Juno has planned and that Aeneas will ultimately
leave Carthage and frustrate Juno's plans. Dido arranges a hunt
for herself and the Trojans. Juno will send a storm that scatters
the hunters, and Dido and Aeneas will arrive at the same cave for
shelter. In this excerpt, Dido and Aeneas prepare to depart.

Vēnātum Aenēās ūnāque miserrima Dīdō
in nemus īre parant,

---

1. Identify the supine in each of the above excerpts.
2. Identify the use of the supine in each of the above excerpts.
3. Finish the translations below by translating the bracketed
   form.

> **Livy:** And defeated by this trick no less than by the
> attack, the Veientes sent ambassadors to Rome
> _____ [*petītum*] peace.

> **Vergil 2:** I will not see the proud seats of the
> Myrmidons or the Dolopes nor will I go _____
> [*servītum, serviō, -īre* = to serve] Greek mothers, as a
> nurse to the Dardanians or to divine Venus;

> **Vergil 4:** Aeneas and miserable Dido both prepare to
> go into the woods _____ [*vēnātum; vēnō, -āre* = to
> hunt].

Supine Texts

Vergil, *Aeneid 1*.110-112. Juno sent the god of the winds, Aeolus,
to unleash a storm on Aeneas' fleet. Aeneas has just spoken for the
first time in the *Aeneid*, wishing that he had died gloriously at Troy
rather than be killed anonymously at sea. In this excerpt, the wind
and waves that batter Aeneas' fleet are described.

tris Eurus ab altō   110
in brevia et Syrtīs urget—miserābile vīsū—
inlīditque vadīs atque aggere cingit harēnae.

Vergil, *Aeneid* **2.172-175.** The Greek Sinon was a "plant" left
by the Greeks to convince the Trojans that the Trojan Horse
was indeed a gift to Athena, and not the ruse that it was. In this
excerpt, Sinon describes how the Palladium, the statue of Athena
in her temple, was taken by the Greek warriors Ulysses and
Diomedes back to the Greek camp, and gave a forboding omen of
their destruction.

Ārsēre coruscae
lūminibus flammae arrēctīs, salsusque per artūs
sūdor iit, terque ipsa solō—mīrābile dictū—
ēmicuit parmamque ferēns hastamque trementem.   175

Vergil, *Aeneid* **4.181-183.** When Dido and Aeneas begin their
relationship, rumors abound in and around Carthage. Vergil
describes the personified Rumor that flies around the city and
reports: she is a multi-eyed, multi-mouthed, multi-eared monster.

…cui quot sunt corpore plūmae,
tot vigilēs oculī subter—mīrābile dictū—
tot linguae, totidem ōra sonant, tot subrigit aurīs.

---

1. Identify the supine in each of the above three excerpts.
2. What use of the supine is illustrated here?
3. Translate each of them.

126. *Ut* + the Indicative

1. What are the two English clause markers that *ut* can translate?
2. What are the two categories into which these clause markers fall?

- When *ut* is used to show comparison ("as"), it can be used with
  or without a verb: "I fell like a rock" or "I fell as a rock falls."
  English will use "like" when *ut* is used without a verb and "as"
  when *ut* is used with a verb.

Ut + the Indicative Text

The Province of Ontario Motto

Ut incēpit fidēlis, sīc permanet.

---

1. Translate the motto.

Ut + the Indicative Text

Ovid, *Metamorphoses* **1.530-534.** Apollo has been chasing the fleeing Daphne, asking her to stop, offering to slow down so that she might slow down and flee more safely, and pursuing her in as playful a tone as is possible. In the excerpt below, however, the tone of Apollo's chase changes. He pursues more quickly, and with increased fervor, and is compared to a dog pursuing a hare.

> 　　　　　Sed enim nōn sustinet ultrā　　530
> perdere blanditiās iuvenis deus, utque monēbat
> ipse Amor, admissō sequitur vēstīgia passū.
> Ut canis in vacuō leporem cum Gallicus arvō
> vīdit, et hic praedam pedibus petit, ille salūtem;

---

1. Choose the correct translation of *utque monēbat ipse Amor* in lines 531-532.
   a. so that Amor himself might encourage him
   b. as Amor himself was encouraging him
   c. with the result that Amor himself encouraged him
2. Explain your answer.
3. Choose the correct translation of *Ut canis…vīdit* in lines 533-534.
   a. With the result that the Gallic dog saw a rabbit in an empty field.
   b. So that the Gallic dog might see a rabbit in an empty field.
   c. Because the Gallic dog saw a rabbit in an empty field.
   d. Just as when a Gallic dog saw a rabbit in an empty field.
4. Explain your answer.

Ut + the Indicative Text

Ovid, *Metamorphoses* **10.277-286.** Ovid's Pygmalion has just prayed to Venus that he find a wife similar to the statue that he sculpted; he did not dare to ask Venus for what he really wanted, that the statue itself come to life. The excerpt below describes Venus' reaction to his prayer and the physical manifestations of that reaction.

Sēnsit, <u>ut</u> ipsa suīs aderat Venus aurea fēstīs,
vōta quid illa velint; et, amīcī nūminis ōmen,
flamma ter accēnsa est, apicemque per āera dūxit.
<u>Ut</u> rediit, simulācra suae petit ille puellae   280
incumbēnsque torō dedit ōscula. Vīsa tepēre est.
Admovet ōs iterum, manibus quoque pectora temptat.
Temptātum mollēscit ebur, positōque rigōre
subsīdit digitīs cēditque, <u>ut</u> Hymettia sōle
cēra remollēscit, tractātaque pollice multās   285
flectitur in faciēs, ipsōque fit ūtilis ūsū.

There are three occurrences of *ut* in the above excerpt; they are underlined.

1. All three instances of *ut* begin their clauses; identify where their clauses end.
2. Determine whether each *ut* clause has an indicative or a subjunctive verb.
3. Complete the following translations with the correct translation of *ut*.

    277-278: *Sēnsit…velint*: Golden Venus sensed what those prayers wanted, _____ she herself was present at her festival.

    280: *Ut…puellae*: _____ he returned home, he sought that likeness of his girl.

    283-285: *positōque…remollēscit*: and with her stiffness put aside, she yielded to his fingers and he believed, _____ Hymettian wax softens in the sun…

4. What is the subjunctive verb in line 278?
5. In what construction is it used (*quid* is your clue)?

127. More on Relative Pronouns

1. What are the three most common additional uses of relative pronouns?
2. What two things does the connecting relative often refer to?
3. How is the connecting relative translated?

- The difference between the connecting relative and a demonstrative or personal pronoun in Latin is often the difference between the semicolon and the period in English, i.e. the former creates a closer connection between the two clauses that it connects.

---

4. What does a relative clause of characteristic do?
5. What kind of verb does a relative clause of characteristic use?

- The relative clause of characteristic is most often used with a form of *sum*. Relative clauses with a subjunctive verb that are not used with a form of *sum* sometimes can be interpreted as either relative clauses of characteristic or relative clauses of purpose.

---

6. What word does the relative clause replace in a relative clause of purpose?

More on Relative Pronouns Text

Ovid, *Metamorphoses* 10.238-252. Ovid transitions into the Pygmalion story with the briefly described transformation of the Propoetides. These were women who, because they denied the divinity of Venus, became the first prostitutes, and ultimately were changed to stone as an outward reflection of their hardened inner emotional state.

Sunt tamen obscēnae Venerem Prōpoetides ausa
esse negāre deam, prō quō sua nūminis īrā,
corpora cum fāma prīmae vulgāsse feruntur;　240
utque pudor cessit sanguisque indūruit ōris,
in rigidum parvō silicem discrīmine versae.
Quās quia Pygmaliōn aevum per crīmen agentēs
vīderat, offēnsus vitiīs quae plūrima mentī
fēmineae nātūra dedit, sine coniuge caelebs　245
vīvēbat, thalamīque diū cōnsorte carēbat.

Intereā niveum mīrā fēlīciter arte
sculpsit ebur, fōrmamque dedit, quā fēmina nāscī
nūlla potest: operisque suī concēpit amōrem.
Virginis est vērae faciēs, quam vīvere crēdās,   250
et, sī nōn obstet reverentia, velle movērī:
ars adeō latet arte suā.

---

1. Identify the five relative pronouns in the above excerpt.
2. Identify the case, number, and gender of each.
3. Identify which of the five is/are a connecting relative. Explain your answer.

More on Relative Pronouns Text

Plautus, *Miles Gloriosus* **1301-1303.** The plan to reunite Philocomasium and Pleusicles hinges on the Miles Gloriosus, Pyrgopolynices, falling in love with another woman, and then agreeing to have Philocomasium rejoin her mother and sister, who happen to be in town that day. Pleusicles, disguised as a sailor, has just come to take Philocomasium to the docks. In this excerpt, the Miles Gloriosus sends Palaestrio to fetch her things.

Pyrgopolynices. Iam dūdum rēs parātast. Ī, Palaestriō,
[aurum, ornāmenta, vestem, pretiōsa omnia]
dūc adiūtōrēs tēcum ad nāvim quī ferant.

Vocabulary

ornāmentum, -ī. furniture
vestis, -is (*f.*). clothes
pretiōsus, -a, -um. delicate, valuable
adiūtor, -ōris (*m.*). helper

nāvim = nāvem [*The* -im *ending is an archaic third declension accusative singular ending.*]

---

1. Identify the relative pronoun in the above excerpt.
2. Is its verb indicative or subjunctive?
3. Translate the excerpt. Because the Latin word order is particularly convoluted, a reordered Latin sentence has been provided.

> Ī, Palaestriō, [et] dūc adiūtōrēs tēcum quī aurum, ornāmenta, vestem, pretiōsa omnia ad nāvim ferant.

   4. The Latin word *Ī* is of course not the English pronoun. From what verb does it come? What form of this verb is it?

128. Additional Uses of the Subjunctive

   1. What does the potential subjunctive indicate?
   2. What is its negative?
   3. Which verbs are commonly used in the potential subjunctive? Often, in what person?
   4. How is the potential subjunctive translated?
   5. When is the subjunctive used in indirect speech?

   • The impersonal construction in English (e.g. "It is permitted to go") is a semantic adjustment for a subjective infinitive, i.e. the subject of "permitted" is "it" but the pronoun "it" replaces the infinitive "to go": what is permitted? to go.

Additional Uses of the Subjunctive Text

   Ovid, *Amores* 1.6.39-40. Ovid here offers an extended address to the door that bars him from his love. In the couplet before this excerpt, he has just mentioned with what "arms" he comes to the door. He then addresses the door in regard to these "arms."

   Arma quis haec timeat? Quis nōn eat obvius illīs?
      tempora noctis eunt. Excute poste seram!   40

   1. Complete the translation of line 39 below by translating the subjunctive verbs in brackets.

        Who _____ [*timeat*] these weapons? Who _____ [*nōn eat*] in the face of these arms?

   2. Explain your translation of the subjunctives above.
   3. Complete the translation above with a different translation of the subjunctives.

Additional Uses of the Subjunctive Text

   Plautus, *Menaechmi* 962-963. The father of Menaechmus' wife brought a doctor to check Menaechmus over because of how strangely he has been acting. The doctor and the father have just left Menaechmus. In the excerpt below, he wonders about what just happened.

An illī perperam insānīre mē āiunt, ipsī insāniunt?
Quid ego nunc faciam? Domum īre cupiō: uxor nōn sinit.

---

1. Complete the translation below by translating the Latin in brackets.

   Or do they wrongly say that I am crazy, when they themselves are crazy? _____ [*Quid ego nunc faciam?*] I want to go home: my wife does not allow it.

Additional Uses of the Subjunctive Text

Cicero, *In Catilinam* 1.6.15. Cicero has just tried to convince Catiline to leave Rome of his own volition. In this excerpt, he reviews the evidence against Catiline, that he stood armed before the senate on January first.

Potestne tibi haec lūx, Catilīna, aut huius caelī spīritus esse iūcundus, cum sciās esse hōrum nēminem, quī nesciat tē prīdiē Kalendās Iānuāriās Lepidō et Tullō cōnsulibus stetisse in comitiō cum tēlō, manum cōnsulum et prīncipum cīvitātis interficiendōrum causā parāvisse, scelerī ac furōrī tuō nōn mentem aliquam aut timōrem tuum sed Fortūnam populī Rōmānī obstitisse?

---

1. Does the relative clause above contain an indicative or subjunctive verb? Explain your answer in terms of its grammatical function.

129. Impersonal Constructions

Impersonal Constructions Text

King's College (PA) Motto

Oportet eum regnāre.

---

1. Translate the motto.

Impersonal Constructions Text

Martial 4.54. Martial here recalls a theme common to Horace, that of *carpe diem*. He advises Collinus, the addressee of the poem (line 3) to not concern himself excessively with honor or wealth because neither is a concern of the Fates; their thread is spun the same length no matter what.

Ō cui Tarpeiās licuit contingere quercūs
    et meritās prīmā cingere fronde comās,
sī sapis, ūtāris tōtīs, Collīne, diēbus
    extrēmumque tibī semper adesse putēs.
Lānificās nullī trēs exōrāre puellās   5
    contigit: observant quem statuēre diem.
Dīvītior Crispō, Thraseā constantior ipsō
    lautior et nitidō sīs Meliōre licet:
nīl adicit pensō Lachesis fūsōsque sorōrum
    explicat et semper dē tribus ūna secat.   10

---

1. Identify the three impersonal verbs in the above poem.
2. Identify the tense of each.

Impersonal Constructions Text

Catullus 70. Catullus is frustrated by the disparity between what Lesbia says to him and how she apparently acts. He discounts any words of women speaking to their lovers as inherently distrustful.

Nullī sē dīcit mulier mea nūbere malle,
    quam mihi, nōn sī sē Iuppiter ipse petat.
Dīcit: sed mulier cupidō quod dīcit amantī,
    in ventō et rapidā scrībere oportet aquā.

---

1. Identify the impersonal verb in the above poem.
2. Identify the infinitive that functions as its subject.

Impersonal Constructions Text

Seneca, *Phaedra* **105-109.** Seneca opens the play proper (i.e. after the prefatory speech by Hippolytus) with a long speech by Phaedra in which she describes the extent to which her life has been disrupted by her illicit passion for Hippolytus. In this excerpt, she describes how she has lost interest in her sacred and domestic duties because of this passion.

Nōn <u>colere</u> dōnīs templa vōtīvīs libet,   105
nōn inter ārās, Atthidum mixtam chorīs,
<u>iactāre</u> tacitīs consciās sacrīs facēs,
nec <u>adīre</u> castīs precibus aut rītū piō
adiūdicātae praesidem terrae deam:

---

1. On what verb are each of the underlined infinitives dependent?

CITATIONS BY AUTHOR

Alcuin, *Farewell to his Cell* 1-2 (6)
Anonymous, *The Alleluiatic Sequence* 23-28 (7)
Anonymous, *Ave maris stella* 9-12 (9)
Anonymous, *Carmina Burana, In taberna* 9-16 (23)
Anonymous, *Carmina Burana, In taberna* 33-48 (1)
Anonymous, *Carmina Burana, Return of Spring* 11-20 (9)
Anonymous, *Carmina Burana, Return of Spring* 21-30 (23)
Anonymous, *Conflictus veris et hiemis* 32-33 (8)
Anonymous, *Conflictus veris et hiemis* 42-48 (27)
Anonymous, *De lupo ossa corrodente* 1-4 (11)
Anonymous, *In Praise of Wine* 1-4 (5)
Anonymous, *Miraculum Sancti Nicholai* 30-34 (13)
Anonymous, *Miraculum Sancti Nicholai* 50-58 (5)
Anonymous, *Miraculum Sancti Nicholai* 66-73 (9)
Anonymous, *Miraculum Sancti Nicholai* 80-83 (6)
Archipoeta, *Aestuans intrinsecus ira vehementi* 73-76 (3)
Caesar, *De bello Gallico* 1.2 (13)
Cato, *De agri cultura* 2 (17)
Catullus 1.1-5 (13)
Catullus 2.1-4 (19)
Catullus 4 (22)
Catullus 4.1-4 (3)
Catullus 5 (11)
Catullus 8.13-18 (11)
Catullus 8.15-18 (13)
Catullus 9.6-9 (11)
Catullus 9.10-11 (26)
Catullus 23.7-11 (2)
Catullus 23.24-27 (21)
Catullus 29.1 (8)
Catullus 34.9-12 (7)
Catullus 43.1-4 (5)
Catullus 49.1-3 (7)
Catullus 49.4-7 (5)
Catullus 55.3-5 (4)
Catullus 62.11-18 (13)
Catullus 62.20-31 (13)
Catullus 63.1-11 (4)
Catullus 63.58-60 (4)
Catullus 63.63-73 (9)
Catullus 64.19-21 (7)
Catullus 64.86-99 (24)
Catullus 64.143-144 (27)
Catullus 64.154-157 (13)

Catullus 64.171-176 (27)
Catullus 64.205-206 (7)
Catullus 65.10-12 (11)
Catullus 67.1-8 (22)
Catullus 68.20-24 (9)
Catullus 70 (23, 32)
Catullus 76.1-6 (22)
Catullus 92 (9, 30)
Catullus 101.1-2 (4)
Catullus 101.1-4 (28)
Catullus 109 (29)
Cicero, *In Catilinam* 1.2 (10)
Cicero, *In Catilinam* 1.6.15 (32)
Cicero, *In Catilinam* 1.9 (15)
Cicero, *In Catilinam* 1.10 (23)
Cicero, *In Catilinam* 1.12 (18, 30)
Cicero, *In Catilinam* 1.13 (13)
Cicero, *In Catilinam* 1.16 (28)
Cicero, *In Catilinam* 1.17 (30)
Cicero, *In Catilinam* 1.20 (23)
Cicero, *In Catilinam* 1.21 (18)
Cicero, *In Catilinam* 1.30 (13, 19)
Cicero, *In Catilinam* 1.32 (27, 28)
Cicero, *In Catilinam* 2.18 (13)
Cicero, *In Catilinam* 2.21 (7)
Cicero, *In Catilinam* 3.4 (28)
Cicero, *In Catilinam* 3.8 (28)
Cicero, *In Catilinam* 3.13 (28)
Cicero, *In Catilinam* 3.16 (7)
Cicero, *In Catilinam* 4.6 (17, 31)
Cicero, *In Catilinam* 4.12 (24)
Cicero, *In Catilinam* 4.18 (13)
Cicero, *Pro Archia* 1 (30, 31)
Cicero, *Pro Archia* 4-5 (16)
Cicero, *Pro Archia* 5-6 (18)
Cicero, *Pro Archia* 6 (17, 28)
Cicero, *Pro Archia* 8 (22)
Cicero, *Pro Archia* 12 (27)
Cicero, *Pro Archia* 14 (31)
Cicero, *Pro Archia* 16 (26)
Cicero, *Pro Archia* 17 (16)
Damian, Peter, *On the Paradise of God* 1-3, 13-21 (2)
Eugenius of Toledo, *Carmen Philomelaicum* 1-10 (9)
Gellius, *Noctes Atticae* 4.10.8 (17)
Gellius, *Noctes Atticae* 14.5.1 (31)
Gellius, *Noctes Atticae* 17.9.16-17 (15)

Gellius, *Noctes Atticae* 17.9.3 (31)
Gellius, *Noctes Atticae* 18.2.9 (5, 15)
Horace, *Carmina* 1.7.1-4 (11)
Horace, *Carmina* 1.8 (29)
Horace, *Carmina* 1.8.1-7 (27)
Horace, *Carmina* 1.9.1-4 (27, 29)
Horace, *Carmina* 1.10.5-8 (3)
Horace, *Carmina* 1.24.5-8 (5)
Horace, *Carmina* 1.36.10-16 (27)
Horace, *Carmina* 1.37.1-4 (31)
Horace, *Carmina* 3.2.13 (8)
Horace, *Carmina* 3.30.1-5 (19, 26)
[Inscription], CIL IX 2128 (10)
[Inscription], CIL I 1210 (29)
[Inscription], CIL VIII 9691 (29)
Livy, *Ab urbe condita* 1.5 (22)
Livy, *Ab urbe condita* 1.12.2-3 (16)
Livy, *Ab urbe condita* 1.13.1-2 (24, 29)
Livy, *Ab urbe condita* 1.15.5 (32)
Livy, *Ab urbe condita* 1.15.1 (31)
Livy, *Ab urbe condita* 1.15.3 (28)
Livy, *Ab urbe condita* 1.15.6 (31)
Livy, *Ab urbe condita* 1.16.1 (5)
Martial 1.1 (19)
Martial 1.5 (9)
Martial 1.8 (21)
Martial 1.9 (5)
Martial 1.19 (11)
Martial 1.21.5-6 (8)
Martial 1.23 (29)
Martial 1.41.14-17 (13)
Martial 1.46 (29)
Martial 1.49 (6)
Martial 1.68.1-4 (18)
Martial 1.71 (11)
Martial 1.75 (21)
Martial 1.89 (1)
Martial 1.90 (6)
Martial 1.109.1-5 (26)
Martial 2.1.1-2 (28)
Martial 2.2 (26)
Martial 2.5.1-2 (12)
Martial 2.7 (4)
Martial 2.27 (4)
Martial 2.33 (5)
Martial 2.44.7-9 (3)
Martial 2.44.7-12 (11)
Martial 2.48 (2)
Martial 2.53 (18)
Martial 2.90.1-4 (6)
Martial 3.9 (19)
Martial 3.44.10-18 (24)
Martial 3.63 (19)
Martial 3.86 (29)
Martial 3.89 (23)

Martial 4.5.1-2 (13)
Martial 4.6 (17)
Martial 4.10 (25)
Martial 4.54 (32)
Martial 5.2.1-2 (6)
Martial 5.17 (18)
Martial 5.29 (12)
Martial 5.37.1-17 (19)
Martial 5.42 (6)
Martial 5.43 (5)
Martial 5.48 (24)
Martial 5.83 (23)
Martial 6.7.1-2 (20)
Martial 6.14 (8, 22)
Martial 6.40 (10)
Martial 6.60 (1)
Martial 6.70.7-14 (17)
Martial 6.75 (11)
Martial 6.87 (3)
Martial 6.88 (15)
Martial 7.3 (3)
Martial 7.60 (1)
Martial 7.20.1 (26)
Martial 7.34.1-5 (26)
Martial 7.71 (5)
Martial 7.72.1-6 (12)
Martial 7.77 (21)
Martial 7.85 (8)
Martial 8.31.5-6 (14)
Martial 8.54 (26)
Martial 8.55.21-24 (7)
Martial 8.61 (17)
Martial 8.65.5-6 (16)
Martial 8.73 (10)
Martial 8.74 (15)
Martial 8.81 (10)
Martial 9.1 (18)
Martial 9.1.1-2 (5)
Martial 9.10 (21)
Martial 9.42 (27)
Martial 9.65 (28)
Martial 9.75 (4)
[Motto], Albertson College of Idaho (7)
[Motto], Appalachian State Univ (NC) (26)
[Motto], Beloit College (WI) (5)
[Motto], Brevard College (NC) (28)
[Motto], Bryn Mawr College (15)
[Motto], College of the Holy Cross (11)
[Motto], Columbia University (6)
[Motto], Cumberland College (KY) (26)
[Motto], Johns Hopkins University (6)
[Motto], King's College (PA) (32)
[Motto], Marist College (NY) (1)
[Motto], MGM Studios (7)
[Motto], New England College (31)

[Motto], New Mexico (State of) (31)
[Motto], Niagara University (NY) (28)
[Motto], Olympics (26)
[Motto], Ontario (Province of) (32)
[Motto], Roberts Wesleyan College (NY) (6)
[Motto], Rockhurst University (MO) (8)
[Motto], Syracuse University (13)
[Motto], Tottenham-Hotspur (Soccer) (8)
[Motto], Tulane University (13)
[Motto], University of Chicago (27)
[Motto], University of Leicester (UK) (28)
[Motto], University of Michigan (7)
[Motto], University of Waterloo (Ontario) (5)
[Motto], Wellesley College (17)
Ovid, *Amores* 1.1.1-4 (15)
Ovid, *Amores* 1.1.5, .13, .19, .27 (7)
Ovid, *Amores* 1.3.21-24 (19)
Ovid, *Amores* 1.5.1-2 (31)
Ovid, *Amores* 1.5.1-12 (24)
Ovid, *Amores* 1.6.39-40 (32)
Ovid, *Amores* 1.8.1-2 (5, 23)
Ovid, *Amores* 1.9.11-14 (31)
Ovid, *Amores* 1.9.17-20 (10)
Ovid, *Metamorphoses* 1.1-4 (9)
Ovid, *Metamorphoses* 1.452-453 (5)
Ovid, *Metamorphoses* 1.457-458 (5)
Ovid, *Metamorphoses* 1.468-473 (10)
Ovid, *Metamorphoses* 1.481-482 (3)
Ovid, *Metamorphoses* 1.510-511 (26)
Ovid, *Metamorphoses* 1.527-530 (6)
Ovid, *Metamorphoses* 1.530-534 (32)
Ovid, *Metamorphoses* 1.533-539 (11)
Ovid, *Metamorphoses* 4.63 (4)
Ovid, *Metamorphoses* 4.65-77 (20)
Ovid, *Metamorphoses* 4.73 (3)
Ovid, *Metamorphoses* 4.83-90 (29)
Ovid, *Metamorphoses* 4.91-92 (17)
Ovid, *Metamorphoses* 4.99-104 (18)
Ovid, *Metamorphoses* 4.152-153 (8)
Ovid, *Metamorphoses* 8.200-202 (23)
Ovid, *Metamorphoses* 8.686 (11)
Ovid, *Metamorphoses* 10.8-10 (18)
Ovid, *Metamorphoses* 10.25 (22)
Ovid, *Metamorphoses* 10.50-52 (29)
Ovid, *Metamorphoses* 10.56-59 (17, 31)
Ovid, *Metamorphoses* 10.64-71 (24)
Ovid, *Metamorphoses* 10.72-74 (12)
Ovid, *Metamorphoses* 10.238-252 (32)
Ovid, *Metamorphoses* 10.250-251 (17)
Ovid, *Metamorphoses* 10.256-258 (30)
Ovid, *Metamorphoses* 10.267-269 (10)
Ovid, *Metamorphoses* 10.277-286 (32)
Petronius, *Satyricon* (Matron of Ephesus) 111 (3, 6)
Plautus, *Menaechmi* 17-50 (10)
Plautus, *Menaechmi* 26-40 (16)

Plautus, *Menaechmi* 72-73 (17)
Plautus, *Menaechmi* 75-76 (7)
Plautus, *Menaechmi* 110-124 (27)
Plautus, *Menaechmi* 143-159 (9)
Plautus, *Menaechmi* 208-212 (22)
Plautus, *Menaechmi* 238-241 (30)
Plautus, *Menaechmi* 266-267 (30)
Plautus, *Menaechmi* 387 (28)
Plautus, *Menaechmi* 398-400 (8)
Plautus, *Menaechmi* 420-421 (30)
Plautus, *Menaechmi* 469-470 (24)
Plautus, *Menaechmi* 551 (1)
Plautus, *Menaechmi* 639-648 (9)
Plautus, *Menaechmi* 716-717 (15)
Plautus, *Menaechmi* 860-861 (31)
Plautus, *Menaechmi* 879-881 (29)
Plautus, *Menaechmi* 962-963 (32)
Plautus, *Menaechmi* 966-967 (1)
Plautus, *Menaechmi* 976-980 (23)
Plautus, *Menaechmi* 1009-1019 (9)
Plautus, *Menaechmi* 1031-1034 (25)
Plautus, *Menaechmi* 1100 (27)
Plautus, *Menaechmi* 1107-1108 (7)
Plautus, *Menaechmi* 1126-1136 (20)
Plautus, *Menaechmi* 1162 (9)
Plautus, *Miles Gloriosus* 42-46 (11)
Plautus, *Miles Gloriosus* 55-67 (10)
Plautus, *Miles Gloriosus* 79-80 (31)
Plautus, *Miles Gloriosus* 126-128 (4, 22)
Plautus, *Miles Gloriosus* 189-189a (2)
Plautus, *Miles Gloriosus* 206-210 (1)
Plautus, *Miles Gloriosus* 496-513 (13)
Plautus, *Miles Gloriosus* 718-722 (30)
Plautus, *Miles Gloriosus* 1301-1303 (32)
Plautus, *Miles Gloriosus* 1394-5 (9)
Pliny, *Epistulae* 1.6.1 (23)
Pliny, *Epistulae* 1.13.1-2 (31)
Pliny, *Epistulae* 1.13.3 (28)
Pliny, *Epistulae* 1.13.5 (31)
Pliny, *Epistulae* 2.17.3 (12)
Pliny, *Epistulae* 2.17.8 (31)
Pliny, *Epistulae* 5.19.3 (4, 28)
Pliny, *Epistulae* 7.20.1 (31)
Pliny, *Epistulae* 9.23.1 (29)
Pliny, *Epistulae* 9.23.6 (30)
Pliny, *Epistulae* 9.36.1 (12)
Pliny, *Epistulae* 9.36.4 (17)
Pliny, *Epistulae* 10.39.2 (31)
Pliny, *Epistulae* 10.96.1, 9-10 (17)
Pliny, *Epistulae* 10.96.5 (22)
Pliny, *Epistulae* 10.97 (31)
Scholiast on Juvenal 6.117 (308.29) (28)
Seneca, *Phaedra* 1-8 (9)
Seneca, *Phaedra* 54-59 (19)
Seneca, *Phaedra* 70-72 (16)

Seneca, *Phaedra* 105-109 (32)
Seneca, *Phaedra* 110-111 (23)
Seneca, *Phaedra* 296-316 (15)
Seneca, *Phaedra* 370-372 (17)
Seneca, *Phaedra* 448-451 (9)
Seneca, *Phaedra* 463-465 (28)
Seneca, *Phaedra* 530-539 (15)
Seneca, *Phaedra* 568-573 (11)
Seneca, *Phaedra* 640-644 (12)
Seneca, *Phaedra* 665-669 (10)
Seneca, *Phaedra* 736-757 (24)
Seneca, *Phaedra* 854-855 (16)
Seneca, *Phaedra* 882-893 (20)
Seneca, *Phaedra* 1050-1056 (16)
Seneca, *Phaedra* 1123-1125 (26)
Seneca, *Phaedra* 1211-1212 (7)
Seneca, *Phaedra* 1226-1237 (24)
Vergil, *Aeneid* 1.1 (2)
Vergil, *Aeneid* 1.110-112 (32)
Vergil, *Aeneid* 2.10-13 (1)
Vergil, *Aeneid* 2.27-30 (8)
Vergil, *Aeneid* 2.45-49 (24)
Vergil, *Aeneid* 2.108-109 (11)
Vergil, *Aeneid* 2.146-147 (21)
Vergil, *Aeneid* 2.172-175 (32)
Vergil, *Aeneid* 2.185-188 (22)
Vergil, *Aeneid* 2.203-205 (4)
Vergil, *Aeneid* 2.232-233 (22)
Vergil, *Aeneid* 2.298-303 (16)
Vergil, *Aeneid* 2.353 (27)
Vergil, *Aeneid* 2.531-532 (5)

Vergil, *Aeneid* 2.533-534 (3)
Vergil, *Aeneid* 2.687-688 (5)
Vergil, *Aeneid* 2.730-734 (6)
Vergil, *Aeneid* 2.757 (15)
Vergil, *Aeneid* 2.774 (15)
Vergil, *Aeneid* 2.785-787 (32)
Vergil, *Aeneid* 4.1-2 (17)
Vergil, *Aeneid* 4.50 (2)
Vergil, *Aeneid* 4.6-7 (15)
Vergil, *Aeneid* 4.24-29 (13)
Vergil, *Aeneid* 4.117-118 (32)
Vergil, *Aeneid* 4.181-183 (32)
Vergil, *Aeneid* 4.208-210 (1)
Vergil, *Aeneid* 4.215-217 (5)
Vergil, *Aeneid* 4.232-237 (27)
Vergil, *Aeneid* 4.288-295 (27)
Vergil, *Aeneid* 4.311-313 (30)
Vergil, *Aeneid* 4.331-332 (11)
Vergil, *Aeneid* 4.333-336 (6)
Vergil, *Aeneid* 4.333-336 (16)
Vergil, *Aeneid* 4.340-344 (30)
Vergil, *Aeneid* 4.356-359 (23)
Vergil, *Aeneid* 4.361,381 (23)
Vergil, *Aeneid* 4.419-420 (8)
Vergil, *Aeneid* 4.421-423 (16)
Vergil, *Eclogues* 4.11-14 (24)
Vergil, *Eclogues* 6.31-40 (29)
Vergil, *Eclogues* 6.43-51 (28)
Vergil, *Eclogues* 8.69-71 (4)

CITATIONS BY CHAPTER

Chapter 1

Anonymous, Carmina Burana, In taberna 33-48
Vergil, *Aeneid* 4.208-210
Plautus, *Menaechmi* 551
Plautus, *Menaechmi* 966-967
Martial 1.89
Plautus, *Miles Gloriosus* 206-210
Martial 6.60
[Motto], Marist College (NY)
Martial 7.60
Vergil, *Aeneid* 2.10-13

Chapter 2

Vergil, *Aeneid* 1.1
Catullus 23.7-11
Martial 2.48
Plautus, *Miles Gloriosus* 189-189a
Damian, Peter, *On the Paradise of God* 1-3, 13-21
Vergil, *Aeneid* 4.50

Chapter 3

Archipoeta, *Aestuans intrinsecus ira vehementi* 73-76
Catullus 4.1-4
Horace, *Carmina* 1.10.5-8
Martial 2.44.7-9
Martial 6.87
Martial 7.3
Ovid, *Metamorphoses* 1.481-482
Vergil, *Aeneid* 2.533-534
Petronius, *Satyricon* (Matron of Ephesus) 111
Ovid, *Metamorphoses* 4.73

Chapter 4

Martial 2.7
Martial 2.27
Pliny, *Epistulae* 5.19.3
Ovid, *Metamorphoses* 4.63
Catullus 63.1-11
Martial 9.75
Plautus, *Miles Gloriosus* 126-128
Vergil, *Aeneid* 2.203-205
Catullus 55.3-5
Catullus 101.1-2
Catullus 63.58-60
Vergil, *Eclogues* 8.69-71

Chapter 5

Catullus 49.4-7
Martial 1.9
Horace *Carmina* 1.24.5-8
Martial 7.71
Catullus 43.1-4
Ovid, *Metamorphoses* 1.452-453
Ovid, *Metamorphoses* 1.457-458
Martial 5.43
Martial 9.1.1-2
Gellius, *Attic Nights* 18.2.9
Ovid, *Amores* 1.8.1-2
Martial 2.33
Anonymous, *Miraculum Sancti Nicholai* 50-58
[Motto], Beloit College (WI)
[Motto], University of Waterloo (Ontario)
Vergil, *Aeneid* 2.531-532
Vergil, *Aeneid* 2.687-688
Vergil, *Aeneid* 4.215-217
Livy, *Ab urbe condita* 1.16.1
Anonymous, *In Praise of Wine* 1-4

Chapter 6

Petronius, *Satyricon* (Matron of Ephesus) 111
Martial 1.90
Vergil, *Aeneid* 2.730-734
Ovid, *Metamorphoses* 1.527-530
[Motto], Columbia University
[Motto], Johns Hopkins University
Martial 5.42
Vergil, *Aeneid* 4.333-336
Martial 1.49
[Motto], Roberts Wesleyan College (NY)
Alcuin, *Farewell to his Cell* 1-2
Anonymous, *Miraculum Sancti Nicholai* 80-83
Martial 5.2.1-2
Martial 2.90.1-4

Chapter 7

[Motto], MGM Studios
[Motto], University of Michigan
[Motto], Albertson College of Idaho
Plautus, *Menaechmi* 75-76
Catullus 64.19-21
Cicero, *In Catilinam* 3.16
Catullus 34.9-12

Anonymous, *The Alleluiatic Sequence* 23-28
Cicero, *In Catilinam* 2.21
Seneca, *Phaedra* 1211-1212
Catullus 64.205-206
Martial 8.55.21-24
Catullus 49.1-3
Plautus, *Menaechmi* 1107-1108
Ovid, *Amores* 1.1.5, .13, .19, .27

Chapter 8

[Motto], Rockhurst University (MO)
Plautus, *Menaechmi* 398-400
Martial 1.21.5-6
Catullus 29.1
Ovid, *Metamorphoses* 4.152-153
Martial 6.14
Vergil, *Aeneid* 4.419-420
[Motto], Tottenham-Hotspur (Soccer)
Anonymous, *Conflictus veris et hiemis* 32-33
Vergil, *Aeneid* 2.27-30
Martial 7.85
Horace, *Carmina* 3.2.13

Chapter 9

Anonymous, *Carmina Burana, Return of Spring* 11-20
Eugenius of Toledo, *Carmen Philomelaicum* 1-10
Plautus, *Menaechmi* 1162
Ovid, *Metamorphoses* 1.1-4
Plautus, *Miles Gloriosus* 1394-5
Seneca, *Phaedra* 1-8
Seneca, *Phaedra* 448-451
Anonymous, *Ave maris stella* 9-12
Plautus, *Menaechmi* 1009-1019
Plautus, *Menaechmi* 143-159
Catullus 63.63-73
Catullus 68.20-24
Anonymous, *Miraculum Sancti Nicholai* 66-73
Catullus 92
Martial 1.5
Plautus, *Menaechmi* 639-648

Chapter 10

Cicero, *In Catilinam* 1.2
Martial 6.40
Martial 8.81
Plautus, *Miles Gloriosus* 55-67
Ovid, *Amores* 1.9.17-20
Ovid, *Metamorphoses* 1.468-473
Plautus, *Menaechmi* 17-50
[Inscription], CIL IX 2128
Seneca, *Phaedra* 665-669
Martial 8.73
Ovid, *Metamorphoses* 10.267-269

Chapter 11

Vergil, *Aeneid* 4.331-332
Anonymous, *De lupo ossa corrodente1-4*
[Motto], College of the Holy Cross
Catullus 9.6-9
Martial 6.75
Catullus 8.13-18
Seneca, *Phaedra* 568-573
Catullus 65.10-12
Martial 1.71
Martial 2.44.7-12
Plautus, *Miles Gloriosus* 42-46
Martial 1.19
Catullus 5
Vergil, *Aeneid* 2.108-109
Ovid, *Metamorphoses* 1.533-539
Ovid, *Metamorphoses* 8.686
Horace, *Carmina* 1.7.1-4

Chapter 12

Martial 7.72.1-6
Seneca, *Phaedra* 640-644
Martial 2.5.1-2
Pliny, *Epistulae* 9.36.1
Pliny, *Epistulae* 2.17.3
Martial 5.29
Ovid, *Metamorphoses* 10.72-74

Chapter 13

Catullus 1.1-5
Catullus 8.15-18
Catullus 62.20-31
Cicero, *In Catilinam* 1.13
Catullus 64.154-157
Cicero, *In Catilinam* 1.30
Martial 1.41.14-17
Vergil, *Aeneid* 4.24-29
Plautus, *Miles Gloriosus* 496-513
[Motto], Syracuse University
[Motto], Tulane University
Caesar, *De bello Gallico* 1.2
Anonymous, *Miraculum Sancti Nicholai* 30-34
Martial 4.5.1-2
Cicero, *In Catilinam* 2.18
Cicero, *In Catilinam* 4.18

Chapter 14

Martial 8.31.5-6
Catullus 62.11-18

Chapter 15

[Motto], Bryn Mawr College
Martial 6.88
Vergil, *Aeneid* 2.774
Seneca, *Phaedra* 296-316
Gellius, *Noctes Atticae* 18.2.9

Cicero, *In Catilinam* 1.9
Seneca, *Phaedra* 530-539
Martial 8.74
Plautus, *Menaechmi* 716-717
Vergil, *Aeneid* 4.6-7
Vergil, *Aeneid* 2.757
Gellius, *Noctes Atticae* 17.9.16-17
Ovid, *Amores* 1.1.1-4

Chapter 16

Vergil, *Aeneid* 2.298-303
Vergil, *Aeneid* 4.333-336
Vergil, *Aeneid* 4.421-423
Cicero, *Pro Archia* 17
Seneca, *Phaedra* 70-72
Seneca, *Phaedra* 854-855
Seneca, *Phaedra* 1050-1056
Martial 8.65.5-6
Livy, *Ab urbe condita* 1.12.2-3
Cicero, *Pro Archia* 4-5
Plautus, *Menaechmi* 26-40

Chapter 17

Martial 6.70.7-14
Martial 8.61
Vergil, *Aeneid* 4.1-2
Pliny, *Epistulae* 9.36.4
Ovid, *Metamorphoses* 10.250-251
Ovid, *Metamorphoses* 4.91-92
Plautus, *Menaechmi* 72-73
[Motto], Wellesley College
Martial 4.6
Pliny, *Epistulae* 10.96.1, 9-10
Cicero, *In Catilinam* 4.6
Gellius, *Noctes Atticae* 4.10.8
Seneca, *Phaedra* 370-372
Ovid, *Metamorphoses* 10.56-59
Cato, *De agri cultura* 2
Cicero, *Pro Archia* 6

Chapter 18

Martial 1.68.1-4
Martial 2.53
Cicero, *In Catilinam* 1.12
Martial 5.17
Ovid, *Metamorphoses* 4.99-104
Martial 9.1
Ovid, *Metamorphoses* 10.8-10
Cicero, *In Catilinam* 1.21
Cicero, *Pro Archia* 5-6

Chapter 19

Horace, *Carmina* 3.30.1-5
Catullus 2.1-4
Seneca, *Phaedra* 54-59
Martial 1.1

Martial 3.63
Cicero, *In Catilinam* 1.30
Martial 5.37.1-17
Ovid, *Amores* 1.3.21-24
Martial 3.9

Chapter 20

Martial 6.7.1-2
Ovid, *Metamorphoses* 4.65-77
Plautus, *Menaechmi* 1126-1136
Seneca, *Phaedra* 882-893

Chapter 21

Martial 1.8
Martial 1.75
Martial 7.77
Martial 9.10
Catullus 23.24-27
Vergil, *Aeneid* 2.146-147

Chapter 22

Ovid, *Metamorphoses* 10.25
Vergil, *Aeneid* 2.185-188
Livy, *Ab urbe condita* 1.5
Cicero, *Pro Archia* 8
Martial 6.14
Catullus 76.1-6
Catullus 4
Catullus 67.1-8
Plautus, *Miles Gloriosus* 126-128
Plautus, *Menaechmi* 208-212
Vergil, *Aeneid* 2.232-233
Pliny, *Epistulae* 10.96.5

Chapter 23

Pliny, *Epistulae* 1.6.1
Vergil, *Aeneid* 4.356-359
Catullus 70
Ovid, *Metamorphoses* 8.200-202
Anonymous, *Carmina Burana, In taberna* 9-16
Ovid, *Amores* 1.8.1-2
Anonymous, *Carmina Burana, The Return of Spring* 21-30
Martial 5.83
Plautus, *Menaechmi* 976-980
Seneca, *Phaedra* 110-111
Cicero, *In Catilinam* 1.10
Cicero, *In Catilinam* 1.20
Vergil, *Aeneid* 4.361, 381
Martial 3.89

Chapter 24

Catullus 64.86-99
Vergil, *Aeneid* 2.45-49
Ovid, *Amores* 1.5.1-12
Martial 3.44.10-18

Seneca, *Phaedra* 736-757
Seneca, *Phaedra* 1226-1237
Ovid, *Metamorphoses* 10.64-71
Cicero, *In Catilinam* 4.12
Vergil, *Eclogues* 4.11-14
Martial 5.48
Plautus, *Menaechmi* 469-470
Livy, *Ab urbe condita* 1.13.1-2

Chapter 25

Plautus, *Menaechmi* 1031-1034
Martial 4.10

Chapter 26

[Motto], Cumberland College (KY)
Cicero, *Pro Archia* 16
Martial 7.34.1-5
Martial 2.2
Martial 8.54
[Motto], Appalachian State University (NC)
Horace, *Carmina* 3.30.1-5
Catullus 9.10-11
Martial 1.109.1-5
[Motto], Olympics
Martial 7.20.1
Ovid, *Metamorphoses* 1.510-511
Seneca, *Phaedra* 1123-1125

Chapter 27

Plautus, *Menaechmi* 1100
Martial 9.42
Vergil, *Aeneid* 4.288-295
Plautus, *Menaechmi* 110-124
Cicero, *In Catilinam* 1.32
Horace, *Carmina* 1.9.1-4
Cicero, *Pro Archia* 12
Horace, *Carmina* 1.8.1-7
Catullus 64.143-144
Vergil, *Aeneid* 2.353
[Motto], University of Chicago
Vergil, *Aeneid* 4.232-237
Horace, *Carmina* 1.36.10-16
Catullus 64.171-176
Anonymous, *Conflictus veris et hiemis* 4248

Chapter 28

Martial 2.1.1-2
Livy, *Ab urbe condita* 1.15.3
Cicero, *In Catilinam* 3.4
Vergil, *Eclogues* 6.43-51
Martial 9.65
Cicero, *In Catilinam* 3.13
Pliny, *Epistulae* 5.19.3
Pliny, *Epistulae* 1.13.3
Cicero, *In Catilinam* 3.8
[Motto], Brevard College (NC)

[Motto], Niagara University (NY)
[Motto], University of Leicester (UK)
Plautus, *Menaechmi* 387
Seneca, *Phaedra* 463-465
Catullus 101.1-4
Scholiast on Juvenal 6.117 (308.29)
Cicero, *In Catilinam* 1.32
Cicero, *In Catilinam* 1.16
Cicero, *Pro Archia* 6

Chapter 29

Horace, *Carmina* 1.9.1-4
Martial 1.23
Plautus, *Menaechmi* 879-881
Horace, *Carmina* 1.8
Vergil, *Eclogues* 6.31-40
Martial 1.46
Martial 3.86
Ovid, *Metamorphoses* 4.83-90
Livy, *Ab urbe condita* 1.13.1-2
[Inscription], CIL I 1210
[Inscription], CIL VIII 9691
Pliny, *Epistulae* 9.23.1
Catullus 109
Ovid, *Metamorphoses* 10.50-52

Chapter 30

Pliny, *Epistulae* 9.23.6
Ovid, *Metamorphoses* 10.256-258
Plautus, *Menaechmi* 266-267
Plautus, *Menaechmi* 420-421
Plautus, *Menaechmi* 238-241
Plautus, *Miles Gloriosus* 718-722
Cicero, *In Catilinam* 1.17
Vergil, *Aeneid* 4.311-313
Vergil, *Aeneid* 4.340-344
Cicero, *Pro Archia* 1
Catullus 92
Cicero, *In Catilinam* 1.12

Chapter 31

[Motto], New Mexico (State of)
Ovid, *Metamorphoses* 10.56-59
Pliny, *Epistulae* 1.13.1-2
Livy, *Ab urbe condita* 1.15.1
Cicero, *Pro Archia* 1
Livy, *Ab urbe condita* 1.15.6
Cicero, *Pro Archia* 14
Plautus, *Miles Gloriosus* 79-80
Ovid, *Amores* 1.5.1-2
Ovid, *Amores* 1.9.11-14
Pliny, *Epistulae* 7.20.1
Pliny, *Epistulae* 10.97
Gellius, *Attic Nights* 14.5.1
Gellius, *Attic Nights* 17.9.3
Pliny, *Epistulae* 2.17.8

Gellius, *Attic Nights* 4.10.8
Pliny, *Epistulae* 1.13.5
Cicero, *In Catilinam* 4.6
[Motto], New England College
Horace, *Carmina* 1.37.1-4
Pliny, *Epistulae* 10.39.2
Plautus, *Menaechmi* 860-861

Chapter 32
Livy, *Ab urbe condita* 1.15.5
Vergil, *Aeneid* 2.785-787
Vergil, *Aeneid* 4.117-118
Vergil, *Aeneid* 1.110-112
Vergil, *Aeneid* 2.172-175

Vergil, *Aeneid* 4.181-183
[Motto], Ontario (Province of)
Ovid, *Metamorphoses* 1.530-534
Ovid, *Metamorphoses* 10.277-286
Ovid, *Metamorphoses* 10.238-252
Plautus, *Miles Gloriosus* 1301-1303
Ovid, *Amores* 1.6.39-40
Plautus, *Menaechmi* 962-963
Cicero, *In Catilinam* 1.6.15
[Motto], King's College (PA)
Martial 4.54
Catullus 70
Seneca, *Phaedra* 105-109